*Acclaim for Ted Halstead and Michael Lind's*

# THE RADICAL CENTER

"A provocative, thoughtful, and timely message for the political establishment and the governing class, *The Radical Center* should be mandatory reading for everyone in office and for those of us who cover them."　　　　　　　　　　—Tom Brokaw, NBC News

"A milestone in political thinking. Nowhere else has the case for the irrelevance of the old categories of Left and Right been put so forcefully. *The Radical Center* is required reading for anyone who aspires to political literacy."　　　　　　—John Gray, author of *False Dawn*

"Halstead and Lind have done a superb job of outlining a provocative starting point for the radical center."　　—*The American Prospect*

"In this brilliant book, Halstead and Lind capture a new center visible to the next generation but never before expressed. Regardless of your political party, your future is here."

—Eric Schmidt, chairman of Google

"A fresh and intelligent roadmap for America's future."

—Fareed Zakaria, *Newsweek*

"A clear and coherent program of innovative policy ideas adapted to the Information Age. With a creative drive and passion . . . Halstead and Lind offer a bold vision of institutional transformation."

—Eric Benhamou, chairman of 3Com Corporation

"Subtle, clear, and provocative. . . . The authors present a remarkably coherent vision for the renewal of America."　—*Publishers Weekly*

"Halstead and Lind represent important and refreshing new voices of the generation to come, whose work will challenge received opinion about public policy."

—Francis Fukuyama, author of *The End of History*

"Halstead and Lind offer us a new progressive center. I hope this book starts the wide-ranging debate that we need."

—Bill Joy, cofounder of Sun Microsystems

"*The Radical Center* represents new thinking, combining lessons learned from the past with an optimistic view of the future. This book deserves to be read by thoughtful Americans of all generations."　—John C. Whitehead, former chairman of Goldman Sachs

"The curse of modern politics is what the technology world calls 'legacy code'—inherited taboos, biases, and blinders that prevent most public figures from expressing, or even thinking, original thoughts. *The Radical Center* shows us how we could deal with a number of intractable public issues if we were willing actually to think about them rather than just operating by reflex and rote."

—James Fallows, chairman of the New America Foundation

"Persuasive . . . clear, succinct. . . . This book adds many fresh insights to our currently stale political discourse."　—*Library Journal*

*Ted Halstead and Michael Lind*

# THE RADICAL CENTER

Ted Halstead is the founder and president of the New America Foundation (www.newamerica.net), one of the nation's most successful public policy institutes. He writes frequently for *The New York Times, The Washington Post, The Atlantic Monthly,* and *Los Angeles Times.*

Michael Lind, a senior fellow of the New America Foundation, is the author of a number of books, including *The Next American Nation* (1995). He has been an editor or staff writer at *The New Yorker, Harper's Magazine,* and *The National Interest.*

ANCHOR BOOKS
A Division of Random House, Inc.
New York

# THE
# RADICAL
# CENTER

·  ——

*The Future of
American Politics*

·  ——

TED HALSTEAD *and*
MICHAEL LIND

*To my parents Roy and Kate,*
*for their never-ending love and encouragement;*
*and to my sister Libby, for her bravery and joie de vivre.* —TH

*To the memory of my father, Charles R. Lind.* —ML

FIRST ANCHOR BOOKS EDITION, NOVEMBER 2002

*Copyright © 2001 by Ted Halstead and Michael Lind*

All rights reserved under International and Pan-American Copyright Conventions.
Published in the United States by Anchor Books,
a division of Random House, Inc., New York, and simultaneously
in Canada by Random House of Canada Limited, Toronto.
Originally published in hardcover in the United States by Doubleday,
a division of Random House, Inc., New York, in 2001.

Anchor Books and colophon are registered trademarks
of Random House, Inc.

The Library of Congress has cataloged the Doubleday edition as follows:

Halstead, Ted.
The radical center: the future of American politics / Ted Halstead and
Michael Lind.—1st ed.
p.   cm.
Includes bibliographical references and index.
ISBN 0-385-50045-9
1. United States—Politics and government—2001–   2. United States—
Economic policy—1993–   3. United States—Social policy—1993–
I. Lind, Michael, 1962–   II. Title.
JK275.H35 2001
320.5—dc21
2001028285

**Anchor ISBN: 0-385-72029-7**

*Author photographs © A. Little and Sigrid Estrada*
*Book design by Jennifer Ann Daddio*

www.anchorbooks.com

Printed in the United States of America
10   9   8   7   6   5   4   3

# CONTENTS

———— • ————

# DIGITAL

# DISJUNCTURE

By the dawn of the twenty-first century, more Americans identified themselves as independents than as either Democrats or Republicans. Astonishing as it may seem, a clear plurality of Americans have become so hostile to the two parties that have defined our nation's politics for the past century that they prefer "neither of the above," even in the absence of a serious alternative. Political analysts like to talk about electoral "realignments" in favor of one party or another, but what is occurring here is something altogether different—we are experiencing a large-scale political "dealignment."

This striking dealignment suggests that our Democratic and Republican Parties have failed the two most important tests of American politics: the ability to unite a majority of citizens in a lasting coalition, and the ability to find workable solutions to the problems of our era. Our nation's politics are dominated by two feuding dinosaurs that have outlived the world in which they evolved.

In ordinary times, a dysfunctional political order may be less of a cause for concern. But these are no ordinary times. In the first two years of the twenty-first century, America suffered the worst terrorist attack in its history, experienced the collapse of the NASDAQ bubble that had spawned such wealth and euphoria in the preceding years, and witnessed the meltdown of Enron, one of its most celebrated companies. Meanwhile, long-term technological, economic, and demographic transformations were remaking our nation and world. In such extraordinary times, America needs a compelling vision of national renewal and a concrete program of national reform, capable of guiding the way forward while unifying the American people.

Sadly, neither political party has supplied either a vision or a program. There are two reasons for this failure. First, both parties have been captured by their own extremes and special interests, which prevent them from promoting majority views across a wide range of issues. Second, and more important, both remain so wedded to the ideas and institutions of the last century that neither has proven itself capable of rising to the challenges of the next. Together, these two factors have deterred either party from championing the type of forward-looking reforms that would serve the broader public interest in this new century.

Let us consider each of these shortcomings of our two-party cartel in turn.

Despite concerted efforts over the past decade, both the Democratic and Republican Parties have failed to build new majority coalitions. Instead of expanding their voter bases, both parties have allowed themselves to be taken hostage by narrow pressure groups on certain defining issues. These groups include social conservatives and economic libertarians in the case of the Republican Party, and a constellation of aggrieved minority groups and public employee unions in the case of the Democratic Party. Naturally, this consolidation of power at the extremes has further alienated growing numbers of Americans from either party.

The ascendancy of these well-organized factions in their respective parties has given them a level of political power far out of proportion to their actual numbers in the general electorate. Nowhere is this more apparent than in the presidential nominating process, where the religious Right has effective veto power over any Republican nominee, just as defenders of affirmative action and opponents of school choice have in the case of the Democratic nominee. This is not to suggest that the parties do not espouse centrist positions on some issues or that neither has centrist members; to the contrary, both do have centrist wings. But these centrists are constantly overshadowed and overpowered by the more extreme elements in their own camp.

This basic reality leads to a fundamental disjuncture between what the American people want and what the leading parties offer. As Harvard political scientist David C. King explains, "Both political parties have been growing more extreme . . . they are increasingly distant in their policies from what the average voter would like." While the conservative wing of the Republican Party and the liberal wing of the Democratic Party have become ever more powerful, the American people themselves have become ever more moderate in their views. During the 2000 election, for instance, a national poll revealed that only 29 percent of Americans actually view themselves as conservatives, and an even smaller number, 20 percent, view themselves as liberals, with a full 50 percent describing themselves as moderates.

It is this moderate majority of Americans—composed of self-identified independents, along with significant numbers of centrist Republicans and Democrats—who feel most alienated by today's increasingly dogmatic two-party system. Although their numbers in the electorate far outweigh those of the special interest groups on the Right and Left, the latter nevertheless continue to wield more political power as a result of the archaic design of our electoral process, which in effect limits political choices to an option between two extremes. This not only fuels popular resentment against the political system as a whole, it perpetuates the illusion of a sharply divided nation when in fact the alienated majority of Americans are far more interested in finding common ground than in fighting culture wars.

Further fueling this sense of political alienation, our current two-party cartel forces many voters to sacrifice one important value for another. Suppose that, like many Americans, you believe in reproductive choice as well as school choice. In an ideal world, you could vote for a presidential candidate and political party that reflects both of these positions. In today's political system, however, any American holding these two views must confront the uncomfortable dilemma of choosing one at the expense of the other. Likewise, voters are now routinely forced to choose between the party that stands for treating all citizens equally regardless of racial origin and the party that stands for treating all citizens equally regardless of sexual orientation; between the party in favor of tax fairness and the party in favor of tax simplification; and between the goal of a more competitive marketplace and that of a more sustainable environment. In addition to imposing these artificial trade-offs on the public, several items most Americans say they favor—such as amending our electoral system to increase voter choice—are not on offer from the major parties, which are less interested in pleasing voters than in colluding to maintain rules that preserve their comfortable cartel.

Given the degree to which our major parties are captured by their extremes, is it really that surprising that an unprecedented number of Americans feel they no longer have a party to call their own? This striking political dealignment has not escaped the attention of politicians. Indeed, during recent presidential races, analysts from both parties agreed that the election would turn on a candidate's ability to win the support of the growing pool of undecided and independent-minded swing voters. But this presented presidential aspirants with a genuine dilemma, given the stark dichotomy between their increasingly rigid parties and an increasingly heterodox electorate. In an effort to escape from this dilemma, recent presidential candidates and victors have developed the dubious art of political triangulation.

The two-term presidency of Bill Clinton from 1992 to 2000 was unusual in that Clinton, a Democrat, borrowed heavily from the ideas of the Republican establishment, often to the consternation of his own party's rank and file. His dominant strategy, which came to be known as triangulation, was premised on applying what were widely seen as conservative policy ideas to achieve progressive ends. George W. Bush used the same strategy in reverse during the 2000 presidential race: In an effort to appropriate what are traditionally viewed as Democratic issues (such as concern about poverty and education) to his advantage, he coined the clever campaign slogan of "compassionate conservatism."

With the benefit of hindsight, it seems clear that this two-way triangulation, far from providing a genuine alternative to conservative Republicans or liberal Democrats, only reinforced the shortcomings of our two-party system, and will accelerate the political dealignment already under way. Interestingly, Clinton's and Bush's versions of triangulation failed for different reasons.

To his credit, President Clinton did forge a new middle ground on some issues, such as fiscal policy and welfare reform, though he often had difficulty bringing the Democratic Party along with him. Yet the more fundamental fact is that Clinton never so much as tried to challenge his party's most powerful special interest groups, which have maintained their lock on issues like affirmative action, Social Security, and education policy. After eight years of Clintonian triangulation, then, the Democratic Party remains as dominated as ever by its most entrenched interest groups.

President Bush's early experimentation with triangulation was also a failure, but mostly because it was disingenuous. Indeed, to Bush, triangulation appears to have been little more than a game of bait and switch. During the campaign, he promised the American people that he would be a different kind of Republican, tear down the walls that kept America divided, and even fight to reduce our emissions of carbon dioxide (the main culprit in the global warming equation). Yet during his first months in office Bush did just the opposite: He angered many centrist voters by tapping a far-right conservative, John Ashcroft, as his attorney general; he pushed through a large tax cut that would overwhelmingly benefit the well-to-do and return the government to long-term deficits; and he reversed himself completely on his global warming pledge.

The tragic terrorist attacks of September 11, 2001, confronted President Bush with a whole new set of challenges, to which he responded admirably by waging a swift and decisive war against al Qaeda and Taliban forces in Afghanistan. Shaken by the crisis, the American people rallied behind their government and president, expecting both parties to work together and set their differences aside. But the rare period of bipartisan détente following the attacks on New York and Washington proved to be short-lived; within months of America's victory in Afghanistan, partisan politics had returned with a vengeance, with each party playing to its narrow constituencies rather than to the broader public interest. Once again, the alienated majority of Americans had nowhere to turn.

If the first way in which our two-party duopoly has failed the American people is by succumbing to extremes, then its second and more profound failure is its imprisonment in the past. Underlying the growing political disengagement and dealignment is a widespread, if largely unspoken, sense on the part of the American people that the parties, ideologies, and institutions that have defined our social and political order in the past are simply incapable of addressing the challenges and opportunities awaiting us in the Information Age.

By the turn of the twenty-first century, the sources of America's next major transformation were in full view: the twin revolutions in information technology and biotechnology, the graying and browning of our population, and the increasing globalization of knowledge and commerce. Yet for all these new developments, our dominant political parties have failed to rise to the occasion by genuinely reinventing themselves or updating their programs. Indeed, our leading parties are now relics of a bygone era.

Many of the tenets of Democratic liberalism, now commonly called progressivism, were developed during the New Deal era, beginning in the 1930s, while most of the orthodoxies of today's Republican conservatism were developed during the 1960s or 1970s. Both ideologies are vestiges of the Second Industrial Revolution of the twentieth century and are ill suited to the new challenges and opportunities of the information era. History provides innumerable examples of technological and demographic changes driving broader social change, and reveals that tectonic transformations in the economic and social spheres usually precede those in the political sphere. As a nation's technological, economic, and demographic circumstances evolve, so must its political landscape.

To varying degrees, today's Republican and Democratic Parties recognize the need for upgrading their political programs to meet the new circumstances of the twenty-first century, but neither has come anywhere near realizing this goal. Instead, they have mostly endeavored to dress up their old thinking to make it look new and innovative. For instance, former House Speaker Newt Gingrich famously claimed that "Third Wave" technological change requires us to enact the agenda of the Republican Right, while the "New Democrats" of the Democratic Leadership Council have made the "new economy" the centerpiece of their political platform. In both cases, the perception that technology-driven change requires a new political and social agenda is accurate. But all too often, the conclusions have been determined in advance on the basis of antiquated partisan dogma.

Rhetoric aside, both major parties remain surprisingly wedded to the programs, if not the principles, of New Deal America. Ever since

the charismatic presidency of Ronald Reagan in the 1980s, denouncing the goals of the New Deal has become a major rallying cry
of the Republican Party. Yet the GOP has nevertheless cooperated in
not only maintaining but expanding virtually all of the New Deal and
Great Society programs: Social Security, Medicare, Medicaid, and
unemployment insurance. While the Republican establishment has
been schizophrenic in renouncing the ends but embracing the
means of the New Deal, the Democratic Party has been steadfast in
its support of both, priding itself as the defender of the New Deal
legacy.

There can be no question that the New Deal was a tremendous
success from its inception in the 1930s until the early 1970s: It
brought America out of its worst depression, created the world's first
mass middle class, allowed us to overcome the worst forms of racial
injustice, all but wiped out poverty among the elderly, and helped
save humanity from political tyranny and economic stagnation by defeating two separate totalitarian challenges worldwide. During its
heyday, the New Deal consensus also served as America's dominant
public philosophy, providing a broadly shared national narrative to
inspire and guide the nation. In the 1970s, however, the New Deal
consensus began to collapse, as did the efficacy of its trademark programs. For lack of a better alternative, however, we remain stuck in a
New Deal paradigm, even when it has ceased to serve its original
purposes: unifying the nation, ensuring basic economic security for
all, and broadening America's middle class.

Many of the New Deal programs of the industrial era are now as
obsolete as they are entrenched in our two-party structure. To appreciate the depth of this disjuncture, we need only take a quick look at
many of the inherited assumptions and institutions that both parties
take for granted, and ask ourselves: Does it still make sense to go on
organizing our society this way in the twenty-first century?

Let's begin with our basic social contract—an arrangement inherited from the mid-twentieth century—which is premised on an

intergenerational public pension program and an employer-based health care system. At the birth of the New Deal, it made sense to structure Social Security as a transfer program in which current workers pay for current retirees—so long as the working-age population greatly outnumbered the elderly whom they subsidized. Indeed, the system worked remarkably well for the first generation of retirees to benefit from it. Today, however, the rapid growth in the ratio of retirees to workers threatens to bankrupt both Social Security and Medicare, or to impose crippling taxes on the young and the employed. What was the proudest achievement of the New Deal era is fast becoming a sobering liability in the information era.

At the height of the Second Industrial Revolution, when most employees aspired to lifetime employment with a single firm, it also might have made sense to link the provision of health care benefits to one's employer (although even then a series of American presidents tried and failed to create a single-payer universal health care system). In the turbulent economy of the early twenty-first century, however, when average job tenure is only three to five years and the proportion of contingent and part-time workers is high, does it really make sense to maintain this industrial era linkage between health insurance and employers? Doing so only makes changing jobs that much more disruptive, and breeds a profound sense of insecurity in a workforce that is increasingly oriented toward a free-agent model. Our basic social contract, then, is being undermined by the inescapable forces of demographics and economic change.

In a similar fashion, our nation's education and tax systems are held hostage to the past. For all the partisan rhetoric over the future of primary and secondary education, neither the Democratic nor the Republican Party dares to tackle what is arguably the most pressing education problem of all—the way we fund our public schools. The archaic link between local and state taxes and school funding perpetuates dramatic disparities in per pupil funding both within and between states. As the premium on education continues to rise, these vast inequities become harder to tolerate. Like our school hours and long summer breaks, which harken back to the bygone rhythms of our agricultural past, the local nature of school finance is a relic of the preindustrial agrarian era.

Meanwhile, the rapid spread of e-commerce threatens the sales tax systems that fund our state and local government services. This is hardly surprising, given that these taxes were introduced as emergency measures during the Depression, when commerce was far more localized. Likewise, the accelerating pace of globalization is undermining the rationale for corporate income taxes. Even the progressive income tax, a worthwhile legacy of the New Deal period, is corroded by countless loopholes added over the decades.

More broadly still, the general direction of our nation's economic policies betrays an obsession with the past at the expense of the future. From the Great Depression onward, political leaders from both parties have sought to subsidize consumption (through the tax code and through our retirement program) in order to create a mass consuming public for industrial era manufacturing, and to help our cold war partners run large trade surpluses with us. But with the retirement of the baby boom generation now imminent and the growing economic weight of the rest of the world, this industrial era emphasis on consumption at the expense of savings and investment may be precisely backward. Indeed, we probably have more to fear from the fact that personal savings rates have dipped below zero less than a decade before our nation's largest generation begins retirement, than we do from a temporary economic downturn caused by falling personal consumption. Obviously, our reigning political duopoly has yet to come to terms with the new economic dynamics of Information Age America. Neither party has adequately confronted the pro-consumption bias in our current economic incentives, and neither has proposed a way to increase personal savings that does not favor the rich.

Our approaches to race relations and immigration are no less anachronistic. In the area of civil rights, the large-scale immigration of nonwhites and rising rate of interracial marriage are destroying the rationale for the policies of racial preferences that presupposed a society forever polarized between white and black. For instance, the most recent census demonstrated that Latinos are rapidly overtaking African-Americans as the nation's largest minority group. For that matter, our whole system of racial classification has itself become obsolete, now that the growth in numbers of multiracial Americans is blurring racial categories that were pseudoscientific to begin with. These developments make it clear that America needs a whole new approach to civil rights. It is also high time a new approach to immigration was instituted, as there is a fundamental mismatch between our economy's need for more high-skilled workers and the bias in our current immigration policies in favor of unskilled labor.

For all these disjunctures between our nation's past and future, nowhere is reform more necessary than in our electoral system. Here, our current arrangement dates back not to the New Deal but rather to eighteenth-century Britain. In the 2000 presidential election, the combination of our archaic two-party cartel and our electoral college system produced a political fiasco. But the problems of our electoral system are far greater: It generates a binary two-party system that limits the choices available to the American public and the consideration of serious new policy ideas (other than in moments of national crisis, when partisanship is sometimes set aside). As we enter the information era, the increasingly heterodox pluralism of the American public is in direct conflict with the dogmatic duopoly of our two parties. This not only leads to political alienation and dealignment, as we have seen, but it also constrains the ability of our government to respond to the tectonic shifts taking place in our private, public, and communal sectors.

The two national parties, along with the liberal and conservative ideologies they invoke, have failed, then, to provide an agenda that reflects the moral outlook and economic interests of most Americans,

or responds to our changing conditions with innovative policy reforms. As a result of this deficit of intellectual and political leadership, we live in a time of profound confusion, despite our superpower
status and dynamic economy. As a nation, we have become, for the
moment at least, the world's predominant technological, military, and
economic power, but we have yet to figure out what we want to do
with this awesome opportunity, or how to use it to further unify and
strengthen our nation. What America needs at this historic moment
is a compelling national vision to guide us into a postindustrial future,
along with a coherent program for how to get there. Instead of providing such a vision or program, our reigning political duopoly has
only fueled a false sense of national division while sending a large portion of the electorate into temporary hiding.

This is not the first time that America has found itself in this
predicament. Twice before, technological and economic progress,
along with demographic change, have forced American society to
struggle to adapt to a transformed environment. The story of the evolution of the United States from a small agrarian republic into the
world's dominant superpower is at the same time the story of America's ability to periodically reinvent itself in order to take full advantage of new technological breakthroughs, such as the introduction of
the steam engine in the 1800s and the emergence of electricity and
the internal combustion engine in the 1900s. Profound technological innovations of this type tend to occur in concentrated bursts and
have a destabilizing impact on virtually all facets of society—giving
rise to a remaking of established social, economic, and political institutions (the economic sector is typically the first to undergo large-
scale change). These critical technologies have transformed entire
nations in relatively short periods of time.

In the United States, our Founding Fathers created a decentralized
agrarian republic, which the second Founders of the Civil War/Recon-

struction period replaced by harnessing the power of steam to create an urbanizing America of factory towns. Then, in the twentieth century, the third Founders of the New Deal era enlisted the new technologies of electricity and the internal combustion engine in their successful campaign to establish the world's first nation with a mass middle class—a third United States characterized by a service-oriented economy, a suburban majority, a greatly expanded welfare state, and a military capable of prevailing in two world wars and one cold war.

Although technological advances make periodic reinventions of our nation necessary and inevitable, the actual outcome of technologically driven change owes as much to public philosophies and political alliances as to technology itself. If the Confederacy had successfully seceded from the United States, it would have industrialized and urbanized—but with results far different from those that followed its defeat. Likewise, the New Deal consensus of the twentieth century was only one of a number of competing visions of twentieth-century America; its rivals included socialism, laissez-faire libertarianism, and even neoagrarian populism.

America will be reinvented again. At some point in the early twenty-first century, the modern equivalents of Abraham Lincoln and Franklin Delano Roosevelt will once again remodel the inherited institutions of our republic in order to adapt them to the rapidly emerging technologies and circumstances of the Information Age. At each stage in our evolution from a nation of farmers to a nation of urban and suburban service workers, our market economy, system of governance, and civic society have been remade—sometimes voluntarily, sometimes against bitter resistance.

Whatever form it finally takes, Information Age America will be as different from New Deal America as New Deal America was from Reconstruction America—and as different as Reconstruction America was from the America of the Founding Fathers. But the creation of a new Information Age America will force us to confront a variety of difficult dilemmas from which there is simply no escape, even though our two parties seem intent on delaying the day of reckoning for as long as possible.

On what basis, then, are we to make the decisions that will shape America in the twenty-first century? To answer this all-important question, we must first identify the timeless values that have guided our nation since its inception, and should continue doing so. Only then can we craft a new political program that is tailored to the particular circumstances of the Information Age, yet grounded in the perennial values that have guided America at its best.

In the words of Supreme Court Justice Oliver Wendell Holmes, Jr., "Continuity with the past is not a duty, only a necessity." The great civic reformers of the American past changed what was ephemeral and secondary in the America tradition in order to conserve what was permanent and important. In our opinion, America's unique ability to remake itself and thrive during each successive wave of technological change—past and future—stems from its core commitment to a division of social authority among three distinct realms of society: the market, the state, and community. Our nation's history reveals that these three sectors—the private, the public, and the communal—are interdependent, complementary, and mutually supporting. For our nation to flourish, all three must be in relative balance with one another, so that each may perform its unique functions, and provide its unique form of freedom.

The core value of the market is liberty, and its core functions are to promote wealth creation and the efficient allocation of resources. The core value of the state is equality of opportunity, and its core functions are to promote the public good, maintain civil liberties, and preserve law, order, and national defense. And the core value of community—which encompasses the realm of organized religions, voluntary organization, customs, and traditions—is solidarity; its core functions are to preserve communal bonds and national unity and to nurture civic virtues. Each provides a unique form of freedom: The market provides freedom *to* enrich oneself through hard work, the state provides freedom *from* oppression and destitution, and the community provides freedom *of* association with like-minded people. The precise form and makeup of each of these three sectors have changed dramatically throughout our nation's history, but their core values and functions, as well as the freedoms they confer, have remained constant and, it may be hoped, will for the foreseeable future.

Rather than to any particular ideology, it is to our nation's ongoing commitment to this unwritten division of authority between the private, public, and communal spheres that we owe our historic success both in balancing and expanding our competing goals of liberty, fairness, and unity. This is not to suggest that American history has been unidirectional—to the contrary, we have progressed in fits and starts, at times moving forward and at other times moving backward. But taken as a whole, there is little question that our nation's relatively short history has been characterized by an unmistakable upward mobility on the axes of individual freedom, social equality, and national unity. Any particular political program must be judged on the basis of its success in promoting improvement in all three realms of American society, not just one.

From this vantage point, the New Deal political program was a resounding success from its inception at the height of the Second Industrial Revolution until roughly the 1970s. Since then, however, while our individual freedoms have continued to expand, the same cannot be said for the material equality of our people, or for the unity of our nation. Indeed, since the collapse of the New Deal consensus in the 1970s, we have witnessed a three-decade eruption of narrow particularism—featuring the identity-group politics of the multicultural Left and the religious Right, and the libertarian glorification of the market above all other sectors of society. As we have also seen, a great many of the programs and institutions of New Deal America are beginning to crumble under the weight of their own obsolescence. All of this suggests that it is high time for a new political program, one tailored to the new realities of Information Age America yet anchored in our nation's timeless values.

We call our new political program the Radical Center. We chose this name to differentiate our principles and policies from those of the Democratic Left and the Republican Right. To us, it seems obvious that the familiar varieties of liberalism and conservatism, developed as they were in response to the Second Industrial Revolution, are largely irrelevant in the fundamentally different environment of the first half of the twenty-first century. "Centrism" itself has become something of a shallow mantra in recent American politics. It is usually invoked in a tactical effort to bridge the differences between the existing Left and Right—yielding a "Squishy Center" that lies between Left and Right, rather than a "Radical Center." We use the word *radical*—in keeping with its Latin derivation from "radix," or "root"—to emphasize that we are interested not in tinkering at the margin of our inherited public, private, and communal institutions but rather in promoting, when necessary, a wholesale revamping of their component parts.

The underlying purpose of this Radical Centrist program is to further expand America's perennial goals of individual liberty, equality of opportunity, and national unity in the new circumstances of the Information Age. We begin by outlining the guiding principles of a Radical Centrist agenda, which are grounded in an understanding of what differentiates this period in our nation's history from previous ones. Next, we put forth a series of concrete reform proposals that follow from—and give substance to—these principles.

What, then, are the defining characteristics of the Information Age? The technological breakthroughs of the First and Second Industrial Revolutions were large and physically imposing. By contrast, the defining breakthroughs of the Information Revolution tend to be either invisible to the naked eye—like the silicon chip, genetic therapy, or prototypes of nanotechnology—or intangible altogether—like the World Wide Web and the map of the human genome. Whereas the agrarian era was based on human and animal muscle power, and the First and Second Industrial Revolutions were based on machine power, the Information Revolution is based on brainpower. And the primary currency in this latest technological revolution is not physical matter but digitized information.

Despite their unimposing appearance or ethereal nature, the technologies of the information era promise to be just as revolutionary as those of earlier eras and to catalyze social transformations that may be even more profound. Indeed, the interesting part of this story does not revolve around the new technologies per say, but rather around their manifold impact on virtually all facets of our society. It would be a mistake, however, to assume that Information Age America will only be shaped by the latest technologies, for several of the most profound technological innovations of the twentieth century are only now beginning to exert their full social impact. For instance, it is largely due to early advances in biomedical technology—the introduction and widespread adoption of antibiotics and contraceptives in the last century—that America's demographic profile is now graying so rapidly. These demographic changes may only foreshadow what is to come, especially if our birthrates remain low and scientists succeed in extending average human life spans to 120 years or beyond.

Already, the new technologies of the information era have redefined the nature, pace, and organization of commerce in our nation and much of the world. Over the past decade, thanks largely to new information technologies, our economy has undergone a fundamental shift from standardization to customization, from centralization to decentralization, and from reliance on intermediary institutions to more direct relationships between buyers and sellers. To appreciate the magnitude of these changes, one need only compare a model twenty-first-century corporation to its Industrial Age counterpart, and consider how foreign the ideas of flat organizational charts, just-in-time production, niche marketing, electronic mail, and mass outsourcing would seem to a mid-twentieth-century business executive. Likewise, the sheer speed and global scope of commerce and capital mobility today would have been almost unimaginable fifty years ago. This increased velocity, in turn, requires today's workers, managers, shareholders, and communities to withstand far more frequent fluctuations in their fates and economic prospects. Many who are inadequately prepared to weather such abrupt and wrenching changes find themselves in a chronic state of insecurity.

The Information Age has also brought significant changes to our political and community spheres. These include a recent devolution of political power and authority, a twenty-four-hour news cycle that often blurs the lines between substance and entertainment, the advent of instant-poll-driven politics, the general shift from broadcasting to narrowcasting, and the birth of on-line communities as well as chat rooms. Meanwhile, the unresponsiveness of our two-party system has caused an increase in the proportion of our political life that now takes place outside the formal political arena—in hyperactive citizen groups and nongovernmental organizations focused on narrowly defined causes, interests, and grievances.

More profound still are the recent shifts in our nation's economic and political geography, as various high-tech centers across the country have accumulated vast new wealth—and hence cultural and political power—in a short amount of time, and as demographic changes have empowered and emboldened a rapidly growing voting block of senior citizens who have a self-interest in maintaining and even expanding our largest entitlement programs. At the same time, the increasing geographic segregation of our population by age and wealth has caused a decline in the health of many of our neighborhood institutions, from the town square to the public school.

Yet for all these changes in the economic, political, and community spheres, it is probably in the personal sphere that the Information Age has exerted its greatest impact. The archetypical citizen of the Information Age is a professional and, increasingly, a free agent. It might be objected that professionals are and will remain a minority of the population, but this misses the point. We are witnessing a mass professionalization of society—the spreading of norms, values, and knowledge to most members of our society that were once the limited purview of a small elite. For example, the vast majority of adult Americans now own credit cards and their own homes, and approximately half have money invested in financial markets. Likewise, most Americans now have access to the unlimited repository of free information available on the World Wide Web. As a result, contemporary citizens are far more sophisticated than their parents and grandparents in making financial choices and sifting through the mass media. Even in the realm of politics, polls consistently reveal that Americans are extremely thoughtful as well as duly skeptical.

America's increasingly competent citizens are capable of flourishing in a system that permits far more individual choices and responsibilities. Unfortunately, the sophistication of our citizens has surpassed that of our dominant institutions, as well as the ideologies that maintain them. Our basic social contract, our political parties, our governmental programs, and our educational and even charitable institutions are designed on the premise that highly educated experts should be in charge of relatively passive, ignorant, and incompetent people. A century ago this paternalistic approach may have promoted progress. Today it retards progress.

What then should be the organizing principle of an Information Age political program? In redesigning our nation's public, private, and communal institutions once again for the new conditions of the early twenty-first century, we believe that one design criterion above all others should guide us: increasing the amount of choice available to individual citizens. So far, the information era has enabled most Americans to enjoy newfound choices only as consumers in the economic and entertainment spheres. Any new political program worthy of the Information Age must be capable of translating this so far narrow expansion of choices to many other spheres of society: voting choices, educational choices, medical choices, retirement choices, lifestyle choices, and career choices.

Our Radical Centrist philosophy therefore begins from the premise that American citizens in the twenty-first century deserve more choices in—and discretion over—the decisions that shape their lives. While this emphasis on expanding individual choices may seem obvious, its implications are profound. For one thing, if individual citizens are to be empowered with greater decision-making authority, then many of today's institutions must be redesigned so as to become citizen-based. For example, today's employer-based programs (such as health care), group-based programs (such as Social Security), and place-based programs (such as locally financed public schools) must undergo a radical reinvention if the locus of decision making is to be transferred to the individual. Such a shift would not only empower individuals but also protect them from many of the uncertainties associated with relying on intermediary institutions that are themselves at the whim of today's fast-changing economy. A citizen-based reform program of the Radical Center not only offers the greatest promise for addressing the emerging challenges of the Information Age but, just as important, enables all Americans to take the fullest possible advantage of the new opportunities afforded them by the century ahead.

Broadening individual choice by means of a citizen-based reform agenda represents a significant departure from the past two reinventions of the American republic. In the early years of our republic, the options of Americans were narrowly defined by the race, gender, and class roles to which they were assigned by a highly traditional community. Later, during the First and Second Industrial Revolutions of the nineteenth and twentieth centuries, most social thinkers and reformers insisted on a significant degree of standardization and hierarchy, and the institutions they gave birth to tended to be quite paternalistic. In the first industrial era of the nineteenth century, for instance, the prototypical citizen was a factory worker who sometimes doubled as an army conscript. In the second industrial era of the twentieth century, factory work gave way to factory-like office environments. The "organization man"—the clerk or manager—and his wife—the homemaker, teacher, or secretary—replaced the proletarian. But the nature of work and government programs remained top-down and standardized. So did the organization of politics. The very term *political machine* speaks volumes about the nature of civic life during the first 150 years of technological civilization.

The homogenized and paternalistic institutional models of the United States in its industrial heyday may well have been necessary to create a large-scale middle class and to supply the armed forces which were needed to defeat totalitarian empires. But these old industrial structures have now become victims of their own success. Their goal was to produce a New Citizen, and they have.

In 1997, President Bill Clinton observed, "The era of big government may be over, but the era of big challenges in our country is not. And so we need an era of big citizenship." By *big citizenship,* however, Clinton meant merely what his predecessor George Bush, Sr., had referred to as "a thousand points of light"—namely, a higher level of volunteering by Americans. Subsequently, President George W. Bush has continued to emphasize this theme of voluntarism. We agree that America needs a new era of big citizenship, but believe that the concept should encompass far more than greater rates of volunteer work, important as that may be.

A second guiding principle of Radical Centrism is that the citizens of the twenty-first century can and should be held to a higher personal standard. In this new era of big citizenship, greater choice and freedom must go hand in hand with greater responsibility. Formerly, civic duty was identified primarily with military service, jury duty, and the act of voting. But the definition of civic duty now needs to be expanded, especially in a society in which most citizens receive transfer payments or subsidies from their fellow taxpayers. In such a society, self-reliance must become a civic duty as well as a private virtue. If Americans want more discretion over the decisions that affect their lives, then they will need to be more self-sufficient. For example, if our health care and pension systems are to become citizen-based and personally managed, then it seems only reasonable to require those who can to pay for their own health care insurance and save for their own retirement. Doing otherwise would inhibit personal freedom at the broadest level, by forcing our least fortunate citizens to subsidize the irresponsibility of those who are capable of fending for themselves. Likewise, certain types of personal free-dom—the ability to use genetic engineering to create designer ba-bies, for example—must be limited when they risk undermining the broader common good. In short, freedom and responsibility must ex-pand in tandem.

Implicit in this Radical Centrist philosophy is a new conception of the role of government. There are, in essence, two models through which a government can provide basic economic security to its citizens: the safety net model and the universal provider model. The former assumes that public benefits should only go to help the neediest, while the latter assumes that public benefits should accrue to all citizens, regardless of need. The New Deal philosophy, in its most familiar version—epitomized by programs like Social Security and Medicare—is based on the universal provider model. The Radi-cal Centrist philosophy, by contrast, is premised on the safety net model.

At this stage in our nation's history, the universal provider model not only inhibits personal choice and responsibility, but economic security as well. For instance, the very design of our Social Security system creates a powerful disincentive for personal savings, which is the exact opposite of what the nation needs as the retirement of the baby boom generation approaches. Meanwhile, many of today's youngest workers fear for the future of our Social Security system. More worrisome still is the threat that the rapidly escalating costs of Social Security and Medicare will turn our government into little more than an intergenerational transfer agency, while crowding out government's ability to fund and invest in other critical public functions, ranging from education to infrastructure to national defense.

To criticize the New Deal welfare model that is routinely defended by today's Democratic Party is not to side with today's Republican Party, which has established a troubling record of slashing funds to the neediest and youngest Americans. The Radical Centrist alternative is a true safety net model, under which public benefits would be provided to those who need them the most, while those who can afford to pay their own way would be required to do so. The overwhelming advantage of this approach is that it would enable our nation to increase individual choice, responsibility, and security simultaneously.

A final implication of this new emphasis on individual choice relates to our notion of federalism, or the balance between state and federal authority. Typically, debates over federalism are viewed as zero-sum games pitting the power of local or state bureaucracies against those of federal bureaucracies. Ensuring greater individual choice in public policy, however, will sometimes require a greater federal role at the expense of local or state governments. For example, any equitable plan for nationwide school choice would require nationwide equalization of school funding on a per pupil basis, which in turn can only be accomplished through greater federal involvement in school funding. Interestingly, however, the terms of such a debate would not so much pit federal control against local control as they would pit control by local bureaucracies against control by individual citizens (in this particular case, parents). Hence a final principle of Radical Centrism is cooperative federalism: the principle that local and state jurisdictions should sometimes cede authority to federal jurisdictions in cases where the outcome is the expansion of individual freedoms and choices. As we shall see, this principle has strong precedents in U.S. Constitutional thought.

Combined, these various principles for a Radical Centrist public philosophy for Information Age America—expanding individual choices and responsibilities through citizen-based programs, the notion of big citizenship, a safety net approach to public benefits, and cooperative federalism—serve as unifying threads that weave together the various proposals that animate these pages.

We begin our book by summarizing the remarkable story of how a series of technological, economic, and demographic revolutions, combined with farsighted leadership, transformed America from a nation of farmers into the world's foremost superpower in a mere two hundred years. In particular, we highlight how technology-driven change has led to a periodic remaking of America's market, state, and community sectors in order to draw lessons for the next remaking of our nation, which will result from the emergence of the Information Age. We caution, however, against technological determinism. Although America has succeeded in adapting itself to previous waves of technological innovation—and expanding the freedom, equality, and unity of our citizens in the process—this does not guarantee that we will be able to do so again, especially if we lack a compelling vision or dynamic leadership.

The remainder of the book is devoted to specific proposals for reinventing the institutions of the American economy, American government, and American community in accordance with the new realities of the Information Age, the guiding principles of the Radical Center, and the enduring values that have inspired America since the beginning of the republic.

In the realm of the market, if American citizens are to welcome a highly dynamic global economy and tolerate continuous waves of technology-driven change, then the prerequisite will be a new citizen-based social contract. In the twenty-first century, the flexibility of business and the security of individuals alike require severing the traditional link between employers and the provision of benefits, and doing away with the old distinctions between full-time and contingent workers altogether. Done correctly, this would free businesses from the burden of benefit administration, and give rise to a very dynamic new workforce able to enjoy the freedoms of today's contingent workers and the security of today's full-time employees. Specifically, we propose a mandatory private health care system for all Americans that would ensure that the poorest and least healthy are fully covered.

In the area of retirement policy, we recommend "progressive privatization" of our Social Security system, to be based on mandatory retirement savings for all workers, public subsidies to top off the personal savings accounts of low-income workers, and a guaranteed safety net for those who fall through the cracks. Both reforms—severing health care insurance from employment, and increasing reliance on personal savings accounts for retirement—embody the principles of citizen-based policies, of big citizenship and greater self-reliance, and of a safety net approach to public benefits.

In the twentieth century, the objective of our basic social contract was to protect all Americans from destitution. In the twenty-first century, however, we must go one step further by adding a major new clause: universal capitalism. The key to upward mobility and personal wealth creation in the so-called new economy is ownership of capital assets, which explains why the gap between the very wealthy (who own most of our nation's financial assets) and the rest of Americans (who rely primarily on their wages for income) is growing to frightening heights. The solution is to broaden the ownership of financial capital so that all Americans can benefit directly from our growing economy, and have access to the resources required to invest in their own skills development and futures. We therefore propose endowing every American child with individual financial assets from birth.

When it comes to our public sector, the challenge is not so much to shrink or expand government as it is to radically modernize it. As we have seen, much of the popular resentment against government and elected officials stems from our lack of true electoral choices. We therefore propose overhauling our political system via changes that would provide more options to voters, whether they choose to support our existing parties or new parties. Most modern democracies have upgraded their electoral systems in the past half century, and there is no reason why the United States shouldn't follow suit. No less important would be modernizing and revising some of the internal procedures of the House and Senate.

Next, we turn to the one feature of the government that most impacts the daily lives of all Americans: the tax code. In order to solve the Internet sales tax problem and boost national savings rates, we propose eliminating the antiquated patchwork of state sales taxes altogether and replacing it with a simple and progressive national consumption tax, whose revenues would be rebated to all states. The centerpiece of our proposed new federal tax structure is a radically simplified progressive income tax. By eliminating virtually all the tax deductions, expenditures, and loopholes that render our current system so unwieldy, we could create a much fairer tax system for the twenty-first century that is so simple and transparent that most Americans could file their tax returns in a matter of minutes.

As for the all-important task of educating future generations, we favor various ways to broaden school choice and, in the process, increase accountability. But for this to be done in an equitable manner, we argue for the national equalization of school funding on a per pupil basis, and for doing away once and for all with the archaic link between school financing and state and local taxation. This fundamental change could dramatically improve the quality of public education across our land, and pave the way for numerous educational improvements to follow.

In the penultimate chapter, we turn to the future of America's community, and the upcoming challenges to our nation's unity. Whereas our private sector is driven primarily by market forces and our public sector by rules of law, our communal sector is driven more by custom, tradition, and charitable impulse. As this difference in kind suggests, most efforts to rebuild or redirect our communal sector through social engineering of various forms are doomed to failure. Not only does our national community evolve in its own organic way, but it is actually more vibrant and resilient than many social critics would suggest. In our opinion, then, the best way to reinforce the health of our communal sector in the future is indirectly—by removing the primary threats to our national unity so that a healthy community sector can evolve in as unencumbered a manner as possible.

In our opinion, the three greatest risks to our national cohesion in the decades ahead stem from a racial divide, a generational divide, and a potential genetic divide. Starting with the first, we believe the United States should aspire to be a unified melting-pot nation instead of a polarized multicultural one, and we therefore argue for replacing our twentieth-century race-based civil rights paradigm with a new citizen-based model geared to the Information Age. The emerging generational divide arises from two factors: the fiscal pressures that the retirement of the baby boom generation will place on its successors, and the caregiving crises that will accompany an aging America. Part of the solution to the latter problem, we believe, is a permanent expansion of the nonprofit institutions—religious and secular—that provide care for the elderly as well as for the young and the most needy. Looking into our future, one of the most frightening potential divides could be a genetic one, created by the ability of elites to permanently enhance the genetic characteristics of their descendants, permanently locking in advantages that otherwise would last only a generation or two. The best remedy to this threat, we believe, is to carefully distinguish between the types of genetic interventions and biomedical advances that ought to be pursued and embraced, and those that ought to be banned outright.

This book covers a lot of ground. Even so, there are several important topics that we do not address directly. The most prominent relate to the major issues of U.S. foreign policy. Doing justice to the challenges of international trade, the threats of international conflict, and the need for new institutions of global governance in the decades ahead would require another book in itself—if not a series. For all the international forces reshaping the United States, moreover, the nation-state remains the locus of power when it comes to the majority of public policy decisions affecting the daily lives of U.S. citizens. Where these topics are relevant to our discussion, we raise them in the context of specific domestic policy choices.

Our concluding chapter explores the forces that have engendered political transformations and realignments in America's past in order to understand the prospects for comprehensive national reform in the future. Major renovations of our society have usually resulted from a combination of three factors: an external shock to the system (be it economic or military), the emergence of new political alliances, and the availability of compelling new ideas for social reform. In the absence of a crisis, new alliances and new ideas have not always proved to be sufficient.

We are cautiously optimistic, however, for several reasons. First and foremost, the dissatisfaction of the American electorate in recent years has given rise to a broad and diverse base of independent-minded voters who, we argue, might be particularly receptive to the principles and programs of the Radical Center. Next, a new generation and a new elite are ascending in America. Both lack a well-formed political worldview, and could prove to be a ready audience for the institutional and ideological metamorphosis that we propose. In addition, the sheer speed and magnitude of the technological revolution under way could further destabilize today's archaic political and institutional arrangements far sooner than many of us might expect.

Already, the current coalitions that form the bases of the Democratic and Republican Parties are beginning to fissure, perhaps irreparably. For Democrats, the issue of school choice is pitting two of the party's core constituencies against one another: teachers unions, which are overwhelmingly opposed to school choice, and African-Americans, who are overwhelmingly in support. The emerging biotech revolution may have much the same effect on the Republican side, pitting social conservatives, who tend to oppose the genetic modification of human beings, against the free-market libertarian camp, which views genetic technology as the next big commercial bonanza.

Each of these developments suggests that America's next major political realignment may not be far off. That realignment may take the form of the emergence of one or more new national parties. More likely, however, it will result from the transformation of either or both of today's leading parties. The future of American politics may well belong to the major party that is first to renounce its more extreme positions, and embrace a new Radical Centrist agenda.

The time frame for this book is not the next presidential or congressional cycle, but rather the next ten to twenty-five years. Our goal is not to predict the policies of the next administration but to propose the policies of the next generation. We have sought to articulate a coherent, pragmatic, and forward-looking vision of how America's private, public, and communal institutions *should* be transformed and modernized if all Americans are to enjoy the full promise of the Information Age.

Our ultimate hope is that this book will help unite a new set of allies who wish to join together in remaking our nation.

# One

•

# THE FIRST
# THREE AMERICAS

Consider the contrast between three countries. One is a preindustrial, agrarian nation with a population the size of Eritrea's. Nine out of ten people live on farms. The cities—scarcely more than villages by our standards—have arisen chiefly along the coasts and rivers. Roads and other forms of overland transportation are primitive. The distribution of wealth is highly unequal. A small number of landowning families and a few urban merchant families are extremely rich. The majority of the population consists of small farmers and farmworkers laboring on the estates of the rich landlords. The central government is weak and dependent on customs duties for its limited revenues. National politics is constantly agitated by talk of rebellions, and rival politicians—mostly members of the tiny upper class—accuse one another of plotting to dismember the country and planning military coups d'état.

Now consider a second country. This one is much larger, with a population the size of today's Philippines. Its economy is that of a newly industrializing nation. Much of its population is still rural, but the number of urban factory workers and city dwellers is growing rapidly. Primitive, polluting "smokestack industries" are ravaging the landscape while enriching a new elite of millionaires who display their wealth by building palaces and importing fine art from abroad. The national politics of this country is agitated by both sectoral and class struggle. Leaders of the impoverished farming sector denounce those of the booming industrial sector. The government has to send troops to quell violence between striking workers and thugs hired by the corporations. The ruling class, fearing insurrection by those who work in the urban sweatshops and live in filthy, crowded tenements, is building arsenals in the big cities. The standard of living in this country is higher than in the first, and it is steadily rising, but the society is deeply fissured.

The third nation is one of the most populous in the world, with more than a quarter of a billion people. The nation's farming and manufacturing have been almost completely mechanized. Four out of five workers are employed in the service economy. A majority live in single-family homes in spacious suburbs, and the mass possession of automobiles, refrigerators, televisions, and computers has become so commonplace that many families own multiples of each. This country has an enormous, centralized national government that takes in approximately one quarter of the national income, using the largest share to finance public pensions and health care for the retired. The biggest political problem is the alienation of the citizenry, manifest in low rates of voter turnout. This high-tech superpower is also a military superpower, with a ring of worldwide bases coordinated by orbiting satellites.

Three countries as different as these might seem to have little in common. But all three are the United States—in 1800, 1900, and 2000.

In a little more than two centuries, the United States has evolved from an agrarian republic with 4 million inhabitants to a high-tech continental nation with more than 280 million citizens. American history has been marked by catastrophes like the Civil War and by injustices like racial discrimination and extreme social inequality. Nevertheless, by comparison with other countries, the United States has been a remarkable success. What is the secret of America's success, and what kind of society is the United States?

Some argue that the central value of the American tradition is liberty; others, equality; still others, communal solidarity. These schools of thought are all partially correct, but ultimately wrong. The perennial American tradition cannot be defined in terms of any single value. Rather, it consists of a complex of values—values that are complementary, not contradictory. The more accurate formulation would therefore be liberty *and* equality *and* community—each in its appropriate sphere of the market, the state, and civil society.

Most political theories tend to view only a single aspect of society, focusing on just one of its particular sectors and using it to define the totality. For example, socialists have long described the United States as a "capitalist" or "bourgeois" regime, while libertarians are equally focused on the "market," though far more favorably. Yet both capture only the economic dimensions of American life. Likewise, describing the United States as a "democracy" or "liberal democracy" captures only the political aspect. In recent years, it has become fashionable to portray America as a "market democracy," but this neglects the equally important "third sector" of religious, charitable, and voluntary associations that cannot be assigned either to the state or to the market.

Since its inception, the United States has been committed to a division of social authority between three distinct yet interdependent realms of society—market, state, and community—each of which has been governed by its own norms. In the realm of the state, for instance, people should be treated the same on the basis of their common citizenship; to distinguish among them on the basis of their wealth or their personal characteristics is wrong. In the realm of the market, however, what counts most is how much wealth a person has; citizenship is irrelevant, and so are personal characteristics like race and gender. The very personal characteristics that are illegitimate in the realm of governance and the marketplace, however, are central to identity in the realm of the community. The fact that you are a Baptist should not influence how you are treated by the IRS or Wal-Mart, but if you want to go to a summer camp run by and for Mormons, then you can be rejected legitimately because of your religion. One can argue about where to draw the boundaries between these three realms of society and the norms that should govern each. But there is little question that America has been defined since its beginning by its preservation of relatively autonomous public, private, and communal spheres.

The United States is hardly unique in its commitment to a division of social authority between the market, state, and community. To the contrary, we inherited this tripartite arrangement from Britain and other liberal democracies, which developed it in the seventeenth and eighteenth centuries. Nor is the United States unique in its territorial expanse, in its bounty of natural resources, or in the size of its population—these, too, have counterparts elsewhere. If not to these defining features, then to what does the United States owe its remarkable success in progressing from a small agrarian republic into the world's predominant superpower in a mere two hundred years?

The secret to America's success has been its capacity for continuously reinventing its private, public, and communal sectors as circumstances change. These changing circumstances have included technological, demographic, geopolitical, and cultural transformations. Of these, it is the technological changes that have served as the greatest catalysts in each of the previous remakings of America.

Since the founding of the American republic in 1776, there has been one "great transformation" (to use the historian Karl Polanyi's term) and, as lesser waves within that tidal wave, three "revolutions" (to use the conventional word for dramatic technological and economic change). The great transformation has been the shift from an agrarian world order to an industrial world order—from a civilization powered by wood, wind, water, and animal and human muscle, to a civilization of machines powered by minerals (first coal, then, increasingly, petroleum). This transformation has taken place in three phases of technological change: the First Industrial Revolution, the Second Industrial Revolution, and the Third Industrial Revolution (now usually called the Information Revolution). The First Industrial Revolution was based on coal-powered steam engines, while the Second Industrial Revolution was based on the widespread use of electricity and internal combustion engines. The Information Revolution is based not on a new energy source but on a combination of computer information and genetic technologies.

These successive waves of technological and economic change, originating in the North Atlantic nations, have reverberated across the globe. Most of the political, economic, and social structures that existed at the beginning of the industrial era—empires, hereditary monarchies and aristocracies, slavery and serfdom—have been obliterated in the past two centuries. In much of the world, the collapse of the old order under the stress of change produced wars, revolutions, and tyrannies. Two abortive attempts to create a high-tech civilization along illiberal lines, fascism and communism, plunged the world into a series of wars and resulted in the deaths of tens of millions as a result of deliberate genocide or artificial famines.

Unlike most of the polities that existed in 1776, the United States has not only survived and expanded, it has retained its defining character in the process. The secret of our republic's survival and progress has been the ability of the American people to reinvent our institutions repeatedly in order to take full advantage of new technological breakthroughs, such as the introduction of the steam engine in the 1800s and the emergence of electricity and the internal combustion engine in the 1900s. Without the steam-powered factories and railroads that Lincoln used to defeat the Confederacy, for instance, the American republic may well have dissolved. Indeed, the survival of the United States and the end of slavery owe as much to James Watt's invention of the steam engine as to James Madison's theory of federalism.

To simplify a complex history, we might speak of three previous American republics. Each of these was adapted to a particular set of technological, economic, and demographic circumstances; each emerged after a period of political and social turmoil. The first American republic, formed in the aftermath of the American War of Independence, was in place by the early nineteenth century. It was a decentralized agrarian republic that lasted until the Civil War. The Civil War and Reconstruction produced the second republic, a regime better suited to the conditions of the First Industrial Revolution. The next wave of change, the Second Industrial Revolution of the late nineteenth century, gave birth to a third American republic, defined by the New Deal consensus that coalesced between the 1930s and the 1960s.

America's historic challenge has been to continuously reinvent all three sectors of society—market, state, and community—without allowing any one of these to overpower or stifle the others. Despite occasional disasters and failures, we Americans have proven ourselves to be remarkably successful in periodically remaking our republic in response to changing conditions, while simultaneously improving all three sectors of our society—making our government more democratic, making our economy more dynamic and inclusive, and making the associational life of the American community richer and more diverse. It is this dynamic capacity for institutional reinvention that has enabled us to not only take full advantage of new technologies and circumstances, but, increasingly, to ourselves become a seedbed of technological and social innovation.

It is time now for another historic remaking of our nation's private, public, and communal realms. As we have seen, the New Deal version of the American republic under which we still live is rapidly being rendered obsolete by the new technological, economic, and demographic circumstances of the twenty-first century. The challenge of sketching a fourth republic suitable to the new realities of Information Age America is the subject of the following chapters. In this chapter, we will sketch the historic evolution of American society from 1800 to 2000. Only when we understand how America has reinvented itself in the past will we be prepared to reinvent America in the future.

By one of the ironies of history, the thirteen colonies that became the United States seceded from the British empire at the very moment that Britain was becoming the laboratory of the Industrial Revolution. Far from being one of the first societies of the dawning industrial era, however, the first republic of the United States—in the late eighteenth and early nineteenth centuries—was one of the last countries to be born in the final years of agrarian civilization. A few visionaries—among them Alexander Hamilton, George Washington's Secretary of the Treasury—understood the importance of the new, steam-powered industrial economy arising in Britain, and wanted the United States to become a great manufacturing power. But the Hamiltonian vision of America's future was defeated by the rival vision of Thomas Jefferson and his allies, whose hopes that the United States would remain a republic of farmers resonated with America's rural majority.

The American economy was almost wholly agrarian well into the nineteenth century. In 1790, only 5 percent of the 4 million inhabitants of the United States (including 757,000 nonwhites, most of them slaves) lived in urban areas with 2,500 or more residents. When Alexis de Tocqueville visited the United States in 1831, 10 out of every 11 Americans lived on family farms. In its technology and economy, the United States of 1800 was closer to ancient

Greece and Rome or medieval Europe than it was to the United States of 1850 or 1900 or 1950. The major sources of energy were still wind and water. Mills still had to be located on streams, and just as in Antiquity and the Middle Ages, canals were the major infrastructure projects. Before 1840 inland waterways like the Erie Canal were much more important than railroads in providing transportation. Steamboats made it possible to extend commerce up previously unnavigable rivers; between 1817 and 1840 the number of steamboats in the trans-Appalachian West grew from 17 to 536. Nonetheless, travel remained so difficult that Jefferson believed it would take centuries to settle the territory of the Louisiana Purchase, and speculated that Anglo-American settlers on the remote Pacific coast would form new countries.

The market in the first American republic was rudimentary and weak. Modern capitalism is based on national and international markets, a complex division of labor among workers, and large-scale economic enterprises. All of these were missing or poorly developed from the 1780s until the mid-nineteenth century. Corporate capitalism and banking were stuck at a primitive stage. Joint-stock corporations usually had to be chartered for specific public purposes by state legislatures—a relic of the medieval idea of the corporation as a monopoly chartered by the king. The formation of an integrated national market was retarded by the powerful tradition of states' rights localism. Despite the political independence of the United States from Britain, the southern plantation economy in effect was part of the British economy. Cotton, which displaced wool as the chief raw material for the British textile industry by 1801, could only be grown in tropical climates like that found in the Caribbean and the American South. The South became Britain's principal supplier, and before the Civil War the South got most of its capital from Britain.

In the first republic of the United States, the government sector was as undeveloped as the business sector. Indeed, in most respects the state governments were more important than the federal government. The main source of federal revenue was the tariff, a tax on imported goods. The largest federal government agency was the post office, which provided presidents with a source of patronage appointments. The federal presence in the economy was minor. The states, rather than the federal government, paid for most infrastructure projects like canals and early railroads.

The United States greatly expanded its continental territory during this period—usually by means that did not require a powerful federal army. For example, in 1804, Jefferson bought the Louisiana Territory from Napoleon, and filibusters (American settlers covertly encouraged by U.S. leaders) detached Florida and then Texas from Spanish and Mexican rule. There was a small, highly competent U.S. military, but Jefferson and his successors rejected Hamilton's plan for a federal military academy; West Point was a scaled-down institution that focused on civil engineering. The American military effort in the Mexican War of 1846–48 was handicapped by reliance on the militias, whose members tended to be disorderly and insubordinate.

In civil rights, localism prevailed. The federal Bill of Rights—the first ten amendments to the 1787 federal Constitution—bound only the federal government. There was no uniform standard of U.S. citizenship, which meant that one had to be a citizen of a specific state to be a citizen of the republic. This enabled the southern states to exclude black slaves from citizenship. Among the white population, citizenship and voting rights were gradually extended by the individual states. By the 1840s, most states had abolished property qualifications for voting and religious tests for holding public office. But suffrage was still limited to adult white men. Racist immigration laws, meanwhile, limited legal immigration and naturalization to "free white persons." The informal conception of American identity in this era held that the United States was an Anglo-American Protestant nation.

The first American republic, then, was a largely agrarian society in which extensive development, in the form of expansion of the plantation and family farm economy to the South and West, took the place of intensive development, in the form of industrialization. This suited the interests and values of the southern slave-holding elite, which succeeded in adding to its southern base enough allies among the electorate in the North and Midwest to dominate federal politics between 1800 and 1860.

Nevertheless, long-term technological, economic, and demographic trends were working slowly to undermine the first American republic and to prepare for the emergence of the second. The most important of these trends were regional industrialization and large-scale European immigration, which steadily shifted the balance of power in American national politics away from the conservative, agrarian South and toward the modernizing North.

By the eve of the Civil War, both manufacturing and agriculture were being industrialized in the northern states. Eli Whitney pioneered the use of interchangeable parts in making small arms in the 1790s; a decade earlier, another New Englander, Oliver Evans, had pioneered assembly-line techniques in a water-powered flour mill. During its industrialization, which began to accelerate in the 1840s and 1850s, the United States followed the British pattern: The textile industry was the first to be dominated by large-scale factories. The number of people employed in New England textile factories rose from one in a hundred in 1816 to one in seven by 1840. After the 1840s, factories powered by steam rather than water began to be used in the manufacture of iron, glass and distilling, machines and machine tools. Many of these factories were located in Pennsylvania, where anthracite coal, a cheap fuel for steam engines, began to be mined in the 1830s. Railroad construction, which accelerated in the 1850s, began to connect factories with their markets and their sources of raw materials.

The Industrial Revolution was also applied to agriculture. By the 1850s, John Deere was mass-producing plows while Cyrus Mc-

Cormick was mass-producing mechanical reapers. The fact that northern agriculture depended on expensive free labor rather than on cheap slave labor stimulated mechanization. In the wheat-growing North, horse-drawn machines were being used in every stage of farming by 1860. Between 1840 and 1860, the share of agricultural workers declined, while the share of workers in manufacturing and construction rose. By 1860, the Northeast had 71 percent of U.S. manufacturing capability.

Demographic shifts were just as important to the outcome of the Civil War. In the decades before the Civil War, the North gained an advantage in population, thanks to European immigration, to which Germany and Ireland contributed the most. Although the birthrate in the United States declined steadily between 1800 and 1860, the overall U.S. population increased to 31 million. In part this was the result of growing immigration from western Europe, which rose from 250,000 between 1782 and 1819, to 700,000 between 1820 and 1840, and then skyrocketed to 4.2 million between 1840 and 1860, inspiring a political backlash in the form of nativism by Anglo-American Protestants.

Because almost all of the German, Irish, and other European immigration went to the northern states, the share of the U.S. population accounted for by southern whites steadily declined. The election of Abraham Lincoln—a regional Greater New England candidate who did not receive a single southern electoral vote—convinced many southerners of the danger that a new northern-midwestern majority would marginalize the South in politics and move to abolish southern slavery. When the South attempted to secede, the North's combination of superior industry and demographic advantage proved decisive in the Civil War. Without the steam-powered factories and the steam-powered trains that Lincoln used to defeat the Confederacy, and without federal armies swelled by German and Irish immigrants, the feeble central government in Washington might have been unable to hold the United States together.

As the most powerful elite in national politics, the southern ruling class was replaced by a new northern elite based in New England and the Midwest. From 1865 until 1932, Lincoln and his heirs in the northern Republican Party renovated the United States, turning the agrarian first republic into a second republic adapted to the first industrial era. During the Reconstruction Era of 1865–76, the American republic was reformed to strengthen individual liberty and federal authority at the expense of the autonomy of state and local communities.

"As I would not be a slave, so I would not be a master. This expresses my idea of democracy," Lincoln had declared during his debates with Stephen A. Douglas. The transformation of the United States from a loose confederation of semiautonomous communities into a nation-state based on individual rights was symbolized by the transformation of former slaves into American citizens. Slavery was abolished by the Thirteenth Amendment, and the Fourteenth Amendment established a national law of citizenship for the first time, retroactively bestowing citizenship on all persons born on American soil. By the 1870s, however, the attempt to use federal power to defend the rights of black Americans in the South was abandoned. Formal and informal racial segregation became the rule. But the cause of women's suffrage slowly advanced in the states, finally succeeding on the federal level with the adoption of the Nineteenth Amendment in 1920, which provided all American women with the vote.

The limited progress in the federal enforcement of civil rights was accompanied by a permanent expansion of the authority and capability of the federal government. Although the Grand Army of the Republic was the largest and most powerful army in the world when Lee surrendered to Grant at Appomattox, the deep distrust of standing armies by the American people led to the demobilization of the federal forces, so that by the end of Reconstruction in 1877, there were only 24,000 U.S. troops. The number of federal civilian employees in 1871—6,222—was only twice the prewar number. Nevertheless, the Civil War had permanently changed the federal government.

Before the war, more than 80 percent of federal revenue came from tariffs; after 1865, the amount coming from internal sources like excise taxes and inheritance taxes never dropped below 32 percent. Although the wartime income tax was abolished in the 1870s, the Bureau of Internal Revenue, created by the Internal Revenue Act of 1862, remained. The federal government also began to issue bonds. The federal veterans pension program became the first comprehensive federal social welfare program before the New Deal. Largely as a result of expenditures on pensions, the percentage of U.S. government spending at all levels accounted for by federal expenditures rose from 13 percent in 1860 to around 30 percent in the last decades of the nineteenth century.

Even as federal armies were clashing with Confederate troops, the Lincoln Republicans and their allies in the North founded a number of new federal departments—among them, the Department of Agriculture in 1862 and the Bureau of Immigration in 1863. Congress passed the Homestead Act in 1862 and the Morrill Agricultural College Act in the same year. The modernization of the federal government was accompanied by increases in the budgets and activities of the state and municipal governments. The state and local police forces were modernized and professionalized. The federal government grew in size and sophistication. By today's standards, government in the post–Civil War United States was still small in scale and limited in scope, but by the standards of Jefferson's first republic, Lincoln's second republic was ruled by a Leviathan state.

In the economic sector, the Lincoln Republicans rebuilt the United States as a successful nation-state of the first industrial era. High tariffs, by blocking British and European competition, helped

America's infant industries develop. In addition, reforms in the "software" of capitalism aided American industry. The rise of corporate capitalism was as much the cause as the result of the Second Industrial Revolution of the late nineteenth century. Before the Civil War, most corporations were chartered by state legislatures to perform a specific purpose, such as operating turnpikes or toll bridges. Only in the second half of the nineteenth century did reforms in corporate law encourage the formation of corporations that could grow into enormous industrial enterprises. These giant corporations, directed by managers distinct from shareholders, were able to raise the vast pools of capital needed to invest in new industries like electric power generation, automobile manufacturing, and petrochemicals and to modernize railroads and factories.

The success of industrial capitalism depended not only on innovative corporate law but on the modernization of the U.S. banking system. In 1815 there had been only two hundred commercial banks in the United States; in 1900 there were twelve thousand. The ability to raise funds from commercial banks and other sources made possible the exploitation of new technologies: the refrigerator car (the basis of Philip Armour's meat-packing fortune), the Bessemer process in steel production (the basis of Andrew Carnegie's success), and improved technology in oil recovery (the foundation of John D. Rockefeller's fortune).

The economic success of the second American republic was remarkable indeed. By the early twentieth century, the United States had emerged as the leading industrial nation of the world. The new national economy, as much as the enhanced federal government, gradually integrated Americans across the continent into a single society, vindicating the vision of the Unionists of the Civil War era, like Henry Bellows of New York: "This American people is not a set of civilized squatters upon a common territory, a school of wriggling fish accidentally caught in the federal net—an aggregation of petty communities, confined to some political kaleidoscope, to which a strong hand at every election may give a shake that alters its whole aspect and identity; but instead of this, it is a *Nation*."

The very success of Lincoln's generation and those who followed in building a second American republic adapted to the Industrial Age created new problems for American society. If the greatest weakness of the first American republic had been the majoritarian tyranny of caste-ridden rural communities unchecked by an adequate central government or an emancipatory market economy, following the Civil War the major domestic threat to our nation's stability and harmony was an expanding industrial economy and the growing urban population that served it. The resulting social and political crises threatened to overwhelm the institutions of the other two sectors of society, the community and the state.

This period of crisis had been foreseen. In the 1820s, former president James Madison, one of the few survivors of the founding generation, had turned his thoughts to the implications of economic development and demographic change for America's future. Eventually, he predicted, the supply of cheap farmland on the frontier would be exhausted, and a growing number of Americans would move to the cities and find work in manufacturing. At some point, most Americans would be "without landed or other equivalent property and without the means or hope of acquiring it." Madison predicted a dangerous increase in social inequality between "the great Capitalists in Manufactures and Commerce" and "indigent labourers." The great challenge to republican government caused by urbanization and industrialization, he predicted, would come in "a century or a little more." He made that prediction in 1829. Exactly a century later, in 1929, the stock market crashed, causing the Great Depression and the end of the era of laissez-faire industrial capitalism in the United States and the world as a whole. The historian Drew R. McCoy writes that "as Madison understood it, the challenge of future generations of Americans would be to redefine the republican revolution by adapting its basic spirit and principles to a form of society" that was radically different from that of the past.

The technological transformation was the Second Industrial Revolution. Even as the United States was perfecting the technologies of the British-derived First Industrial Revolution, the Second Industrial Revolution, pioneered largely in the United States and Germany as well as Britain, began in the 1880s and 1890s. The key innovations of the Second Industrial Revolution were two energy technologies: electricity and the internal combustion engine.

The electrical revolution depended on several kinds of machines: electricity-generating turbines, electric motors, and electric batteries. Combined with electrical transformers, which permit voltages and currents to be modified and transmitted long distances, these devices produced the basic infrastructure of contemporary civilization—the electrical power grid, which permitted factories to be located far from sources of power, and enabled streetcars and electric trains to begin to disperse populations to growing suburbs.

The other transformative technology of the Second Industrial Revolution was the internal combustion engine. Despite rivalry from electric cars and even steam-powered cars, the gasoline-powered internal combustion engine became the major power source for cars, trucks, motorcycles, aircraft, and watercraft in the twentieth century. Completing the ensemble of Second Industrial Revolution technologies were new communications media. To the telegraph, an invention of the first industrial era, were added the telephone and the wireless media of radio and television.

The demographic changes of the late nineteenth and early twentieth centuries were just as dramatic. America's immigration regime—made even more exclusive by a series of Asian exclusion acts—continued to limit immigration to whites. As a result, waves of immigration from Europe filled the continental domain. The "new immigrants" from eastern and southern Europe—Italians, Greeks,

Jews, Poles, Czechs, and others—came to eclipse the "old immigrants," the Germans and Irish. Just as a wave of German and Irish immigration that began in the 1840s had produced a nativist backlash, so the new immigrants produced hostility, not only among Anglo-Americans but among many assimilated German- and Irish-Americans as well. Before large-scale European immigration was cut off by a political alliance of Anglo-Americans and Old Immigrants in the 1920s, however, it had transformed the United States not only in its ethnic makeup but in its size. In 1791, the U.S. population of 4 million had been only 2 percent of that of Europe and Russia; by 1860, the American population of 32 million had surpassed that of Britain, Italy, and Spain and was 11 percent of the population of Europe and Russia combined. As a result of European immigration in addition to native fertility, between 1860 and 1900 the U.S. population more than doubled to 76 million.

Another migration was just as important—the migration of native Americans from farms into towns and cities. The Census of 1930 was the first to show that more than half of all Americans lived in urban areas rather than on farms. In 1880 more than half the American workforce had been employed in agriculture; by the 1930s fewer than one in five Americans still worked in agriculture. The growing number of factory and office workers, unlike farmers, had no economic resources to fall back on during economic downturns. As natives from farms and European immigrants poured into crowded cities, the United States experienced a wave of social breakdown and disorder and crime.

These technological changes and demographic shifts came at a time when American leaders were still struggling with the consequences of the last reinvention of the American republic. The industrialization of the United States following the Civil War had been accompanied by enormous human suffering. In the South, blacks along with the white rural poor were reduced to debt peonage. In the industrial areas, workers found that the courts and politicians usually sided with employers to battle union organization. The 1870s and 1880s saw the greatest labor violence in American history. At the same time, farmers were hurt by global depressions and victimized by the railroads on which they depended for their livelihoods. The attempts of some industrialists to manipulate prices by means of trusts provoked outrage and fear that American democracy would give way to plutocracy.

Reformers in both the community sector and the government sector in the late 1800s and early 1900s struggled to devise new ways to deal with the problems created by the dynamism of industrial capitalism, and by the mass migration to the cities. In the community sector, new organizations like the YMCA and Boy Scouts and Girl Scouts helped to assimilate enormous populations of immigrant and rural children and youth to middle-class norms, while amateur baseball, football, and bowling leagues provided working-class and rural Americans with new forms of recreation and community. This period also saw the rise of fraternities and sororities for college students and for adults—the Lions Club, the Elks Club, the Rotary Club and the rest of the menagerie (the Shriners or Masons had been around since the early republic). Charitable organizations like the Salvation Army along with church-based missions and hospitals proliferated, as civil society expanded to cope with the new problems of the industrial order. The dark side of the American community was epitomized by the Ku Klux Klan, which underwent a renaissance in the 1920s.

Although it could ameliorate some of the ills of society, the community sector could not begin to address all of the problems associated with industrialization and immigration. It was necessary for the government sector as well to expand in order to take on new responsibilities.

One of the earliest governmental responses to industrialization was the extension of the state's responsibility for education. During the early decades of the American republic, educational reformers concentrated in the Northeast promoted the "common school" or

THE FIRST THREE AMERICAS

public school movement. A common school education often ended with the sixth grade. The skills it provided—basic literacy and numeracy—were adequate for an agrarian society but not for an industrial society. As a result, reformers in the late nineteenth and early twentieth centuries sought to extend the period of primary education. Child labor laws and compulsory school attendance laws were combined with the spread of junior high and high schools. The Ivy League universities remained the preserve of the upper class and a few scholarship students, but land-grant universities in the states and local community colleges provided low-cost higher education to growing numbers of Americans, preparing them for the challenges of an urban, industrial society.

But it was not enough for Americans to be prepared by universal, compulsory primary and secondary education to succeed in the new urban, industrial society. They also needed protection from destructive forces in the new industrial economy. On the Right, laissez-faire conservatives believed that government should refrain from interfering with the "laws of the market." On the extreme Left, socialists proposed government control of all large-scale industry. Agrarian populists, led by tribunes like William Jennings Bryan, sought a restoration of the Jeffersonian ideal of a republic of small farmers and craftsmen—through government control of railroads and some industries, if necessary. Progressive reformers like Theodore Roosevelt and Woodrow Wilson, based in the educated middle class, were equally appalled by socialist and populist radicalism and by the brutality of corporations crushing labor organizers. The Progressive answer was strong government carried out by a nonpartisan, educated elite.

The Progressives managed to enact a number of significant reforms. Some took the form of state legislation—the Oregon ten-hour laws, the Massachusetts 1912 minimum wage law, the 1910 New York compulsory workmen's compensation act, and child-labor laws. Progressives also enacted important federal legislation—the 1906

Pure Food and Drug Act, the railroad regulation embodied in the 1906 Hepburn Act, the 1910 Mann-Elkin Act, and the Clayton Antitrust Act and Federal Trade Act, both in 1914. Theodore Roosevelt passed conservation legislation, and Woodrow Wilson established the Federal Reserve. The Progressives also pushed through political reforms, like the secret ballot; the federal income tax amendment, ratified in 1913; and, in the same year, the Seventeenth Amendment, which provided for direct election of senators.

The third major transformation of American government and society, however, came during the New Deal period, between the Great Depression and the 1960s. Franklin Roosevelt's original New Deal programs such as Social Security began the third founding of the American republic. Then in the 1940s, Harry Truman's Fair Deal gave us the G.I. Bill and the first federal civil rights reforms. And in the 1960s, Lyndon Johnson's Great Society gave us not only Medicare, Medicaid, Head Start, and student loans but also the most sweeping civil rights legislation since Reconstruction. Combined, these programs of the New Deal era, ratified by Republican presidents including Eisenhower, Nixon, and Reagan, gave rise to a fundamental transformation of all three sectors of American society—in effect, establishing the third republic of the United States.

The New Deal is often misunderstood by both liberals and conservatives who think of it solely in terms of government entitlement programs like Social Security. The New Dealers, however, devoted as much effort to building a new technological infrastructure for industry, agriculture, and housing as they did to projects of social reform. Indeed, the Second Industrial Revolution itself created a need for both federal and state governments to lay down a whole new infrastructure for a changing economy. In the nineteenth century, America's economic progress had depended on the construction of a web of railroads. In the first part of the twentieth century, electric power stations and grids and highways replaced railroads as the basis of a new economic infrastructure upon which business would depend in the future but that only government could establish.

Building on the tradition of Progressive state government supports for massive hydroelectric projects in states like California and New York, the Roosevelt administration promoted rural electrification by means of joint public-private power systems like the Tennessee Valley Authority (TVA) and the Lower Colorado River Authority (LCRA) in Texas. New Dealers also advocated a system of national highways for a new society in which most Americans had the opportunity to own their own homes and their own cars. During the New Deal era, Congress also enacted sweeping reforms of banking laws, which made it easier for consumers and small businesses to acquire capital. In short, the New Deal project for modernizing the national infrastructure of power generation, transportation, and credit was as comprehensive and ultimately successful as the Lincoln Republican program of railroad-building, tariff-based industrialization, and national banking had been.

In the realm of the marketplace, the New Deal produced a national social contract, based on the federal government's assumption of responsibility for welfare. FDR linked social insurance measures to the helplessness of workers in an industrialized economy: "People want some safeguard against misfortunes which cannot be wholly eliminated in this man-made world of ours." Roosevelt made it clear that his goal was to save the industrial market economy from its own excesses: "I am fighting Communism. . . . I want to save our system, the capitalistic system; to save it is to give some heed to world thought of today. I want to equalize the distribution of wealth."

Among the New Deal programs were both means-tested programs for the poor and universal entitlements. The most important of the universal entitlements was Social Security, enacted into law in 1935; it was later joined by Medicare in 1965. By the end of the twentieth century, these two programs had all but eliminated poverty among the elderly—at the unanticipated price of expanding to absorb an ever-increasing percentage of the federal budget. The growth in the number of aged Americans was the primary cause of the rise of federal social spending between World War II and the present. Subsequent efforts to establish government-based universal health care met political defeat; in its place, an employer-based system of health insurance, supported by federal tax law, sprang up in the 1940s, more by accident than by design.

In addition to establishing a federal social contract to protect American citizens against economic turmoil, the Roosevelt administration also solved one long-standing economic problem—the recurrent crises in American agriculture—by instituting a system of price supports. Roosevelt also sided with industrial workers by passing pro-union legislation, but this was gutted by pro-business legislation after World War II, and labor unions, after peaking in the 1950s, began their long decline.

The New Deal and World War II created a modern, centralized, powerful national government in the United States, comparable in scope, if not always in scale, to those of the industrial democracies of Europe and East Asia. Before the New Deal, state and local taxes were higher as a percentage of total government taxes in the United States than the federal contribution, which amounted to only one third of total revenue. Since the 1930s, the proportions have been reversed; two out of every three dollars going to government have gone to the federal government. In 1946, the number of federal civilian employees was more than three times the number in 1929.

The growth in federal authority was even greater than the growth in federal employment or spending. The civil rights revolution eliminated racial segregation in the United States and replaced America's racist immigration policy with a new, race-neutral immigration regime. From the 1960s until the 1980s, when a backlash set in, federal judges used the enhanced legitimacy they had gained during the civil rights era to extend federal authority in many areas previously considered the domain of the states, like family and sexual legislation. The Supreme Court's ruling in *Roe* v. *Wade* in 1973, which established a federal constitutional right to abortion, was the high-water mark of federal judicial activism. While federal judges were extending federal authority, Congress was stealthily expanding federal power by funding more and more state and local programs. By 2000, as much as a quarter of state and local government activities were funded by federal grants. Congress expanded federal authority even further, by means of "unfunded mandates"—federal rules imposed on the states without federal funding to assist in implementation.

In addition to expanding its responsibility for welfare, the U.S. federal government expanded its capability for warfare. Between 1914 and 1989, the world was almost perpetually in a state of hot or cold war. The decline of British imperial power unleashed a competition among the United States, Germany (as Imperial Germany and then as National Socialist Germany), and the Soviet Union to be the leading military power in the world. The United States and its allies defeated the two German bids for global domination, and then withstood the expansionism of the Soviet-led communist bloc between 1945 and 1989. In the course of these struggles, the peacetime military and intelligence capabilities of the American government were permanently enhanced.

The expansion of the office economy at the expense of the factory and farm economies—a process already well under way by the middle of the twentieth century—permitted women to enter the workforce en masse, albeit most frequently as typists, receptionists, executive secretaries, telephone operators, and sales clerks. After World War II, various forces broke down traditional barriers to the presence of women in the professions and politics. By the end of the twentieth century, a majority of married women as well as men worked outside the home—almost all of them in the service sector, which by 2000 provided four out of five jobs. This revolutionary transformation in gender roles owed as much to the control over fertility that contraception gave women and to their liberation from drudgery through the mechanization of the household as it did to feminist philosophy.

Suburban life, once a luxury of the rich, became the norm first for the middle class and then for working-class Americans. By the 1980s, thanks in large part to federal subsidies for home ownership and highway construction, more Americans lived in suburbs than in old-fashioned urban neighborhoods. (Trapped behind in decaying cities that had lost affluent taxpayers to the suburbs was a small and suffering population of the urban poor.) In 1940, only half of the houses lacked complete indoor plumbing, while one in five did not have a telephone. By 1997, however, almost all households owned color TVs, refrigerators, and gas or electric ranges. And by 2000 nearly two in three American households had at least one personal computer. As a result of the successful reinvention of the United States in the New Deal era, the United States produced the world's first mass middle class.

If the second industrial era has a monument that symbolizes it—the way the pyramids testify to ancient Egypt or the palace of Versailles evokes the ancien régime—it is Rockefeller Center in Manhattan. The location is significant; if London was the heart of the first industrial civilization, and California's Silicon Valley the focus of the Information Age, New York was the core of the second industrial era. The Rockefellers, who built the complex, owed their fortune to oil—the indispensable fuel of the internal combustion engines that transformed the economy and society in the second industrial era. The ziggurat skyscrapers of the complex were themselves made possible by electric motors that permitted elevators to go up dozens of floors quickly and safely. Murals inside depict heroic workers building a dam, a source of hydroelectric power that, transmitted through the electrical grids, brought artificial light and energy to countless homes and offices in the United States and abroad. The very name of the entertainment complex housed by Rockefeller Center from its inception refers to one of the communications technologies that transformed civilization in the twentieth century: Radio City Music Hall.

The Soviet dictator V. I. Lenin famously declared: "The age of steam is the age of the bourgeoisie, the age of electricity is the age of socialism." He was mistaken; the age of electricity turned out to be the age of national and multinational corporate capitalism and the liberal democratic welfare state. Fortunately for humanity, Franklin Roosevelt's United States, not Lenin's and Stalin's Soviet Union or Hitler's Germany, was the model of the technological society that prevailed.

During the 1932 presidential campaign, Roosevelt gave a remarkable speech at the San Francisco Commonwealth Club in which he outlined his view of the stages of American history. The idea of minimal government had been plausible, he argued, in the agrarian republic of Jefferson and his successors, in "the day of the individual against the system, the day in which individualism was made the great watchword of American life . . . Depressions could, and did, come and go; but they could not alter the fundamental fact that most of the people lived partly by selling their labor and partly by extracting their livelihood from the soil, so that starvation and dislocation were practically impossible." But industrialization changed everything: "It was in the middle of the nineteenth century that a new force was released and a new dream created. The force was what is called the industrial revolution, the advance of steam and machinery and the rise of the forerunners of the modern industrial plant. The dream was the dream of an economic machine, able to raise the standard of living for everyone; to bring luxury within the reach of the humblest; to annihilate distance by steam power and later by electricity; and to release everyone from the drudgery of the heaviest manual labor."

Roosevelt made it clear that industrialization, for all its costs, was preferable to the alternative of perpetuating an agrarian society: "So manifest were the advantages of the machine age, however, that the United States fearlessly, cheerfully, and, I think, rightly, accepted the bitter with the sweet." As a response to the new challenges of the Second Industrial Revolution, Roosevelt rejected the idea of turning "the clock back, to destroy the large corporations and to return to the time when every man owned his individual small business." On the contrary, "We did not think because national government had become a threat in the eighteenth century that therefore we should abandon the principle of national government. Nor today should we abandon the principle of strong economic units called corporations, merely because their power is susceptible of easy abuse." Instead, "the task of government in its relation to business is to assist the development of an economic declaration of rights, an economic constitutional order." Roosevelt's term for this economic order was the "social contract."

The future four-term president understood, as James Madison had understood a century earlier, that our republic and its institutions must be fundamentally reinvented as our nation's circumstances change. Were he alive today, he might be the first to argue that the New Deal consensus of which he was the original architect has now outlived its usefulness. Indeed, the very words he used back in 1932 to describe the central disjuncture of his time, and to call for a remaking of the American republic, are once again as timely and urgent at the dawn of the twenty-first century: "New conditions impose new requirements upon government and those who conduct government. . . . The terms of that contract are as old as the Republic, and as new as the economic order. . . . Faith in America, faith in our tradition of personal responsibility, faith in our institutions, faith in ourselves demand that we recognize the new terms of the old social contract."

Today, as in the past, technologically driven changes in the economy, as well as long-term demographic shifts, are undermining the assumptions on which our familiar and long-established institutions are based. The tectonic forces shaping Information Age America are by now well known: the twin revolutions in information technology and biotechnology, the globalization of trade and commerce, the latest wave of immigration, and the rapid graying of our population. While these transformations are well under way, our political leaders have barely begun to grapple with their full implications, or to consider how to use our present moment of great-power peace to rebuild the institutions of America's market, government, and community once again.

No more than in the past will the successful renovation of America be the automatic result of technologically driven change in the economy and society. Those technological determinists who believe that the new technologies of the Information Age will inevitably produce more democracy, equality, and prosperity have their theory of history backward. Technology is the result of freedom, not its cause. Political freedom made commercial capitalism possible; commercial capitalism, by encouraging science and technology, made industrial capitalism possible; industrial capitalism, by freeing the majority of people first from the farm and then from the factory, made the enlargement of the citizenry possible. This is a virtuous cycle. But there are vicious cycles of political tyranny and economic stagnation as well.

If we learn anything from the turbulent and bloody history of the first two centuries of the Industrial Age, it is that politics, in the broadest sense of conscious social choice, is constrained by technology but not determined by it. New technologies are inherently neutral and can be used for good and evil alike. Sailing ships were used to transport European settlers to a better life in the Americas, and African slaves to plantations in the Americas. Franklin Roosevelt used radio broadcasts to restore the faith of the American people in democracy during the depths of the Depression; Hitler used radio to rally the Germans for genocidal warfare. The same computer technology that permits Chinese dissidents to communicate with one another permits Chinese authorities to monitor dissent. And biotechnology labs that hold the promise of dramatically improving human life also hold the peril of developing dangerous new bioweapons. All technologies that can enlarge human freedom and prosperity also have the potential to be used in the service of tyranny and exploitation.

It is not sufficient, then, to adapt our nation to the new technologies and circumstances of the twenty-first century—all societies, the bad as well as the good, will eventually do so. The challenge facing us, rather, is to reinvent our republic in the service of perennial American values, so as to expand the liberty, equality, and unity of our people in the new circumstances of the Information Age. The fact that Americans have succeeded in doing so in the past is no guarantee that we will succeed this time. Success was never inevitable. The Founding Fathers might have failed to win independence from Britain, or, having succeeded at that, might have failed to devise a workable constitution for the new country. The Union might have fallen apart in the Civil War. The proponents of the New Deal might have lost the struggle to define mid-century America to their rivals on the libertarian Right or the socialist or populist Left, with greater class and racial division or economic stagnation as the result.

A fourth American republic of some kind will emerge in the decades ahead, but its character and details will be determined by political struggles. Whether emerging technologies bolster or diminish our freedom and security, whether the gains of the new economy are widely shared or narrowly concentrated, whether there is a renaissance in American politics or continued disengagement, whether racial and generational divisions fade or grow sharper will depend on the relative strength of political coalitions, each guided by a vision of the American future. In the chapters that follow, we provide our vision of the new America that we believe should be built on the still-strong foundations of the old.

# Two

•

# New Economy, New Social Contract

In 1707, the French inventor Denis Papin, one of the creators of the steam engine, achieved a major breakthrough by building the first steam-powered boat. On his way through the German state of Hanover to London, where he planned to demonstrate his marvelous invention, Papin was ambushed by the Boatmen's Guild. The rowers, afraid that steamboats would put them out of work, seized Papin's model paddle wheeler and destroyed it. Papin died a few years later. Thanks in part to the Boatmen's Guild, the use of steam power in shipping was delayed for a century.

The fate of Papin's steamboat should remind us of an uncomfortable truth: A society may resist technological innovation and economic progress unless it is capable of mitigating the pain that innovation inflicts on its workers. Recognizing this, every advanced capitalist nation assembled an elaborate system of social insurance by the middle of the twentieth century. The political Left has often justified social insurance by invoking the ideals of social equality and civic solidarity, while the political Right has often attacked it on the grounds that it stifled individual responsibility and initiative. Both sides, however, have missed the point. Social insurance saved capitalism from a political backlash that, in different countries, would have taken the form of populist, fascist, or socialist movements determined to slow or stop technological progress and economic transformation.

This lesson is particularly important to the United States at the dawn of the twenty-first century because our economic prospects and our standard of living depend more and more on constant technological progress and global trade, both of which tend to be highly dislocating. "Creative destruction" is the name that the twentieth-century economist Joseph Schumpeter gave to the "process of industrial mutation . . . that incessantly revolutionizes the economic structure from within, incessantly destroying the old one, incessantly creating a new one."

Since the Industrial Age began in the late eighteenth century, there have been three tidal waves of creative destruction, each generated by a cluster of transformative technologies: the steam engine in the first industrial era, the electric motor and the internal combustion engine in the second industrial era, and now the information-technology and biotechnology revolutions of the emerging information era. During the first industrial era, for instance, railroads put flatboats out of business, while interstate trucking all but wiped out the railroads in the United States in the second industrial era. In the very same way, the invention and diffusion of the newest technologies require the destruction of many techniques, vocations, companies, and even some entire industries. The only difference between past and future waves of creative destruction is that the pace is accelerating. To see why, we need to understand a little more about the basic nature of what is now commonly referred to as the "new economy."

When the term *new economy* was introduced in the 1980s, it referred to the flat, highly decentralized, and networked organizational structures that are best suited to responding to frequent market changes through constant innovation and product customization. Since then, however, the term has taken on a dizzying array of new meanings and connotations, some reasonable, others far less so. Among the more reasonable is the observation that rapid technological change seems to have reduced the historic tradeoff between inflation and unemployment, meaning that in the new economy we may be able to have less of both at the same time. Emboldened by this new finding, however, some in the mid- to late 1990s began espousing the far less tenable proposition that the new economy had somehow eliminated the business cycle altogether, if not the need to be concerned about such "fundamentals" as profitability. By the turn of the century, this line of reasoning was used by many investors to justify outlandish stock valuations—which in turn gave rise to a spectacular run up in the tech-heavy NASDAQ, followed by an equally spectacular crash. Suffice it to say that this particular interpretation of the new economy did not withstand the test of time.

Another common misconception associated with the new economy is the belief that there are "new" and "old" sectors of the economy as such, and that economic progress therefore entails eliminating older ones in favor of newer ones. Much of the conventional discussion of the new economy at the end of the twentieth century seemed to suggest that the high-tech sector was itself the be-all and end-all of economic progress, destined to eventually replace all other sectors, which were considered dinosaurs belonging to the so-called old economy. Several decades from now, this type of thinking will seem as foolish as an argument at the dawn of the Second Industrial Revolution that motor-making industries would somehow take over the whole economy. To the contrary, motors were used to revolutionize all sectors of the economy; likewise, information technology, and eventually biotechnology, will transform all sectors of our twenty-first-century economy. There are no old economic sectors, only sectors with old technologies waiting to be transformed by the application of new technologies. Information technology and biotechnology, then, are not going to replace agriculture, manufacturing, mining, and services; they are going to modernize them radically.

Despite these misconceptions, there are several features of America's early-twenty-first-century economy that are genuinely "new" and lasting. The most important is that rapid technological innovation and diffusion have become ever more necessary in ensuring our economic prosperity. The key factor in improving the standard of living of Americans and everyone else in the world is not the value of the stock market or the trade balance or the inflation rate, but, rather, the rate of productivity growth—meaning the increase in total output per worker. If American productivity after 1973 had grown at the rate that it grew between 1945 and 1973, for instance, the median household income in the United States would have been more than $60,000 by the turn of the century, rather than $37,000. It is now widely believed that technological innovation accounts for at least half of today's productivity growth, if not more.

The greater the pace of creative destruction in the twenty-first century, then, the higher our standard of living will be. In today's new economy, the more rapidly we develop and adopt new and more efficient ways of doing things (services), making things (manufacturing), mining things (extraction), and growing things (agriculture), the wealthier our society will be. But the diffusion of today's technologies and the invention of tomorrow's come at a price: the annihilation of jobs in businesses that survive, and in some cases the annihilation of entire lines of business. This is a price well worth paying for the good of our society, but its costs can be unduly painful to particular families and individuals. Adding to the speed and intensity of technology-induced dislocations are the expansion of global trade and the competitive pressures of globalization, which also make our nation richer at the same time that they make many of our citizens more insecure.

The central challenge of a new Information Age social contract is to destroy less-productive jobs and less-productive businesses, without destroying lives and livelihoods. There are two sides to this challenge: the need of America's employees for greater security in the new economy, and the need of America's employers for greater flexibility in the new economy. A failure to meet either side of this challenge will ultimately hurt all parties involved. That is, if reliable and flexible safety net programs do not make it easy for workers to move from one job to another or one sector to another, without devastating losses in income or gaps in insurance coverage, then voters will pressure politicians to preserve outmoded jobs and antiquated industries, thereby threatening the very engine of our prosperity. Likewise, if our social contract does not afford modern corporations the increased speed and flexibility they so need to succeed in the new economy, then our engine of prosperity will suffer just as seriously.

As the rate of economic and technological change increases, the rationale for a modernized social contract that enhances both the security of American workers and the flexibility of American businesses becomes ever stronger. The most successful societies in the Information Age will be those that combine a Darwinian marketplace with a non-Darwinian social safety net. The more reliable and fair the safety net is, the more flexible and competitive the marketplace can be.

Unfortunately, our current social contract—premised on employer-provided health care and a pay-as-you-go retirement system—fails both of these tests: It provides neither the security that American workers deserve nor the flexibility that American employers require. As we will see, the decline of lifetime employment, the growth of the contingent workforce, and the changing nature of corporations all provide compelling reasons to replace our current employer-based health care system. In a similar fashion, the aging of America (likely to be exacerbated by new biomedical breakthroughs), the recent collapse in personal savings, and the very nature of the new economy all call for a bold new approach to retirement policy, as well as for new ways to help all Americans become owners of financial capital.

What should be the defining characteristic of a sound social contract worthy of the twenty-first century? In our opinion, the flexibility of businesses and the security of individuals both require severing the traditional link between the provision of benefits and employers (though not employment). The guiding principle of an Information Age social contract should be to link all benefits directly to individuals rather than to employers or to other intermediary institutions. In this chapter, we sketch the outlines of a new, citizen-based social contract that pairs mandatory personal insurance for health care and mandatory personal retirement savings with guaranteed government safety nets, thereby creating a flexible new workforce able to enjoy the freedoms of today's contingent workers and the security of today's full-time employees, while simultaneously freeing American companies from the unnecessary burdens of benefit administration.

Modernizing America's social contract in this manner could do much to alleviate the anxieties and insecurities associated with our globalized modern economy, as well as unleash new waves of creative destruction in the marketplace, but it would still leave a crucial challenge unaddressed: ensuring that all Americans actually share in our nation's economic prosperity. In order to get ahead in today's economy, individuals not only need to participate as wage earners, but also as owners of financial assets. As a final component of a new citizen-based social contract, then, we propose updating America's long-standing commitment to broadening asset ownership—such as farms in the nineteenth century and homes in the twentieth century—through a new program of universal capitalism tailored to the circumstances of the twenty-first century.

The case for a new citizen-based social contract becomes clear when we compare it to the alternatives and when we consider the recent changes to the nature of work and employment in the United States. In essence, there are three ways of organizing a social contract in order to give individuals an economic cushion during times of change and hardship: through family ties, through intermediary institutions, and through government-sponsored or -mandated programs.

Before the Industrial Revolution, most people depended on their families for economic support in times of misfortune. This made sense as long as most Americans lived in close-knit communities, primarily on farms. But by the 1930s, when more than half of the population lived in towns or cities rather than on farms and farmers accounted for only one fifth of the workforce, most Americans had few or no resources to fall back on during economic hard times.

The conditions of urban, industrial society stimulated the development of new kinds of economic support systems other than the family and traditional religious and private charities. One option was the assumption of the task of helping individuals during hard times by intermediary institutions, whether fraternal organizations, unions, or corporations. All three options were tried in the United States in the late nineteenth and early twentieth century. Fraternal organizations like the Shriners and Elks provided medical coverage for their members and helped to pay the cost of funerals (a major financial burden for low-income people). Many unions provided similar benefits for their members. Likewise, some business executives experimented with corporate paternalism, going so far as to provide housing and schools for their workers. But at their peak these benefits helped only a small segment of the American public, and were proven by the Great Depression to be inadequate.

By the 1950s, every advanced nation had adopted some kind of government social contract. In most countries, governments provided basic pensions, universal health care, and unemployment insurance. In the United States, however, from the 1930s onward, attempts to institutionalize universal government-provided health care were repeatedly defeated, with the exception of health care for the elderly and the poor (Medicare and Medicaid). In its place, a unique form of "welfare capitalism" has evolved since the 1940s in which American employers provide health care and private pension benefits to some of their workers. At around the same time, the U.S. government assumed responsibility for public pensions (Social Security) in order to alleviate the growing problem of elder poverty— leaving Americans with an oddly bifurcated social contract that is part employer-based and part government-based.

The employer-based portion of America's current social contract is not the product of intentional design but rather of historical accident. During World War II, wage and price rationing prevented American companies from raising wages. In order to attract workers, companies began taking advantage of a loophole in the tax code that gave them a tax break if they provided health insurance for their employees. This minor loophole then expanded to become the basis of the American health care system for the adult workforce, creating a type of welfare capitalism without parallel in other societies. Subsequently, the major reason for the failure of repeated attempts—by Presidents Truman, Johnson, Nixon, and Clinton—to establish a single-payer system like those of other advanced technological societies was the fact that many Americans already had health insurance through their employers.

It is questionable, then, whether America's employer-based social contract made much sense when it first emerged, but there is no question that it has ceased to make sense in the circumstances of America's twenty-first-century labor market. In contrast to the dawn of the New Deal era, when lifetime employment with a single firm was the ideal (though not always the reality), the era of the new economy has brought with it a significant increase in both job mobility and the use of contingent workers, who do not receive health insurance, private pensions, or other benefits from their employers.

By the turn of the twenty-first century, median job tenure for all American workers twenty-five and older was down to five years. In California, the seedbed of the digital revolution and frequently the harbinger of America's future, median job tenure was only three years. And this trend has affected all age groups. Between 1963 and 2000, for instance, median job tenure for male workers aged fifty-five to sixty-four fell by roughly a third, from 14.7 to 10.2 years. By 2000, the same figure for males twenty-five to thirty-four had fallen to 2.7 years, and for males twenty to twenty-four, to 1.2 years. The model of lifetime employment with a single firm has given way to a model of serial employment with many firms.

While the mobility of today's full-time workers has been increasing, so has the overall share of contingent workers. By the end of the twentieth century, the legions of contingent workers—a category not even tracked by the government before 1995—encompassed between a third and a quarter of the entire workforce. Meanwhile, the nation's largest employers had become agencies providing temporary workers.

In years ahead, both job mobility and the number of contingent workers are only likely to increase. Many assume, mistakenly, that globalization will be the primary driver of job dislocation in the future. Given the increasingly service-oriented nature of our economy, however, much of the job dislocation caused by globalization, especially the export of manufacturing jobs, has already taken place. As a result, American workers probably have more to fear from domestic factors than international ones. For instance, the explosion of business-to-business e-commerce in the United States will probably

cause more economic dislocation in our labor market than globalization. This will give rise to a broad new wave of disintermediation,
eliminating the jobs—and profits—of many of today's middlemen. It
is for such reasons that business author Tom Peters predicts that 90
percent of white-collar jobs in the United States will either be destroyed or altered beyond recognition in the next ten to fifteen years.

Given these trends, maintaining our current employer-based
health care and private pension system turns out to be a bad proposition for all parties involved. It leaves employees inherently insecure
because the risk of losing their jobs becomes immediately compounded by the added distress of changing health care and private
pension plans, or of losing them entirely if they aren't fortunate
enough to move to a job that provides these benefits. Our antiquated
employer-based social contract also compromises the quality of our
overall health care system; surely individual citizens would be better
cared for if they were able to maintain long-term relationships with a
single doctor and insurer, rather than being forced to change insurers every couple of years, as is now the case. More broadly still, the
dependency of workers on employers for basic benefits only diminishes the already fragile public support for greater creative destruction in the economic marketplace.

Employers, for their part, do not fare well under our employer-
based social contract either. Indeed, they are forced to shoulder a
number of administrative burdens that distract them from their primary business. As anyone who has run a small business and tried to
set up a health insurance or private pension plan could attest, the
process can not only eat up many months of hard work but produce
quite a number of unexpected headaches. The practice of imposing
welfare provision responsibilities on the marketplace in general and
businesses in particular represents a misallocation of social responsibility. This mistake is the product of a historical accident during the
Second Industrial Revolution, which should now be corrected during the Information Age.

The unintended consequences of relying on employer-based mechanisms for providing health care and private pensions have been nothing short of tragic. To begin with, the oft-cited figure of 43 million currently uninsured Americans provides a stark reminder of just how inadequate our health care model is. Although we spend almost twice as much per capita on health care than the Organization for Economic Cooperation and Development (OECD) average, the United States alone lacks universal coverage. To make matters worse, health care coverage in the United States reflects economic inequality. In 1997, little more than 5 percent of working adults with incomes over $65,000 lacked health care coverage, but 35 percent of those who earned between $16,036 and $19,885 were without health care coverage.

The situation is only deteriorating: Recent U.S. Census Bureau data reveals that between 1988 and 1998, the number of workers receiving health coverage as compensation from their own employer fell significantly, from 64.6 to 54.1 percent—or a drop of over 10 percent. And even those who still receive health coverage through their jobs find that employers are increasingly shifting the cost of coverage to them. As these trends suggest, there is a significant difference between large companies that have the resources to provide generous health care packages, and small businesses that find the costs of doing so prohibitive. But even this dual arrangement is unlikely to last for long, because it is forcing large employers to increasingly cross-subsidize the spouses or partners of their workers. Indeed, an increasing number of employees in the private sector are now receiving coverage under another worker's policy. Sooner or later, more generous firms will realize that they are simply subsidizing the costs of less generous firms, which is hardly in their self-interest and will eventually compel them to join the race to the bottom.

Yet another flaw in our employer-based health care system is that it disproportionately subsidizes high-income workers, in effect discriminating against low-income workers. Our current system, by allowing employers to pay for the health care costs of their employees with pretax dollars, provides a major tax subsidy worth forty cents on the dollar to those in the top tax bracket, while doing nothing for the bottom third of workers who earn too little to incur any income tax liability in the first place.

Similar problems plague our employer-based private pension system, which covers even fewer workers and is even more skewed in favor of the well-to-do. In 1998, for instance, less than half of all workers (43 percent) received private pension coverage. Not surprisingly, the likelihood of coverage rises dramatically along with income. What is most distressing about this employer-based arrangement, however, is that it means that your employment status determines your ability to enjoy tax-advantaged savings. For instance, the minority of workers who benefit from employer-provided 401k plans can put away upward of $10,000 a year of their own money in tax-advantaged savings accounts, but the majority of workers who do not have access to such plans can save only $2,000 a year through their own Individual Retirement Accounts. Why should your employment status limit your ability to save for your own retirement?

Our continued reliance on an employer-based social contract creates a number of perverse incentives of this sort for employees and employers alike. Increasingly, corporations trying to avoid the costs of fringe benefits like health care and private pensions have resorted to the expedients of hiring temporary contingent workers who are not covered under their health care plans, or trimming benefits to their full-time workers. This not only creates a two-tier labor market, divided between full-time employees with benefits and part-time employees with no benefits, but it also sparks painful confrontations between employees and employers. Throughout the 1990s, for instance, major strikes and protracted legal battles erupted between workers and employers at companies ranging from United Parcel Service to Microsoft, which tried to hire large numbers of contingent workers in order to avoid the costs and burdens of providing benefits.

Under our current system, the options are particularly bleak for the 43 million workers who lack health insurance. Because they do not participate in the employer-based pools around which our present system is designed, it is considerably more expensive for them to purchase health insurance, which of course perpetuates the vicious circle. To make matters worse, those who do not have access to health insurance routinely face higher costs than those insured for the very same medical treatments and prescription drugs, since the uninsured do not benefit from the collective bargaining power that enables large insurers to limit the cost of medical procedures for their members. Indeed, many doctors now have two sets of fees: a lower one for insured patients, and a considerably higher one for uninsured patients.

The situation could get even worse for all parties involved thanks to the rapid proliferation of genetic testing. Within the next few years, simple tests will become available to detect your predisposition to a wide range of diseases, such as Parkinson's disease, breast cancer, colon cancer, and many other serious ailments. Given the design of our employer-based health care system, what ought to be a very positive development could turn into a double-edged sword that wounds individuals and insurers alike. While individuals could face genetic discrimination from insurers, the insurers could face financial ruin if they are prevented from accessing the same information that individuals use in deciding whether to purchase health care insurance in the first place. The latter problem would largely disappear if our health coverage was universal.

All things being equal, the advent of genetic testing should be a wonderful new development that enhances the quality of health care by shifting the focus of care from health maintenance to disease prevention. As long as we maintain our employer-based health care model, however, this promise will never be fulfilled. Beyond the problems already mentioned, the combination of our employer-based health care system and the increasingly brief job tenures of today's workers means that most Americans do not stay with the same insurer for more than a couple of years. As a result, insurers have little incentive to focus on long-term disease prevention, since their customers will typically only be with them for the short term. If our health care system permitted Americans to stay with a single insurer for life, however, there would suddenly be a strong incentive for insurers to focus on long-term disease prevention.

All of this begs an obvious question: Why should we maintain our employer-based social contract when it so obviously fails such a large portion of American workers, when it unnecessarily burdens American companies, when it diminishes the quality of health care, and when it retards new waves of creative destruction? Come to think of it, why maintain the distinction between full-time and contingent workers at all?

The obvious answer is to replace our antiquated employer-based social contract with a new citizen-based social contract geared to the circumstances of the Information Age. Sometimes it is best to maintain an existing system and make marginal improvements upon it; at other times it is necessary to throw the existing system out in its entirety and start over. Given the fact that our current employer-based social contract is breaking, if not already broken, we believe the time has come to begin anew.

The overwhelming advantage of a citizen-based social contract is that basic benefits would flow directly to individuals—following them from job to job. In practice, the distinction between full-time and contingent workers would become meaningless. Workers would count on their employers for their salaries and, it may be hoped, for the fulfillment that derives from their jobs—but not for any of their health coverage or other basic benefits. By minimizing the reliance of workers on their employers for benefits, we could maximize the creative destruction in the economy. This is as it should be.

Responsibility for health insurance, then, should be divided between the individual and the government; businesses should play no role. The individual has an interest in affordable and portable health insurance; the public has an interest in guaranteeing that all citizens receive an adequate minimum of medical care. A new citizen-based social contract between governments and individuals would provide both the security that individuals need in our fast-paced new economy, and the flexibility that businesses need. It would also enable citizens to keep the doctors they prefer (unless they move geographically) as well as a single health insurance provider for as long as they like, thereby increasing the quality of care in the process and paving the way for a whole new approach to health care focused on long-term disease prevention.


How, exactly, can America reach the goal of a universal, citizen-based health care system? In essence, there are two models to choose from: a single-payer health care system, or a two-tier system that combines mandatory self-insurance with means-tested government safety nets. The choice, in essence, comes down to the question of who should bear the primary burden for providing health care: the government or the individual? Most advanced democracies around the world have opted for the former, by establishing a single-payer system in which the government itself provides health insurance to all its citizens, paid for through general taxes or payroll taxes. A small minority of modern nations—Switzerland is one—have chosen the second path, by mandating that all citizens purchase their own health insurance, and by limiting the government's role to that of supporting those who cannot afford to cover their full health care costs. We believe that America would be best served by the model of mandatory self-insurance, supplemented by a guaranteed government safety net.

In theory, a single-payer system could meet all the goals of a universal, citizen-based social contract. In the U.S. context, however, it would effectively kill the private health insurance industry, thereby limiting individual choices and setting off a fierce political battle. What is more, adopting a single-payer system would significantly increase the size both of our government and the tax bill facing ordinary Americans. Further, the price of making single-payer systems solvent in most countries that have them will be unpopular and controversial methods of rationing. We do not believe that most Americans would favor the widespread rationing of medical services, nor the significant increase in the size of the federal government that would be required for our nation to adopt a single-payer system.

Another disadvantage of single-payer systems is that they may retard technological progress in medicine. Where there is a private market in medical services, high-end consumption of luxury health care by the rich may subsidize basic research that leads to breakthroughs. Over time, new medical techniques or drugs that only the rich could afford at first have usually fallen dramatically in price, permitting many or most people to share in their benefits. In a single-payer system in which the government purchases medical services on behalf of the citizenry, the government may decide not to finance speculative or costly experiments that might be funded by wealthy individuals. The trade-off between single-payer systems and advanced technology can be seen in Canada's health care system. Canada provides adequate basic coverage for all of its citizens, but Canadians seeking cutting-edge medical treatment come to the United States, if they can afford to.

Despite these defects, a single-payer system, providing universal, portable coverage, would be an improvement over our employer-based health care system. But it would still be far from optimal. Moreover, the failure of many previous attempts to establish a single-payer system by numerous presidents suggests that its enactment is all but impossible in the United States in the foreseeable future.

Is there a way to sever health insurance from employment without eradicating the private health insurance industry and replacing it with government monopoly? Yes. The solution is mandatory self-insurance, with a public health insurance safety net for the genuinely needy. Just as most states require citizens with cars to buy car insurance, so every American would be required by the federal government to purchase a basic private health insurance policy. On top of this basic insurance, all citizens would be able but not required to purchase additional coverage for luxury health insurance, which would help ensure that there is a thriving market in high-end medical services. The federal government, meanwhile, would subsidize the purchase of private health insurance by those unable to cover the full cost of a basic plan. For example, all Americans might be required to devote a certain percentage of their incomes to purchasing their own insurance plans, with the government picking up the rest. This would ensure that all citizens would contribute a significant, though not ruinous, portion of their incomes to defray the costs of their own medical care.

Why should health insurance be mandatory? Some have proposed encouraging voluntary purchase of health care coverage by allowing individuals to share in the tax breaks enjoyed by today's employers with company health care programs. Even the libertarian economist Milton Friedman, however, argues that the purchase of basic, catastrophic health care coverage should be mandated by the government (lesser costs might be met by voluntary medical savings accounts). While self-insurance would be mandatory, each American could choose from among a number of competing private insurance plans, and perhaps even be allowed, as one of many options, to join the federal health insurance program now offered to civil servants.

Adopting a citizen-based approach to universal, portable health care would require some significant changes in our health care system. For one thing, we would no longer need to maintain a separate Medicaid system for the very poor, because all citizens would be covered under the new system. In addition, our current practice of relying on employers to pool health risks would need to be replaced with a new system of community pooling in which risk would be aggregated on a regional or national basis. At the same time, it would be necessary to ban the practice by insurers of discriminating on the basis of genetic tests or other preexisting conditions (insurance companies could take comfort in knowing that the combination of mandatory self-insurance and community pooling would help disperse such risks broadly among their clientele). These provisions would ensure that all Americans could secure basic health insurance at reasonable rates. Ensuring that all citizens comply with the mandatory self-insurance requirement need not be that difficult; for instance, those unable to demonstrate that they had done so on their annual tax return could be enrolled by default into a private insurance plan; depending on their incomes, they would be either billed or subsidized by the government. Any workable system would require complex regulations—but then, the insurance industry is already one of the most highly regulated areas of the American economy. And none of the changes involved in a shift from an employer-based health care system to the model we propose would be as dramatic as those that would be required by a switch to a single-payer system.

Those who are already insured by their employers need not worry that our citizen-based system would present a new financial burden to them. To the contrary, the money employers now pay to insurers would typically be given to workers as part of their paychecks. Most economists agree that firms in effect take the costs of health care policies out of wages, meaning that if firms no longer paid for employee health insurance they would most likely pass the savings directly on to employees in the form of higher wages. Indeed, many employers have already begun to shift the cost of financing health care coverage to their employees: The proportion of individuals whose employers paid the full cost of coverage fell from 45 percent in 1983 to 27 percent in 1998.

Any serious program for universal health coverage will require more government expenditure, but our plan would accomplish this goal while keeping the scale of government far smaller than under a single-payer plan. In terms of the overall cost of this new system to taxpayers, it must be remembered that the public is already subsidizing health care—the problem is that we are subsidizing it erratically and unfairly. For instance, we currently devote approximately $60 billion a year to subsidize employer-based health care (most of which benefits the well-to-do), and approximately $200 billion on Medicaid to subsidize health care for the very poor, but nothing to help the struggling families in between those extremes. These existing expenditures should be redirected toward the new system we propose. Mandatory self-insurance would also help lower the cost of health insurance for average citizens, because a large share of today's 43 million uninsured Americans are young, healthy, and financially capable of covering all or most of the cost of a basic health care package. Broadening the total pool of those insured through the addition of these relatively young and healthy citizens would help lower average health insurance costs for all those who are now covered. Finally, our proposal would offer most Americans a whole new range of choices in the selection of an optimal health plan. The worker who wants a basic plan could save money; the worker who wants additional coverage and is willing to pay for it would have that option.

A citizen-based health care system of the kind we have described would be limited to working-age adults and their dependents. The elderly would continue to be covered by our single-payer Medicare system, because putting the elderly into the same pool as working-age citizens would greatly drive up the premiums paid by the latter. Although Medicare in something like its present form should be retained, the threat that growing Medicare costs will eat up much of the federal budget in the years ahead compels us to propose reforming Medicare as well, by extending the retirement age, and means-testing benefits.

This citizen-based health care system would have numerous advantages over the present employer-based approach. First, it would offer universal coverage, with every American guaranteed a basic package of benefits. Next, it would be fully portable: Workers could change jobs with far less friction in today's fast-paced economy without changing insurers, doctors, or worrying about the loss of benefits. Third, it would enable all citizens to choose their own health insurers. Fourth, it would free companies from the burden of serving as miniature welfare states, giving them the added flexibility they need in the new economy. This reform would also level the economic playing field by removing some of the advantages that large companies now have over small ones, and eliminating the perverse incentives that have driven many of today's employers to substitute contingent workers for full-time employees. Finally, a new, citizen-based health care system would encourage the development and use of new medical technologies, including genetic testing, which could ultimately benefit all citizens, and shift the whole focus of health care to disease prevention.

If the forces compelling us to reinvent our health care system are the changing nature of work and of the corporation in the new economy, then the forces that compel us to reinvent our public pension system are the changing demographics of our nation and the recent collapse in private savings.

Just as the design of America's health care system was an accident of history, so was that of the other major pillar of our basic social contract: our public pension system. Social Security is widely, and rightfully, regarded as the greatest legacy of President Franklin Delano Roosevelt's New Deal, especially among Democrats and Progressives. But all too often it is forgotten that FDR had a very different vision in mind when he set out to create our pension system. He envisioned a public retirement model that would be fully funded over the course of many years before large-scale payouts began. FDR's successors subsequently changed the basic formula in order to hasten the system's payout timetable. As a result, we ended up with what is essentially a "pay as you go" version of Social Security.

Underlying the tension between FDR's original vision of fully funded Social Security and what it eventually became are two very different models of the modern public pension program. We might call them the transfer model and the savings model. Most public pension systems, beginning with Bismarck's welfare state in Imperial Germany in the 1870s (the ancestor of them all), have been transfer programs. By means of taxation, money is transferred from one part of the public to another. In the case of most public pension systems, for example, younger workers have been taxed to pay for the retirement income of the elderly. This is essentially how the American model works (with the added provision that any income not paid out directly to retirees in any given year is carried over as a surplus for future years).

The savings model, by contrast, is an innovation of the second half of the twentieth century. One example is the pension system of Singapore, which was devised by British colonial authorities in the 1950s. The Singaporean model is quite different from the Bismarckian model in that it is based on compulsory individual savings rather than compulsory transfer payments. All citizens are required by law to accumulate tax-free retirement savings in their own names. Because the savings are mandatory, this is a kind of public safety net. Only when individuals exhaust their mandatory savings does the government help with transfer payments paid for out of taxation.

Which model of a public pension system is better? In theory, each is equally capable of providing individual citizens with retirement income. In practice, however, history will prove the savings model to be superior. The main reason is demography. Transfer-based public pensions were devised during the industrial era when every advanced industrial country had an enormous pool of young people and a small pool of old people. The early architects of such systems in most countries assumed that the demographic profile of their nations would always resemble a pyramid or at least a diamond. As late as 1967, economist Paul Samuelson declared in a *Newsweek* article that Social Security was a great success even though "it is actuarially unsound." His reason? "Always there are more youths than old folks in a growing population." He spoke too soon.

What the early backers of transfer-based public pensions failed to foresee were two medical advances that would transform society. The first was safe, effective contraception—the Pill. The second was a cluster of medical advances promoting longevity. Empowered by newfound reproductive choices, most women in America and other advanced societies have chosen to bear only one or two offspring, and many to enter the workforce. Naturally, this led to a significant fall in birthrates. In addition, various breakthroughs in pharmaceuticals and medical science—such as penicillin and antibiotics—lengthened average life spans considerably. The dramatic drop in fertility shrank the size of the young portion of the population in comparison with the elderly portion. The population pyramid or diamond became a population rectangle. And thanks to increases in longevity, the rectangle grew taller, even as it grew thinner. The

Census Bureau now predicts that the elderly—whose numbers were roughly equal to those of eighteen- to twenty-one-year-olds in 1940—will outnumber college-age Americans by almost four to one in 2040.

Obviously, public pension programs based primarily on transfer payments between generations—as our Social Security system is—are much more threatened by the rapid rise in older people relative to younger people than are public pension systems based in large part on mandatory personal savings. In a savings-based system, each generation will pay for much, if not most, of its retirement costs, using money saved during the prime earning years and accumulating interest over time. Had we remained loyal to FDR's original vision of a prefunded Social Security, we wouldn't now be facing the daunting challenge of financing the retirement costs of a huge "baby boom" on the backs of a "baby bust" cohort twenty or thirty years younger.

If the intergenerational transfer model was the typical public pension system of the second industrial era, the savings model, combining compulsory savings with means-tested transfer programs, may prove to be the norm in the information era—not because of the nature of information technology but because of the demographic changes produced by contraception and longevity.

The great debate over Social Security in American politics today is between those who want to preserve the existing pay-as-you-go intergenerational transfer system, and those who favor moving to a citizen-based savings model, premised on a combination of individual retirement accounts and a safety net for those whose retirement savings are inadequate. This is often described as "privatization," but that term is misleading. If the government compels you to save money and tells you how you can spend it, that money is not really "private." What is more, nobody proposes a purely private or one-tier system in which individuals with inadequate private savings in retirement would be abandoned to poverty; rather, those who favor privatization of Social Security really mean *partial* privatization, based on a two-tier system combining tax-favored personal savings with a means-tested safety net.

Although most public pension systems in the world originated as one-tier transfer programs, paid for out of payroll taxes or general revenues, in recent years the prospective bankruptcy of public pensions by the aging of national populations has inspired many governments to consider moving toward two-tier, individual savings-based plans. Australia and Chile have already done so, and Britain is in the process of emulating their example. The World Bank, in its recent study, *Averting the Old Age Crisis,* recommended that all advanced countries adopt two-tier retirement systems. This is no longer a "conservative" idea, inasmuch as social democratic Sweden, worried about its graying population, has based its new pension system on the personal savings model.

In the United States, the debate about this subject has only begun. For decades, Social Security was regarded as the "third rail" in American politics, a reference to the electrified rail of a subway or railroad. Politicians who touched it would die. In the 2000 election campaign, however, Republican presidential candidate George W. Bush made a proposed move toward a two-tier Social Security system ("partial privatization") a central element of his campaign. Predictably, his Democratic opponent, Al Gore, attempted with some success to frighten elderly voters by equating a two-tier system with the destruction of Social Security. The fact that a majority of younger Americans and roughly half of elderly Americans, according to the polls, favored some kind of partial privatization suggests that the "third rail" no longer carries the charge it used to, and that defending an unreformed Social Security system may no longer work for politicians.

Unfortunately, the initial debate about a two-tier Social Security system has turned on the issue of whether individuals could enjoy greater financial returns if part of their Social Security payroll taxes were invested in the stock market. Expert opinion on this subject is divided. As critics of the current program are fond of observing, the rates of return on the money paid into Social Security is exceptionally low for all but the very first beneficiaries of the system. Workers born in 1930 will receive on average around 120 percent of what they would have received if their Social Security taxes had been invested in long-term government bonds. By contrast, workers born in the 1950s will receive only about 75 percent as much as they could have received if their Social Security taxes had been invested in long-term government bonds.

On the other hand, opponents of a two-tier Social Security system raise the specter of economic depressions, stock market bubbles, wars, and other catastrophes. It is not necessary to believe in rosy scenarios about the stock market, however, to favor a two-tier pension system that promotes individual savings. Even if the private market yielded returns no greater than government bonds, the case for a two-tier system based on demography would be compelling.

Unless the system is dramatically reformed, American workers will pay ever higher taxes for ever fewer benefits. Primarily because of demographic changes, combined employee and employer payroll taxes for Social Security have already grown from 2 percent in 1937 to 12.4 percent in 2000. And according to the Social Security Administration, the ratio of payroll tax contributors to Social Security beneficiaries will decline further from 3.3 today to 2.0 in 2030. Meanwhile the percentage of the U.S. population over eighty-five is projected to grow from little more than 1 percent in 1997 to 5 percent in 2050. With continued advances in the biomedical field, it is perfectly conceivable, if not likely, that even these projections are too conservative.

Projections for the solvency of our current Social Security system are notoriously inaccurate, especially since they are quite sensitive to assumptions about the rate of economic growth and other factors that are difficult to predict in advance. As of this writing, the latest official projections are that the Social Security system will start paying out more in benefits than it is receiving in payroll taxes in 2015, and by 2037, it will only be able to pay out 75 percent of current benefits. Perhaps the system could be extended for several more years if economic growth proves to be higher than projected. On the other hand, the situation could be even worse if growth turns out to be slower, or if new medical advances, such as gene therapy or the possibility of replaceable human organs, extend life spans even further.

Although we can put only so much faith in the official estimates, it may be more revealing to ask why we would want to continue a system in which there is a necessary trade-off between the fiscal burdens on our working-age population and the physical health and longevity of our senior citizens. In an ideal public pension system, such trade-offs would be minimized, by design. Even if, by means of periodic tinkering, we could keep Social Security going in something like its present form indefinitely, is this really a good idea? If we maintain the existing system, then every few years Congress will have to intervene to adjust benefits and taxes in response to fluctuations in the working-age population and the population of retirees. Every change will be accompanied by a nasty political battle, often pitting one generation against another. By comparison, a two-tier system based on private savings could proceed more or less on autopilot; the need for frequent, recurrent, and politically divisive tinkering would be greatly reduced, although not completely eliminated. Is it too much to ask that one characteristic of a sound entitlement program be that it is not likely to provoke civil war by means of the ballot box?

There is yet another reason to rethink our whole approach to public pensions. Despite the seriousness of the fiscal challenges awaiting Social Security, there is actually a deeper cause for concern: the collapse of personal savings across the United States, which is occurring at precisely the wrong time. As a population ages and the proportion of workers to retirees falls, families ought to be saving more for their own retirements, not less. Indeed, Social Security was always intended to provide a *supplemental* income for most retirees. However, a frighteningly large number of Americans have few or no pension savings of their own to supplement, meaning that a very large number of tomorrow's retirees are likely to find themselves entirely dependent on the public purse. This could have profound and very unpleasant implications for our nation's overall economic well-being.

It could be argued that the incentives created by Social Security are largely to blame for the recent fall in personal savings. Trusting that Social Security will be there when they retire, this argument goes, many Americans have chosen to consume more and save less during their working years. Surely there is some truth to this argument. But regardless of the exact cause of the precipitous decline in personal savings, there is no question that this will present a major challenge for our nation, which any new retirement policy must respond to. Throughout the first four decades following World War II, personal savings rates in America averaged between 5 and 7 percent of GDP. By the turn of the twenty-first century, they had plunged into negative territory for the first time since the Great Depression.

Some skeptics argue that the personal savings statistics are understated because they fail to take into account unrealized capital gains. They may have a point, but it would not for a minute change the bleak savings picture facing the majority of Americans, who have negligible or no capital gains in waiting. The unpleasant reality is that most American families were in a more vulnerable economic position at the end of the 1990s than they were in the 1980s. For instance, the percentage of households with zero or negative net worth increased from 15.5 percent in 1983 to 18.0 percent in 1998. Moreover, the Consumer Federation of America recently reported that a full half of American households have under $1,000 in net financial assets. The flipside of these statistics is the rapidly increasing indebtedness of average Americans. Household debt service is now at its highest share of disposable income since the late 1980s. Indeed, roughly 45 percent of American families carry credit card debt from month to month.

The major reason for replacing, rather than reforming, the Social Security system inherited from the New Deal era is as much philosophical as it is pragmatic. A public pension system should be based primarily on individual savings rather than on an intergenerational transfer system; it should encourage individual self-reliance, with assistance when necessary from the government, not paternalism by an all-providing government. Many on today's Left, believing that the oversized welfare states of northern Europe should be the model for the U.S. government, defend Social Security on the grounds that it provides a sense of shared citizenship among Americans. This sentiment, common among social democrats, was quite alien to the thinking of the mainstream American liberals who originally devised Social Security. Franklin Roosevelt thought of Social Security as insurance, not as a sacred political expression of egalitarian solidarity, and went to his grave hoping that it could be fully funded like a conventional insurance program. The genuine heirs of FDR are not the old-fashioned leftists who idealize Social Security but the pragmatic reformers who want to achieve the goal of FDR—preventing destitution in old age—by methods better adapted to the Information Age.

For philosophical as well as practical reasons, then, it makes sense to replace today's pay-as-you-go Social Security with one or another version of a two-tier program combining individual savings accounts with a means-tested government safety net. If you accept this premise, then the next question is: What type of two-tier plan is best for the United States? In the recent presidential election, George W. Bush called for dedicating approximately 2 percent of an individual's wages into his or her own individual retirement accounts by diverting that proportion of the Social Security payroll taxes. At around the same time, Democratic Senator Daniel Patrick Moynihan of New York floated a parallel proposal for carving out percentage points of payroll taxes to fund private savings accounts, and to his credit, combined it with various proposals to shrink Social Security expenses. While both proposals point in the right direction, their greatest weakness may be their modesty.

One of the lessons of politics and economics is that size and scale do actually matter. Thus if we really want to help all working Americans accumulate meaningful private savings for retirement, the mandatory savings rate should be set at closer to 5 percent of one's income. Consider the difference between a 2 percent plan and a 5 percent plan: For an American worker with the average median wage of $35,000 per year, the difference would be between saving $700 per year versus $1,750 per year for retirement. Over the course of a fifty-year career—assuming a return of 6 percent on your savings, and an annual 1 percent wage increase, both adjusted for inflation—the former would be left with $250,000 at retirement, while the latter would have $640,000. In other words, the person putting away 2 percent of wages each year would only be able to make a down payment on retirement expenses—and would therefore have to rely on large-scale public subsidies—while the person putting away 5 percent of wages a year might be able to fund his or her retirement in its entirety. Retirement freedom and independence is fully attainable for most Americans, but it won't come cheap.

Would an ambitious national savings plan of this type simply amount to a big new bite out of the wage-earning American's paycheck? No, these private retirement savings accounts would be carved out of existing Social Security payroll taxes. Fully employed workers already have 6.2 percent of their wages automatically deducted to cover the cost of Social Security, with the employer contributing an equal amount—for a combined total of 12.4 percent. The growing number of contingent workers and independent contractors must shoulder both sides of the Social Security payroll tax. Of this combined rate of 12.4 percent, we recommend that approximately 5 percent of each worker's wages go directly into his or her own personal retirement savings accounts.

To be effective, such citizen-based savings accounts would have to be subject to a few basic restrictions. First, individuals would not be able to draw down their individual retirement accounts until they actually reach retirement age, which they would be free to determine, as long as it was above some minimum agreed upon age, such as sixty-seven or seventy. Second, some form of basic annuatization would be put in place to ensure that retirees do not draw down their capital all at once, but rather do so gradually over the course of their retirement. Finally, as in any 401k plans, individuals would have freedom to choose their own investment strategies and exposure to risk, within the context of a range of well-diversified investment instruments. In other words, individuals would have freedom of choice with regard to their investments, but would be prevented from exposing all of their investments to extremely risky and speculative propositions.

The emergence of new financial instruments in the future should help individuals hedge their risks in entirely new ways—meaning that even if the stock market were to decline considerably in coming years, there is no reason why well-diversified portfolios would have to suffer. Yale economist Robert Shiller provides a compelling vision of how to diversify our financial markets in the future. Although he is best known for anticipating the recent stock market crash in his book *Irrational Exuberance,* it is the solutions-oriented part of his recent work that is most interesting. Bemoaning that the stock market today is limited to trading securities that are claims on corporate profits, Shiller and his colleague Allan Weiss call for new "macro markets" that would include "markets for long-term claims on national incomes of each of the world's major countries, for long-term claims on specific occupational groups, and for currently illiquid assets, like single-family homes." The purpose of the new markets would be to enable individuals and nations to greatly diversify their portfolios, and hedge against downturns in their own countries, vocations, pension plans, or home values. As Shiller explains, "People could then take short positions corresponding to their own incomes, whose value would rise if incomes in their professions fell." In fact, ordinary citizens could hedge against all types of financial risks, including those facing their private pension savings, in the very same manner.

A two-tier pension system of the kind we favor, whatever its particular details might be, would be similar to what many Americans mistakenly believe the current Social Security system is today—a private savings program paid out of an individual worker's own earnings prior to retirement. Much of Social Security's current popularity rests on this misconception, when in fact the money workers pay into the Social Security program is long gone by the time they retire.

If more Americans were able to take advantage of higher rates of return on their savings, the need for public assistance during retirement would fall dramatically. In fact, a substantial part of the American population could live comfortably without any Social Security benefits even today. Your dependence on Social Security depends on your socioeconomic level. The poorest fifth of elderly Americans is almost entirely dependent on Social Security and public assistance. However, the top two quintiles of Americans over sixty-five receive a majority of their retirement income from sources other than Social

Security, including income from assets, earnings, and private pensions. Social Security contributes less than 20 percent to the incomes of the richest fifth of Americans over sixty-five, and about 45 percent to those in the fourth quintile. Clearly, then, two fifths of Americans over sixty-five could live comfortably with few or no Social Security benefits—particularly if they had been encouraged to save even more during their working years.

What about those with low incomes, and thus small retirement savings accounts? Under most two-tier privatization plans that have been proposed, the federal government would set an income floor for retirees. Those whose retirement income exceeded the income floor would receive no money from the government. But those whose retirement income, based on personal savings, fell below the floor would receive government help. If liberals accepted the principle of a two-tier system (instead of rejecting it out of hand, for short-run political purposes, as most Democrats have done recently) they could argue for floors higher than conservatives would prefer.

The advantage of a system of mandatory retirement savings backed by government transfer payments is that even at its most expensive such a system would still cost less than Social Security in its present form. If the stock market experienced a downturn for an extended period, the number of Americans qualifying for public subsidies would increase—but that number would always be less than the number who qualify today for Social Security checks, which is virtually all retirees. If returns on investments in the stock market or other areas of the economy rose, then the amount of transfer payments would correspondingly decline. While costing less than Social Security, the combination of mandatory individual savings and means-tested public safety nets would also be more fair. Under our present Social Security system, affluent Americans with personal savings and generous private pension plans get Social Security checks—checks paid for by the taxes of the nonaffluent majority of

American workers. Under a means-tested two-tier system, no affluent American able to live a middle-class lifestyle on the basis of private retirement income would receive retirement assistance from
the federal government.

Some may object that, while the citizen-based savings aspect of
this plan would be popular, the means-tested safety net portion
would suffer the fate of other politically unpopular welfare programs
that chiefly benefit the poor. But we believe this is highly unlikely.
Those who say the public will not support means-tested safety net
programs are basing their experience on programs that benefit only 5
percent of the population. Only a few Americans are poor, or in danger of being poor, during their working lives, but every working
American has retired relatives, and will retire in time. Retirees with
inadequate personal savings who need public supplements will not
be seen as "others," like the inner-city or rural poor; they will be
viewed as "us" by the majority of the American electorate.

A second and more serious objection is that most privatization
plans would favor the well-to-do because their higher incomes
would enable them to contribute larger amounts to their own retirement savings accounts. Fortunately, there is an ingenious way to
solve this problem, as well as the previously mentioned one, and
that is through what economist Maya MacGuineas calls "progressive privatization." By simply topping off the individual savings accounts of low-income workers, any privatization plan could become
far more progressive. During the lifetimes of low-income workers,
the government could supplement inadequate savings through a
"progressive match" that narrows the difference between the
amount a worker is able to save and how much that worker ought to
save to maintain a minimum middle-class lifestyle in retirement.
The model could be the earned income tax credit (EITC), a federal
program that supplements the income of low-wage workers and en-
joys strong bipartisan support. Progressive matches of this type

would not only lessen the fiscal burden awaiting any means-tested component of a retirement safety net, they would also protect needy retirees from the risk that politicians might slash such benefits in the future.

The biggest problem facing any attempt to move from a pay-as-you-go, transfer-based pension system to a two-tier, savings-based pension system has been how to finance the transition. The problem arises from the fact that for the duration of any transition from one system to another, however gradual, it is necessary to operate two systems at once, each of which requires funding. Reliable benefits must be provided to all those retirees who have been counting on Social Security payments, and who will not have had the opportunity to take significant advantage of the mandatory savings program we propose. At the same time, current workers must begin paying into their citizen-based savings accounts right away in order to build up a sizable asset base on which to retire. This objection has been raised to all proposals of partial privatization of Social Security.

It is not a fatal objection. The countries that have chosen to move from single-tier to two-tier pension systems, like Australia and Chile, have found ways to pay for it. In the United States, there are many ways to pay for the transition. Our preference would be to finance most of the transition through a three-pronged strategy. First, we would begin means-testing Social Security benefits immediately, thus reducing the long-term burden of our current system from the outset. Second, we believe that the increased health and longevity of Americans warrants a gradual extension of today's standard retirement age, which would also lessen the fiscal burden of the current system. Third, assuming that approximately 5 percentage points of each worker's current 12.4 percent Social Security payroll taxes were redirected to fund his or her personal retirement savings account, this would leave 7.4 percent to meet existing Social Security obligations. To eliminate the most distorting and regressive features of today's payroll tax, however, we recommend removing the cap on the amount of wages subjected to payroll taxes, and requiring employers to pay their half of payroll taxes regardless of whether their employees are full-time or contingent. This three-pronged strategy alone would enable the United States to cover more than two thirds of the cost of moving to a new savings-based retirement system for the twenty-first century, while fully honoring its commitments to those who most depend on its twentieth-century Social Security system.

Needless to say, a new two-tier retirement system in the United States, if it emerges at all, will develop as a result of compromises after years of debate and discussion. Whatever the details, moving from a system based on intergenerational transfers to one based primarily on mandatory individual savings would solve the biggest problem facing our public pension system—its extreme susceptibility to demographic change. Establishing individual retirement accounts through a mandatory savings plan would also enable all Americans to benefit from the type of tax-deferred savings and retirement plans—such as 401k's—that until now have been limited to the wealthiest half of Americans, and to those fortunate enough to have full-time jobs. In fact, one of the key features of this proposal would be to enable all Americans to participate in such savings vehicles regardless and independent of their employment status—the citizen-based savings accounts would be tied to the individual, not the employer, and thus would be fully portable from job to job. Finally, our proposal for "progressive privatization" of Social Security would reinvent our public pension system while maintaining its progressive character.

The introduction of citizen-based retirement savings accounts could also yield a huge pool of new savings and investment capital that could help American industry and the American economy prosper well into the twenty-second century. But before we can entertain such optimism, there is one final challenge that a new social contract worthy of the Information Age must be able to meet.

By the turn of the twenty-first century, the U.S. economy had experienced its longest economic boom on record. Yet our extraordinary economic success hides a discomforting truth: Mounting inequality of wealth and opportunity has turned the United States into the country with the greatest degree of economic polarization in the developed world.

As we have seen, maintaining public support for a dynamic economic system requires the upgrading and modernizing of the health care and retirement systems that we adopted during the Second Industrial Revolution. But that is not enough. In the older industrial eras, the danger was that the threat of physical destitution would alienate populations from capitalism. Today, there is a new danger, and that is the prospect that a majority of citizens will not share in the prosperity created by our new economy.

Like Janus, the Roman god of transitions, the new economy has two faces: a benign and optimistic one looking forward to the future, and a sinister, backward-looking one. During the long stock market expansion of the late 1990s, almost all of the gains have gone to the minority of Americans who have significant assets in the financial market. Meanwhile, the wages of the working-class majority, until a recent uptick, have stagnated for a generation. The winners in the new economy are relishing their bounty. But for the majority of Americans, who live from paycheck to paycheck, the face of the new economy that they perceive has a scowl; *their* new economy is one characterized by growing economic inequality, mounting insecurity, and dwindling safety nets. Moreover, many of today's young—especially the roughly two thirds who will never receive a four-year college education—are experiencing surprising levels of downward economic mobility, and are earning considerably less than their parents did at a similar age. To make up for stagnating or falling wages, many American families have resorted to working more hours and taking on more debt. As a proportion of the population, the middle class has been shrinking, as some Americans move up, while many others—overworked and overleveraged—have fallen behind.

Our nation's transition to an information-based, service-oriented economy has produced levels of wealth and income inequality not seen here since the 1920s. The numbers speak for themselves. By 1998, the top 1 percent of families in America owned 47 percent of total financial wealth, while the bottom 80 percent owned only 9 percent. Between 1983 and 1998, according to Edward N. Wolff of New York University, the top 1 percent of households saw their average wealth increase by 42 percent. By contrast, the bottom 40 percent of households saw their average wealth *decrease* by 76 percent over the same time period. Almost all the growth in household income and wealth during the 1990s accrued to the richest 20 percent. Not surprisingly, the final decade of the past century saw an explosion of very rich households: Between 1989 and 1998, the number of millionaires climbed by 54 percent (there are now approximately 5 million) and the number of deca-millionaires (with total assets of over $10 million) almost quadrupled.

Rising inequality in America is the result of two trends: wage inequality and asset inequality. The relative stagnation of wages since the 1970s, before a recent increase, has a number of causes: the post-1973 slowdown of productivity growth, particularly in the service sector; the enlargement of the labor market by the entry of women and millions of low-skilled immigrant workers; the decline in unionization and union bargaining power; and the erosion of the minimum wage by inflation. The growth in asset inequality, by contrast, has a much simpler explanation. In fact, the economic boom of the late 1990s was really an asset boom, caused almost entirely by the run-up in the stock market.

When one considers the extremely concentrated nature of capital asset ownership in America, it becomes obvious why those at the top have received the lion's share of economic gains in recent years. Much has been made of the fact that nearly half of all American households now own stocks—either directly or indirectly, through mutual funds or private pensions. But this statistic is highly misleading, because the richest 10 percent of households still own approximately 90 percent of the total value of stocks, bonds, trusts, and business equity.

When critics of capitalism on the far Left are not treating the enrichment of investors as something inherently sinful, they all too often view the stock market boom as directly correlated to the stagnation of wages. The real problem, however, is not that the new wealth of the capital-owning elite has been created unjustly—because, for the most part, it has not. Rather, the problem is that so few Americans are able to partake in this new bounty.

Even if rising inequality results from the rich getting richer rather than from the poor getting poorer, it is still a profoundly destabilizing problem that threatens the social, economic, and political future of our republic. As William McDonough, chairman of the Federal Reserve Bank of New York, recently remarked: "Issues of equity and social cohesion [are] issues that affect the very temperament of our country. We are forced to face the question of whether we will be able to move forward together as a unified society with a confident outlook or as a society of diverse economic groups suspicious of both the future and of each other."

The social inequality produced by extreme concentrations of wealth and income is as much a threat to the legitimacy of the American market economy as to the legitimacy of the American political order. When masses of insecure and underpaid blue-collar workers, along with environmentalists, took to the streets in Seattle during the recent meetings of the World Trade Organization (WTO), they also undermined the very process by which the rules of global trade are shaped. America can no more build a thriving economy on a foundation of insecure and angered workers than it can build a healthy democracy on the back of an alienated citizenry.

That the United States is the most unequal society among the advanced technological nations is ironic, because our republic was founded in the hope of escaping the rigid class divisions that characterized Britain and other European societies, and because our nation's leaders have long understood the relationship between the health of our democracy and the widespread ownership of economic assets. Indeed, our Founding Fathers were heavily influenced by the seventeenth-century writings of John Locke, who argued that all individuals had a right to property ownership by virtue of their individual efforts. After his visit to the United States in the nineteenth century, Alexis de Tocqueville observed: "Nations are less disposed to make revolutions in proportion as personal property is augmented and distributed among them, and as the number of those possessing it is increased."

It was in this spirit that the Founding Fathers, in the U.S. Constitution, abolished primogeniture and entail—the feudal British legal mechanism that preserved huge family estates from generation to generation. It was in the same spirit that Lincoln's Republican Party introduced the Homestead Act in 1862—as a means of broadening property ownership, settling the western United States, and strengthening American democracy. In the twentieth century, our nation's leaders once again enacted major programs to broaden the stake of American citizens in the economy—most notably the G.I. Bill (1944) and the home mortgage interest deduction, which, along with easy credit, helped turn disgruntled proletarians, soldiers, and ex-farmers into solid middle-class citizens.

One reason that socialism—collective ownership of the means of production—never caught on in the United States was the widespread ownership of property. Many people whose equivalents in Industrial Age Europe or Asia belonged to resentful, landless, and propertyless mobs took part in "the American Dream" of economic mobility by owning their own farms, businesses, or homes.

These various policies to broaden capital ownership were not enacted solely for the benefit of individual landowners in the eighteenth and nineteenth centuries or home owners in the twentieth—rather, they were enacted because our political leaders understood that the ownership of economic assets served to build a stable middle class that would become rooted stakeholders in the nation and in its economy. As Jeff Gates, author of the *Ownership Solution*, explains, "People are likely to become better stewards of all those systems of which they are part—social, political, fiscal, cultural, and natural—as they gain a personal stake in the economic system, with all the rights and responsibilities that implies." More fundamentally, Gates points out, "Contemporary capitalism is not designed to create capitalists, but to finance capital. Absent political will, those dramatically different goals will never be combined."

What would be the twenty-first-century American equivalent of the Homestead Act of the nineteenth, and the home mortgage interest deduction of the twentieth? Both were tremendously successful in democratizing access to economic wealth and opportunity, and both did so by broadening ownership of assets in the form of real estate. In the Information Age, however, it is the ownership of financial assets that most needs to be broadened. Those who have benefited disproportionately from the new economy are those with significant assets in the financial markets, not those who derive their income solely from wages. The most obvious solution for lifting all boats in the new economy is to turn all Americans into owners of financial capital. In the twentieth century, public policy cushioned wage earners against shocks from the economy. In the twenty-first century, public policy should go one step further, and give all wage earners a stake in the system.

The recent collapse in personal savings over the past decade is another problem that could be cured in the very same way: helping all Americans build financial wealth through personal savings and development accounts. Through bold new policies to broaden capital ownership, we could, at one and the same time, enable all American citizens to benefit from the most productive parts of the economy, and ensure that there is a large and reliable savings pool to finance continued investments and economic expansion. What better way to ensure our long-term economic future, and gain the support of all Americans for a dynamic high-tech economy, than by enabling all our citizens to partake directly in our nation's prosperity?

Recognizing the need to broaden individual ownership of financial capital, thinkers and politicians of various stripes have begun to put forth a range of proposals to do so. Bruce Ackerman and Anne Alstott, in their book *The Stakeholder Society*, proposed giving every eighteen-year-old a onetime financial stake of $80,000— paid for by the imposition of a new 2 percent tax on the very rich. While Ackerman and Alstott deserve credit for their bravery, the blatant redistributionism underlying their proposal dooms it from the start in the real world of politics. Closer to the target, Senator Bob Kerrey of Nebraska and Senator Daniel Patrick Moynihan of New York proposed a KidSave Program in 1998 that would provide a nest egg of $3,500 for every American child by his or her fifth birthday.

The game Monopoly has been a longtime national hit because people recognize that it mirrors many of the realities of modern-day capitalism. But there is one big difference between the board game and reality. In the former, everyone starts off with an equal amount of assets, after which a combination of skill and luck reallocates them. In reality, Americans start off life with vastly different financial prospects and situations—the fortunate minority have trust funds set up in their names from birth, while the vast majority must begin the game of life with little other than the love of their parents, and a minority cannot even count on that. Equality of opportunity and inequality of outcomes is the American way. But if we are serious about the first part of this proposition, then perhaps we should give every newborn at least some basic assets with which to begin life.

What if each American newborn were given a onetime gift of $6,000, at birth, as a down payment on a productive life? This is the amount that would be required for all Americans to have approximately $20,000 in their own capital accounts by the time they reach their eighteenth birthdays. Given the number of babies born each year in the United States, such a plan would cost surprisingly little—about $24 billion annually—and if the program were means-tested, it would cost even less. But the potential rewards could be astonishing.

Suppose, for instance, that the average child's nest egg is invested in a relatively safe portfolio which yields a real return of 7 percent per year. By the time this child graduates from high school, she would have over $20,000 to invest in a high-quality college education, in addition to conventional student loans, grants, or scholarships. But maybe she does not want to go to college, and instead decides to go straight into the workforce and save her nest egg to build a family down the road. By the time she and her husband reach thirty, let's imagine that they decide to buy their first house and have their first child. If their publicly provided trust funds have remained untouched, each would have accumulated $48,000—for a combined total of $96,000. This should be more than enough for a down payment on that house, and cover the added expenses of their newborn. At the other extreme, let's suppose that a citizen, for whatever reason, decided not to touch her nest egg until she retired, at the age of seventy-five. By then, because of the miracle of compound interest, her nest egg would have increased to well over $1 million, enabling her not only to retire in peace, but to pursue a new hobby as a philanthropist. Not bad for a onetime investment of $6,000.

For such a system to meet its objectives, there would need to be some basic restrictions on what individuals could do with their endowments. First, a personal development account established for each child would accrue interest tax-free. Although parents would serve as the custodians of these development accounts until their children reached the age of eighteen, it would be clearly legislated that parents could in no way touch the money. In fact, no recipients of this childhood trust fund would be able to assign the rights to their money at any point throughout their lives, meaning that no secondary markets in such rights could be established. As in the case of a Roth IRA today, the use of these special trust funds would be restricted to various types of personal investments, such as: paying for the costs of higher education or vocational training, putting a down payment on a first home, covering serious health emergencies, or starting a legitimate business. Absent these uses, the money might simply accumulate toward supplementing a citizen's retirement income. But the obvious incentive would be for Americans to make full use of these funds throughout their working lives, in order to continually upgrade their skills, earning potential, asset base, or health.

The idea of making every American child a trust-fund baby from birth could also have very positive effects on the well-being of our society at large, not to mention our economy. Even if all children received the same $6,000 endowment, it would be of disproportionate help to the poorest in society, who often feel that the system is rigged against them. By telling poor inner-city children that if they make it through high school there will be a pot of money there to help carry them through college, the incentives of life in the inner cities could change dramatically. Putting home ownership within the reach of all Americans, rather than restricting it to those fortunate enough to have or be able to borrow enough for a down payment, could greatly expand the middle class. Likewise, turning every child into a stakeholder could help foster a new sense of national community, and even national pride.

Henry Ford once said that if each of his workers was not prosperous enough to afford one of his automobiles, then his business would ultimately suffer. Likewise, if the problems of rising economic inequality and collapsing personal savings continue to weigh down average American families, the health of our economy will suffer. There is simply no way to maintain the world's most dynamic economy on the backs of a shrinking, undereducated, and insecure middle class. Our challenge is to ensure that all boats rise once again with the broader economic tide. Accomplishing this goal will require resurrecting one of America's most successful historic traditions— that of broadening capital ownership—and updating it in accordance with the dynamics of the new economy.

The promise of this kind of "universal capitalism" is as profound as it is straightforward: By turning all citizens into capital owners, we could not only enable all Americans to partake in the wealth-creating effects of the most productive sectors of our economy, but we could simultaneously create a broad new class of stakeholders who would have a self-interest in seeing that America sustains its dynamic high-tech economy. A new, citizen-based social contract can ensure that all Americans are protected from the unavoidable dangers caused by creative destruction in our dynamic economy. At the same time, a new citizen-based program of broadening capital ownership can ensure that all Americans share in the economic benefits of creative destruction.

If we want the Denis Papins of today to invent and develop the modern equivalents of the steamship, then we must be careful to persuade the equivalents of the Boatmen's Guild that they will not be thrown into destitution as a result of technological change. Even better, we can provide them with a share of the economic gains from the adoption of the new technology by making them stakeholders in capital markets. If we fail to accomplish these two goals, then we can expect a political backlash against creative destruction in the economy, as a result of which technological progress might very well, so to speak, run out of steam.

All of the ideas we have put forth in this chapter share a dual goal: maximizing economic dynamism while minimizing individual economic insecurity. This should be the grand bargain underlying a new social contract for the new economy. The best way to achieve these two goals, in the areas of health care and retirement policy, is to combine mandatory self-insurance and private retirement savings accounts with guaranteed and means-tested government safety nets. And in order to help all Americans to get ahead, and not merely make do, in the new economy, we should also pursue an imaginative new program of universal capitalism.

The reforms we have proposed, by dividing responsibility between the individual citizen and the government, would free companies to do what they do best: compete with one another to make a profit by providing goods or services at lower costs.

Our proposals are also premised on a new conception of the role of government and of the responsibility of citizens. The safety net philosophy that we advocate holds that public benefits should be provided to those who need them most, while those who can afford to save for their own retirements or finance their own health care insurance should be required to do so. As we have argued, the citizens of the twenty-first century can and should be held to a higher personal standard while benefiting from a greater array of choices. Indeed, our proposal would empower all Americans to choose their own health insurers and decide how to invest their own retirement funds. As a result, these reforms would help inaugurate a new era of big citizenship, in which personal responsibility, individual choice, and economic security grow in tandem.

In a market economy organized to encourage the process of creative destruction, hiring and firing should be encouraged, as a natural part of the process of allocating resources to their most efficient uses. It should be easy for employers to add workers when needed and to shed them when necessary. For their part, workers must worry about losses of wage income, but if they had portable health and pension benefits—and better yet, financial assets—then losing their jobs would be far less devastating, and might even provide opportunities for career advancement. Today's policy of linking safety net benefits to particular employers, however, has left many individuals chronically insecure, in addition to retarding commercial and technological progress.

Our proposals for reforming American retirement policy and health care policy have this added advantage: Each would forever eliminate the troubling distinctions between full-time and contingent workers. Since workers would no longer rely on their employers for the provision of health care and pension benefits, there would no longer be an incentive to distinguish between two classes of employees. All workers would be treated the same, and all companies would suddenly have the flexibility they need to flourish in the new economy. Just as important, workers would have the best of both worlds: the freedom and benefits that derive from their own private retirement accounts and portable health care coverage, and the security of knowing that guaranteed safety nets are there to catch them if they fall.

A new American social contract for the new economy is long

overdue. When basic benefits are citizen-based instead of employer-based, when the distinction between full-time and contingent workers has become meaningless, when all Americans have their own retirement savings accounts, and when all our newborns are turned into trust-fund babies from birth—then we will know that we are living in the morning of the Information Age, rather than in the twilight of the Industrial Age.

# Three

•

# DIGITAL ERA DEMOCRACY

"Youth," Oscar Wilde observed, "is America's oldest tradition." Not anymore. At the beginning of the twenty-first century, America's government is coming to resemble its elderly symbol, Uncle Sam.

The success of the American nation in the twenty-first century, as in the nineteenth and twentieth, depends on the proper functioning of all three sectors of society: the market, the state, and the community. We should therefore be concerned by the fact that American government is lagging so far behind American business in adapting to the latest wave of technological change and organizational efficiencies. As the debacle of the 2000 election illustrated for the whole world to see, the United States has one of the most archaic electoral systems in the modern world. Likewise, its structure of federal, state, and local taxation, and its assignment of responsibility among different levels of government, reflect the customs and theories of earlier eras. And its public educational system, once the most advanced in the world, had deteriorated to such a point that many American schools now rank among the worst of all developed nations.

The U.S. government in the twenty-first century does not need radical reduction, nor does it need radical expansion. But in the interests of national vitality, fairness, and individual choice, American government at all levels needs radical renewal. This is particularly the case when it comes to our basic electoral process, our system of taxation, and our system of public education.

All three of these elements of American government are handicapped today by a similar legacy—a legacy of localism reflecting the peculiar way in which the U.S. nation-state originated. The story of American progress is to a large degree the story of the emancipation of the individual U.S. citizen, with the help of the federal government, from the tyranny of the local majority. For instance, Emancipation and Reconstruction established the promise of nationwide civil rights—a promise not fulfilled until the 1960s. As another example, the New Deal helped to modernize the U.S. economy by replacing a patchwork of state and local programs with streamlined federal ones. It is now time, in the twenty-first century, to promote a similar synthesis of national simplification and fairness, with an added emphasis on individual choice, in the areas of electoral rules, taxation, and education.

In the previous chapter we proposed replacing our employer-based social contract, an obsolete legacy of the industrial era, with a new, citizen-based social contract more suitable for the new economy of the Information Age. In the realm of government, as in the realm of the economy, we need to apply the principle of citizen-based reform. Our democracy should put individual citizens first in every dimension of public life by ensuring that electoral rules maximize the choices of citizens, not the power of parties or interest groups. In the realm of taxation, not only should our federal tax system be radically simplified, but the archaic quilt of state and local sales taxes, which is rapidly being undermined by e-commerce, should be replaced with taxes that are collected at the national level and rebated to the states. Perhaps the most damaging relic of localism remaining in America today is the link between local property taxes and public school funding; in the twenty-first century it is imperative to equalize school funding nationwide on a per-pupil basis.

Let us begin with the rusting machinery of American democracy. In the aftermath of the 2000 election, much public attention was focused on ways to improve the mechanisms by which votes are counted in the United States. As the public learned to its dismay, the likelihood that a vote will count depends on where it is cast. In 2000, primitive punch-card systems, like the ones that created all the controversy in Florida, were used in 37 percent of American counties. More efficient optical scan systems using shaded-in ballots were used in 25 percent. Only 7 percent of counties employed high-tech electronic keyboard or touch-screen voting, while the remainder used marked paper ballots in different ways.

When the Supreme Court ruled that using different standards in Florida recounts violated the equal protection clause of the Fourteenth Amendment, this not only put George W. Bush in the White House, it also energized moves to develop a nationwide standard for vote counting. Indeed, it should not be that difficult for the country to agree to a uniform voting system that maximizes the likelihood that every vote will be counted while minimizing opportunities for fraud and ambiguity. Millions of Americans use ATMs and the Internet for complex financial transactions every day; a voting method that uses touch-screen devices for voting in polling places and the Internet for absentee voting would seem to be the obvious answer.

Although modernizing vote-counting equipment is important, this is essentially a technical question rather than a political one. Adopting a foolproof method of counting votes would not resolve the more fundamental flaws of American democracy, which are caused not by antiquated equipment but by antiquated electoral rules.

The deeper crisis revealed by the 2000 election is that only about half of eligible voters even made it to the polls, and many who did were not particularly enthusiastic about either of the two front-runners. It is by now well known that voter alienation has reached worrisome proportions in America. What is at stake is nothing less than the legitimacy of American democracy. Yet even among those most concerned about this situation, there is no consensus as to either the cause or the cure. Instead, there are three explanations of the problem, each of which justifies a different proposed solution: the Beltway Insider theory, the Special Interest theory, and the Lack of Choice theory.

The Beltway Insider theory holds that the elected representatives we send to Washington are inherently corrupt, and become all the more so the longer they spend within the Beltway. The solution of choice is therefore to impose term limits on congressmen and senators (we already have a two-term limit on presidents). The second theory, the Special Interest theory, also identifies corruption as the source of popular disaffection with politics. Unlike the Beltway Insider theory, the Special Interest theory concentrates not on the politicians themselves but on the interest groups that corrupt them—the lobbies, PACs, and rich donors. Here the solution of choice is campaign finance reform, which by freeing politicians from the need to exchange favors in return for campaign contributions, would permit them to revert to the status of civic-minded public servants. The third theory explaining the alienation of American voters is the Lack of Choice theory. This holds that a plurality, perhaps even a majority, of Americans are frustrated with our political order because they do not like the choices offered by our two-party system—namely, liberal Democrats and conservative Republicans.

Which of these theories is correct? Neither the Beltway Insider theory nor the Special Interest theory explains why Americans are now more likely than in the past to distrust politicians. Contrary to popular belief, our elected officials at the federal level, as individuals, are actually less corrupt today than at any time in American history. And although scholars disagree about the precise effect of spending on elections, it is clear that there is little correlation between money spent and how the two parties do in particular districts and states. For instance, in the epochal 1994 election, which gave control of both houses of Congress to the Republicans for the first time in half a century, Republicans outspent Democrats in only twenty-two of the fifty-six seats they captured, and most of those were districts likely to vote Republican anyway.

To be sure, there are good reasons to support campaign finance reform—among others, it would lower the barrier to entry for middle-class and working-class candidates and reduce the influence that special interests have over candidates once elected. The simplest and most effective way to reduce the importance of money in politics is to require TV and radio stations, as conditions of their licenses, to give free media time to the candidates during the campaigns. Unlike attempts to ban spending on political advocacy by individuals and private associations, mandated free media time would raise no constitutional problems, only the political opposition of the telecommunications lobby, which stands to lose advertising revenues.

But reducing the role of money in campaigns would not alter the major problem with American politics—the lack of political options. As we have seen, polls consistently reveal that self-identified independents outnumber partisan Democrats and Republicans. At the same time, polls reveal that up to 50 percent of Americans routinely describe themselves as moderates, rather than as liberals or conservatives. The younger Americans are, the more likely they are to see themselves as independents. Among the eighteen to twenty-nine age group, 44 percent are independents, compared to only 29 percent

Democrats and 26 percent Republicans. When the three categories of Democrats, Republicans, and independents are further divided among liberals, conservatives, or moderates, one finds that between 1984 and 1998, liberal Democrats made up only 10–13 percent of the public, and conservative Republicans only 17–22 percent.

The mystery of voter alienation, then, is solved. Partisan Democrats and partisan Republicans are both minorities in the American electorate; neither amounts to more than about one third of the public. Not only are independents alienated from the Democratic and Republican Parties, but also moderate and conservative Democrats, and liberal and moderate Republicans, are frustrated by the lack of choice in politics. Americans are frustrated with American politics for one major reason: the limitation of their political choices to the Democratic Party, dominated—in Congress at least—by a liberal minority, and the Republican Party, dominated by a conservative minority.

When asked whether our nation should do away with the existing two-party system, a clear majority of Americans say yes. Intuitively, they know that there must be a better way.

American politics is dominated by two parties because we have yet to abandon an outdated electoral system inherited from eighteenth-century Britain. The United States is one of a dwindling number of democracies, most of them English-speaking countries, which use an archaic electoral system known as plurality or first-past-the-post voting. The plurality system elects legislators from single-member districts and can yield perverse results. In a two-way race, the candidate with a majority of votes wins. But in a race with three or more candidates, the candidate who receives the most votes wins, even if that candidate receives less than a majority of the votes. In other words, if there are more than two candidates, the winner may be a politician whom a majority—sometimes an overwhelming majority—of the public voted against. Thus, in a three- or four-way race a candidate with, say, 35 percent of the vote may represent a district, even though 65 percent of the voters wanted somebody else.

You may have heard that a vote for a third party is a wasted vote. Now you see why. Under a plurality voting system like ours, if you vote for a third party in a three-way race you will merely drain off support from the candidate whom you least dislike and promote the election of the candidate whom you would least like to see in office. In the 2000 presidential contest, Ralph Nader siphoned off votes from Al Gore and probably cost him the election, even though most Nader voters would probably have preferred Gore to Bush. In the very same way, Ross Perot might have siphoned off enough votes from George Bush Sr. in 1992 to throw the election to Bill Clinton. In other words, if we had an electoral system that more accurately reflected the true choices of the people, George Bush Sr. would probably have won in 1992, but his son George Bush Jr. would most likely have lost in 2000.

Because voting for a third party so easily backfires, voters in countries with plurality systems like the United States and Britain are offered a stark choice between voting for one of two major national parties or not voting at all. Increasing numbers of Americans have chosen the latter option. The reason seems clear: A plurality of Americans are not satisfied with the political choices that the two-party system provides. And if the two-party system does not fit our multiparty citizenry, then the system, not the citizenry, must give way.

Are there ways to broaden electoral choices in America without amending our Constitution or moving to a parliamentary system? Yes. One of the most promising reforms that is particularly suited to America's single-member legislative districts and to our elections for single offices—like those of U.S. senators, mayors, governors, and presidents—is "instant runoff voting," alternatively called "rank order voting," or "single transferable vote." Whatever name this system goes by, its basic principle is to allow voters to register the order in which they prefer three or more candidates on their ballots. If no candidate receives a majority of the vote, then the second-choice votes are redistributed, and third-choice votes, and so on, until one candidate passes the 50 percent mark. The result would be the same as a runoff election, except that the initial election and the runoff would take place simultaneously—thus the term *instant runoff*.

If, in the 2000 presidential race, the president had been elected by instant runoff instead of by the plurality method in the electoral college, voters would have been asked to put a 1 or a 2 or a 3 or a 4 after the names of George Bush, Al Gore, Ralph Nader, and Patrick Buchanan. Since no candidate won a majority, Nader and Buchanan would have been dropped and the second-choice votes of those who voted for them would have been redistributed to Gore and Bush. In a crude attempt to mimic an instant runoff system, so-called Nader Traders in the 2000 election tried to register their support for Nader without undermining Gore by swapping pro-Nader votes in states safe for Gore with pro-Gore votes in swing states. If instant runoff voting were formally adopted, this kind of contorted strategy would not be necessary.

The benefit of the instant runoff approach is that it would remove some of the barriers that prevent serious third or fourth parties from emerging, while at the same time ensuring that no fringe or extremist parties could win an election with a small plurality of the vote. In short, an instant runoff system would set a high but not insurmountable bar for the election of third-party or independent candidates. At the same time, it would encourage more serious candidates to run on independent or third-party platforms, since they could no longer be tarred or dismissed as spoilers by the guardians of the existing two-party system. New information technologies can make the widespread use of instant runoff voting both practical and efficient.

Instant runoff voting is one of many ways we could move from our current system of plurality voting to a new system of "choice vot-ing" (also known as proportional representation). Most elections in the United States are for single-member districts, but this need not be the case—particularly when it comes to the election of U.S. con-gressmen and state legislators. The advantage of multimember dis-tricts is that they allow for a greater range of candidates and parties. Imagine, for example, if a dozen candidates were running for a five-member delegation in the U.S. House of Representatives, and vot-ers put a 1, a 2, and so on next to the names of the candidates, in order of preference. In this way, voters would be able to mix and match different parties, or to vote for independent candidates on the ballot. This would help ensure that political parties are repre-sented in the government more or less in proportion to their strength in the electorate. The instability that multiparty systems sometimes cause in parliamentary democracies like Israel and Italy could not occur in the United States, where the executive branch is independent of the legislature, and where the president, the House of Representatives, and the Senate are elected by different con-stituencies.

Replacing plurality voting with choice voting in one or more of these ways not only would broaden the options available to all Amer-ican voters, but also could ultimately result in one of two long-term transformations in our political system, both of which would be good for our nation and our democracy.

One possible outcome would be the gradual ascendancy of one or more serious new parties, if indeed they were able to build up plu-rality support. Even if they failed to elect leaders to high offices, such third parties could certainly broaden the range—and perhaps the depth—of political discourse. For instance, although Reform Party candidate Ross Perot lost in the 1992 presidential election, he was nevertheless quite successful in pushing his pet issue—balanc-ing the budget—to the fore of national attention, as candidates from both major parties scrambled to win over Reform Party voters. The other possible outcome of the adoption of choice voting would be the gradual transformation of one or both of today's dominant parties, which would suddenly have an incentive to forge new coalitions with third-party candidates in order to court their second-choice votes. Over time, this could return our two-party system to the more fluid and less polarized dynamics typical of earlier decades.

In earlier generations, the typical compromise between America's multiparty citizenry and its two-party electoral order was an informal system of two coalition parties. For much of American history real parties were not the Democrats, Republicans, Federalists, or the Whigs, but factions within these nominal parties—conservative Democrats, liberal Republicans, Cotton Whigs, and Conscience Whigs. As late as the 1960s, there was a de facto four-party system in the United States. Both the Republican Party and the Democratic Party were divided into liberal and conservative wings. Liberal Republicans collaborated with liberal Democrats on civil rights; conservative Democrats collaborated with conservative Republicans in supporting the cold war.

In recent years, however, even as more Americans have identified themselves as moderates or independents, the two parties have become more consistently liberal and conservative. In the 1970s, according to the League of Conservation Voters, congressional Democrats and Republicans differed in voting scores by around 20 percent. By the 1980s, the gap had grown to around 30 points. In the 1990s, there was a 60 to 70 percent divergence in voting patterns. Today, there are almost no conservative Democrats left, and very few liberal Republicans. In Congress, both of the national parties are now controlled by their extremes.

The attempts by liberal Democrats and conservative Republicans to make the two major parties in the United States more ideologically uniform have had two results. The first result has been the alienation of a growing number of American voters, who cannot find even a faction within a major party with which they can identify. The second has been the debasement of our political discourse and the emergence of a political culture based on partisan scandal-mongering rather than bipartisan achievement.

When the U.S. Congress worked best—from the mid-1930s until the early 1970s—the House and Senate functioned in a fluid, kaleidoscopic manner. Conservative Democrats often sided with conservative Republicans; liberal Republicans voted sometimes with liberal Democrats; sometimes liberals and conservatives, in the same or opposite parties, cooperated. Indeed, if we look at the major congressional achievements of the twentieth century—Social Security, the Marshall Plan, the enabling legislation for NATO and the UN, the G.I. Bill, Medicare, Head Start, the Civil Rights and Voting Rights Acts— we find that they are concentrated in this era of weak parties and strong cross-party coalitions. Democrats may have controlled Congress, with a few brief exceptions, during this period, but much of the credit for these landmark achievements goes to Republican lawmakers. For example, as a result of the number of segregationist Democrats in Congress in the 1960s, Republican members of Congress were more likely to vote for the historic civil rights legislation than Democrats. Moreover, the great House and Senate leaders in this era were relatively bipartisan figures like House Speaker Sam Rayburn and Senate Majority Leader Lyndon Johnson, who worked comfortably with members of the other party as well as with their own.

Since the 1970s, however, the two parties have become highly polarized again, as they were in the period from the post–Civil War era until the 1930s. First, in the early 1970s, party-line liberals took over the Democratic Party in Congress, rewriting the rules to strip conservative and even moderate members of their own party of congressional power. A similar revolution in the Republican Party took place in the late 1980s and 1990s, culminating in Newt Gingrich's consolidation of power during the 1994 election. Since then, power in the Republican Party in Congress has also been centralized in a tiny group of hard-line ideologues and enforced by ruthless party discipline.

If we look at the Congresses in the eras of partisan polarization before and after the mid-twentieth century, we find very little constructive legislation. From the 1970s to the present, Congress has produced no historic legislation on the scale of the Civil Rights Act or Social Security or the Marshall Plan. Instead, Congress has specialized in scandal. The Democratic majority in the 1970s and 1980s, and the Republican majority in the 1990s, have presided over a series of show trials of presidents of the opposite party—Nixon, Reagan, and Clinton. The conversion of Congress into a permanent inquisition is a result of the polarization of the party elites in Congress, and the loss of power and influence by centrists in both parties—moderate Democrats and moderate Republicans.

If choice voting did not lead to the permanent rise of third and fourth parties, it would at a minimum increase the options in American politics by moving our present polarized two-party system toward a looser two-party system in which the parties were once again coalitions of groups. Because disaffected members of a dominant party could run as independent candidates without ultimately undermining the prospects of their party, these disaffected members could gain more influence and autonomy within their own parties—in direct proportion to their actual popular following. As in the past, we could end up with a de facto multiparty system in which caucuses would function much like miniature parties, as the Southern Democrats and Progressive Republicans did in the middle of the twentieth century. The major caucuses could come together at conventions and elections, but function more or less on their own the rest of the time. In this scenario, there would be no plain Democrats or plain Republicans, only hyphenated Democrats and hyphenated Republicans—Liberal Democrats, Populist Democrats, Centrist Democrats, Conservative Republicans, Libertarian Republicans, and Centrist Republicans. In a new era of Caucus Power, comparable to the one between the 1930s and the 1970s, dissatisfied moderates, populists, libertarians, and others could find places in one or another coalition party. Thanks to choice voting, many Americans who now boycott the ballot box might just find reason to return to it.

When it comes to presidential elections, there is another important reform that could help overcome much of the popular alienation of our day. As all Americans were reminded during the 2000 election, we do not elect our president through a popular vote, but rather through the electoral college system. This system has its share of pros and cons, but one of its greatest weaknesses is that it dilutes the influence of voters in many parts of the country, as well as the attention they receive from the candidates themselves. Because most states award their electoral college votes on a winner-take-all basis, a Democratic voter in predominantly Republican Oklahoma has as negligible an influence as a Republican voter has in predominantly Democratic California. For the very same reason, the presidential candidates have little incentive to spend much time in the majority of "predictable" states, and therefore spend most of their time in a small number of so-called swing states. In both of these ways, ordinary voters across the country rightfully feel they are essentially excluded from the process of selecting their president.

The geographic imbalances created by our electoral college system are further exacerbated by the fact that each state gets as many electoral votes as it has members in its congressional delegation (House plus Senate combined). The addition of two electoral votes for the two senators actually triples the electoral weight of South Dakota, which has only one member of Congress. As a result, one South Dakota electoral vote represents 232,000 people, while one New York electoral vote represents 550,000 people. Thanks to the electoral college, Bush won the presidency in 2000, even though Al Gore won the popular vote nationwide—6.1 million people in six small states gave Bush twenty-four electoral votes, while 10.4 million voters provided Gore with only twenty-two electoral votes.

Short of amending the Constitution to eliminate the electoral college, there is a proven way to reduce the dilution of the votes and influence of the majority of Americans who live in populous states. Today, two states, Maine and Nebraska, divide their electoral votes roughly on the basis of the popular vote, instead of allotting all of the state's electoral votes to the plurality winner. Each electoral vote corresponding to one of the state's congressional districts is assigned to the presidential candidate who wins that district, while the state's two electoral votes corresponding to its two U.S. senators are assigned to the winner of the statewide popular vote. The other state legislatures, on their own initiative, could follow the example of Maine and Nebraska. Doing so would empower all voters with the confidence that their vote really counts, and create a strong incentive for presidential candidates to pay attention to all Americans in all states. (Using instant runoff voting instead of plurality voting to determine the top two candidates would reduce the risk that a third party would throw the presidential election into the House of Representatives, in the absence of an electoral college majority for one candidate.)

Most people make two mistakes when thinking about political reform. First, they assume that the U.S. Constitution mandates the details of our present electoral system. Second, they assume that any significant reform has to begin in Washington, D.C. Both of these beliefs are incorrect. Any state, at any time, has the power to replace plurality voting with choice voting for its own elections, whether they be for state offices or federal offices. Likewise, state legislatures have the right to alter the way that they assign electoral college votes in presidential contests.

The point to remember is that the process of overhauling our national political system need not begin in our nation's capital. Most of the democratic reforms of the past—from the abolition of slavery and segregation to the enfranchisement of women and the adoption of the secret ballot—were achieved in particular states decades or generations before they were adopted at a federal level. Our fifty states are often said to be "laboratories of democracy." They need to live up to that reputation once more.

Although the modernization of our political system should probably start at the state level, it should by no means end there. Another dysfunctional element of our democracy is the way Congress goes about conducting its business and organizing itself. Most for-profit and nonprofit corporations are required to have charters that explain, in language the ordinary shareholder can understand, the rules for appointing officers and making high-level decisions. The House and the Senate, by contrast, operate according to a set of customary procedures. The Founding Fathers chose not to include in the Constitution specific rules for organizing Congress. They trusted the members of Congress to behave in a responsible manner. This was a mistake.

Here is an example. In the fall of 1997, Senate Majority Leader Trent Lott (R-Miss.) used his power to prevent the campaign finance reform bill sponsored by Senators John McCain (R-Ariz.) and Russell Feingold (D-Wis.) from being debated by the Senate—for fear that it might actually pass. Political scientist Barbara Sinclair describes what happened: "[Lott] then 'filled the amendment tree'; that is, he used the majority leader's power of first recognition to offer an amendment that the Democrats saw as anti-labor and strongly opposed and then offered the full complement of amendments allowable under Senate rules, thus assuring that his amendment could not be further amended. Lott's purpose was to force a Democratic filibuster of his amendment and thus both stymie action and shift the blame to Democrats. The maneuver did produce stalemate; the legislation was on the floor for several days, but when neither side had the votes to impose cloture, Lott pulled the bill."

Amendment tree? Cloture? Filibuster? What on earth is going

on? Most American voters expect their representatives and senators to debate bills and then to engage in up-and-down votes on them, not to play tricks with antiquated Senate or House rules in order to *prevent* a debate or a vote. Washington insiders, accustomed to this kind of cynical game playing, seldom ask whether this is a rational way to run the legislature of the world's leading republic.

Democrats as well as Republicans have mastered this kind of parliamentary gamesmanship, so that the party in power in Congress always has an incentive to manipulate the rules to its advantage. In the absence of external pressure, neither of our two official parties will ever adopt a simple, straightforward set of rules for both houses of Congress. That pressure should be supplied, then, by a national citizens' movement advocating a new and transparent set of rules for Congress. Let's call them new bylaws for Congress. Such a movement might support an amendment to the U.S. Constitution detailing basic rules for the organization of the House and Senate and for the way in which Congress should conduct its business. The mere prospect of a popular movement in favor of new bylaws for Congress might be sufficient to frighten the two major parties into reforming Congress on their own.

One of the reasons Americans are disgusted with politics is the fact that Congress, which should present civil debates over issues, instead seems to focus on tactics: filibusters, germane and nongermane amendments, and the like. Sensible new guidelines for Congress should not be particularly detailed. But they could set forth a few rules that would abolish the worst practices inherited from the past. The filibuster in the Senate should be abolished; rules for cloture (ending debate) should be reformed; rules for discharging bills for committees should minimize the authority of party leaders and maximize the chance that legislation will be debated and voted upon. Rules for amendments should prevent the attachment of irrelevant riders to omnibus appropriations bills, to prevent the political gamesmanship that led to the budget showdowns of the mid-1990s between the Democratic president and the Republican Congress. Many veterans and observers of Congress have also proposed that budgeting should be done on a two-year rather than an annual basis, to free time for debate and action on other issues.

Among other provisions, new bylaws for Congress might mandate choice voting instead of plurality voting for many routine votes that U.S. representatives and senators have to cast (equivalent bylaws might do the same for state legislatures, city councils, and other public deliberative bodies). For example, the order in which members of the House and Senate must vote on bills now gives partisans a chance to play parliamentary games. Instant runoff voting provides a mechanism by which an up-or-down vote on a series of similar legislative proposals can be replaced by ranking two or three or four slightly different bills in the order in which the majority of the legislators prefers them. Even the Speaker of the House and the Senate Majority Leader might be elected by instant runoff. If they were elected in this way, then candidates would have an incentive to appeal to members of the other party as well as to their own. They would need the second-choice votes of their partisan rivals, as well as the first-choice votes of their fellow party members. Choice voting at all levels, then, would promote the intent of the Founding Fathers, who feared the influence of rigid political parties and hoped that shifting coalitions of factions, divided between two legislative houses, would not coalesce into permanent, disciplined political machines rolling over all opposition.

The advent of the Information Age has led some to speak about the coming of "digital democracy." But the phrase itself is quite ambiguous. Digital democracy could refer to the use of information technology to reinforce representative government—or to undermine it. In fact, the introduction of new technologies reopens an old debate between two wildly divergent views of governance: representative democracy versus direct democracy. As we seek to modernize our political institutions, we must be careful to keep this distinction forever clear in our minds.

Let's begin with the more hopeful scenario. If digital democracy means making voting on-line more common than voting in polling places, if it means finding more efficient ways to deliver government services, or if it means facilitating dialogue between elected officials and their constituents—then it is a splendid idea. For instance, on-line voting could have helped us avoid the disastrous Florida vote-counting debacle of 2000. During the 2000 primary elections, the state of Arizona allowed on-line voting, and the result was a dramatic increase in voter participation. There were a few glitches, but the experiment was judged to be a success. Once adequate technical back-ups and voter authentication systems are in place, on-line voting could all but replace physical voting. This could increase voter turnout and offer citizens the convenience of casting their votes over a period of days, instead of only on Tuesdays—a practice that discourages turnout by many working people.

What is more, on-line voting might even reduce the influence of money in American politics, by reducing the importance of what money buys—radio and TV advertising, which today supply voters with most of the information they have about candidates. What if the virtual ballot were used, not only for the transaction of voting but for the purpose of informing the public about the candidates? Each ballot might become a portal with on-line links to the websites of the candidates. To facilitate citizen access to this information, a common format for candidate websites might be developed. In addition, the ballot portal might also provide links to endorsements and external evaluations of the accuracy of the candidates' statements. All of these features would empower citizens to make more informed choices.

There are countless other ways to leverage the power of new technologies in the service of our democracy. For instance, the on-line provision of various public services—from driver's licenses to passports to voter registration—could simultaneously increase the quality of such services and reduce their costs. Why go stand in a long line to renew your driver's license when you could accomplish the very same thing with far less hassle from almost any computer terminal? Likewise, why shouldn't each American be able to access their public pension balances, government-backed student loan accounts, or other such benefits on-line—in one centralized site? Already, thanks to a groundbreaking private-public partnership, the federal government in 2000 made all federal websites searchable in one centralized site (www.firstgov.gov). It seems only a matter of time before other government services will be streamlined in similar fashion, and eventually customized to the needs, interests, and circumstances of each individual citizen.

If digital democracy is interpreted to mean on-line voting and the on-line provision of services, then it should be welcomed. The problem arises when digital democracy is used to mean something more than enlisting new technology for the transactional and informational aspects of politics. Sooner or later, the day will come when a renegade populist candidate will propose that all political decisions be made directly by the people, through one or another version of on-line direct democracy.

In essence there are only two theories of democracy: representative democracy and direct democracy. Representative democracy is based on the idea that voters do not choose policies, they choose policymakers. It is these policymakers who choose policies—after debate and compromise with other elected leaders. Ideally, elected representatives should act on behalf of the values and interests of their constituents—not on behalf of their opinions, which may be based on ignorance or prejudice. Elected representatives, in this view, are like doctors or lawyers; their duty is to tell those who hire them the truth, even if it's something the client does not want to hear. Great leaders, be they legislators or chief magistrates like presidents and governors, are those who are willing to risk their political careers in order to promote the long-term interests of their constituents and their nation, even when that interest is not yet understood by a majority of the public.

Direct democracy, by contrast, rejects the distinction between the public interest and public opinion—between what the people really need and what they think they want. Proponents of direct democracy hold that at any moment, what a majority believes to be the public interest is in fact the public interest. The flaws in this conception should be obvious. A majority of the public may be partly or wholly ignorant of the facts in a given area of public policy. Even if the public is informed, the majority may neglect the genuine interests and concerns of various minorities. Direct democracy by its nature cannot provide for second thoughts or compromises.

Direct democracy comes in several versions. Initiative and referendum—the direct enactment of legislation or constitutional provisions by the electorate—is the most extreme. But the theory of direct democracy is also invoked by those who hold that a majority political party or a winning presidential candidate has a "mandate" from the voters. The idea of the party mandate or the presidential mandate assumes the existence of a coherent electoral majority capable of endorsing a coherent political platform.

Neither of these assumptions is realistic. In most races, a relatively small group of "swing voters" determines which party wins control of a legislature or which candidate wins a particular office. In these circumstances, to say that a majority chose the party or politician is technically correct but politically false. What really happened is that one coalition of minorities happened to have slightly more members than a rival coalition of minorities. The allied minorities may agree on nothing more than defeating the rival team. It is just as unrealistic to assume that voters endorse the platform of a party or a candidate. Only a minority of the American voters who gave Newt Gingrich's Republicans a majority in the House of Representatives in 1994 knew what the Contract with America was; however, that did not prevent Gingrich and his allies from claiming that the American people had endorsed the Contract. Bob Dole helped illustrate this point when he admitted that he did not even read the Republican platform in 1996, although he was the Republican candidate for president that year.

If the initiative-and-referendum version of direct democracy were legitimate, there would be no need for elected representatives at all, only something like a perpetual polling agency. Lawmaking and opinion-polling would be the same. If the theory of party mandates were correct, then the party that won a majority in House or Senate elections should get 100 percent of the seats; there would be no reason for members of the opposition party to show up, if the voters had already approved everything that the majority party would do in advance for the next session. Most frightening of all is the theory of the presidential mandate. If the president—and the president alone—has a mystical "mandate" from the American people, then disagreement with the president's policies must be rejection of the "will of the people." The logical outcome of the union of our presidential system with the mandate theory of direct democracy is elective dictatorship, on a four-year basis.

The philosophy of representative democracy, which we wholeheartedly defend, rejects the idea of the dictatorship of public opinion, of a party, or of a president. There is no single, coherent, enduring national majority; rather, there are multiple majorities. On one issue, there may be one majority; on another issue, a different majority. Representative democracy treats parties not as disciplined armies marching in unison to enact a program agreed on in advance of the last election, but rather as elements of shifting coalitions that change from subject to subject and bill to bill.

While we oppose the concept of on-line direct democracy, we would certainly welcome the increased use of new information technologies in facilitating two-way interactions between elected officials and their constituents. For most Americans today, politics is a one-way process: other than the occasional opportunity to vote, ordinary citizens seldom have occasion to voice their concerns or opinions. New communications technologies, by their very nature, hold the promise of making politics and policymaking a more interactive process. For instance, elected officials could host electronic town hall meetings on a regular basis to hear and respond to the issues of concern to their constituents. Alternately, the elected officials themselves could solicit commentary from their constituents on a wide range of issues. It will take time and trial and error to determine how interactive technologies can best be utilized in the public policymaking process, but it does seem clear that elected officials and citizens both could benefit from greater two-way interaction.

In evaluating proposals for using new technology to promote "digital democracy," then, we should favor those technical improvements that strengthen representative government. Representative democracy should be digitally enhanced—while direct democracy should not be digitally disguised.

If broadening electoral choices should be the first pillar of any program to modernize our public sector for the Information Age, then reinventing our tax system should be the second. As Oliver Wendell Holmes Jr. observed in 1904, "Taxes are the price that we must pay to be part of a civilized society." They are also the way in which government policy impacts the daily lives of all Americans most directly.

During the final two decades of the twentieth century, America's tax debate revolved primarily around the old question of *how much* to tax, with the traditional Left arguing for more and the traditional Right arguing for less. Although President George W. Bush chose to revive the old debate with his proposal for a large-scale tax cut, twenty years of intense partisan warfare has led to a broad public consensus that the current share of national income going to government at all levels—approximately 30 percent—is just about right. We accept this assumption that the government's portion of national income should remain relatively constant, and focus instead on the far more interesting tax questions of the Information Age, namely: *What* should be taxed? *Who* should be taxed? *Where* should taxes be administered? *How* should public revenues be allocated?

As you would expect in a country that was founded as the result of a tax revolt, our nation's tax system has changed dramatically and frequently during our brief history. Throughout the nineteenth century, for instance, most of our federal revenue came from tariffs on imported goods. Then the bulk of federal revenues shifted to a broad-based progressive income tax during the early part of the twentieth century, and finally, in the second half of the twentieth century, turned increasingly to regressive Social Security and Medicare payroll taxes. Meanwhile, the balance between state and local taxes, on the one hand, and federal taxes, on the other, shifted just as profoundly. Before the New Deal, state and local taxes raised a higher percentage of our total government revenue than federal contributions did, by one third. Since the 1930s, however, the proportions have been reversed; two out of every three dollars flowing to government have been collected at the federal level.

In the twenty-first century, the U.S. tax system is likely to undergo just as profound a metamorphosis. And indeed it should. As antitax conservatives never tire of pointing out, our nation's tax system has become so complicated and burdensome that it fills 9,400 pages, and even trained professionals have difficulty making sense of it. Beyond its unwieldiness, our current tax system also suffers from a number of design defects that make many of its elements highly inefficient, wildly unfair, and increasingly obsolete.

Any tax system worthy of the Information Age should be as simple, equitable, transparent, and efficient as possible. Ideally, our tax system should also be citizen-based instead of place-based or institution-based. The best way to illustrate these points is to begin with one of the components of our present tax system that fails each of these tests: our archaic patchwork of local and state sales taxes. Our state sales tax regime is to our tax system what the punchcard ballot is to our electoral system: the most obvious symbol of its anachronism.

Long before the advent of e-commerce and the emergence of policy problems relating to Internet taxation, our state sales tax system was already a Byzantine mess. Enacted as temporary measures to raise revenue during the Depression, state sales taxes have yet to be repealed. "Rejected by most economists as medieval anachronisms," wrote economist John F. Due in 1950, these taxes were "drawn up hastily, with little thought to their exact aims beyond raising revenue, their economic effects or the best structures in terms of the desired purposes." In fact, it would be difficult to design a more cumbersome system than one in which all fifty states rely on different sales tax regimes, and in which individual businesses are assigned the administrative burden of collecting such taxes.

Even worse, sales taxes are extremely regressive, meaning that they disproportionately burden the less well off. In 1995 the richest 1 percent of households, with an average income of $801,000, paid 1.1 percent of their income in sales and excise taxes, while the poorest families, with an average income of $15,600, paid 6.7 percent of their income. Yet forty-six states collect between one third and one half of their revenue from such taxes. Does it really make sense to penalize some poor people because of geography, and to continue relying on a sales tax system that is the product of inertia rather than strategy?

The proliferation of e-commerce has made the case for replacing the state sales tax system all the more urgent. To a certain extent, state sales tax systems have always been porous: A New Yorker who buys a product from a local vendor must pay the sales tax, but the purchase is exempt if the same product is ordered from a store in New Jersey that has no presence in New York. But the rapid proliferation of e-commerce has dramatically magnified the scale of this problem, which could cost states and localities up to $20 billion a year in lost revenue by 2003. Now imagine that the states try to remedy this problem by coordinating a system in which vendors in the nation's thirty thousand different tax jurisdictions must reimburse tax authorities in all fifty states for purchases made by their citizens. And imagine the headache—not to mention cost and lost time—that this would impose on small business startups. Just as it should not be the job of businesses in the new economy to provide health care and private pensions, it should not be their responsibility to assume cumbersome administrative duties in tax collecting.

While members of Congress may think they were just buying time by enacting an Internet tax moratorium, this moratorium only creates an artificial divide between brick-and-mortar businesses and Internet-based ones, which disadvantages the former in favor of the latter, and threatens the revenue base and hence fiscal solvency of many states. When you reflect that much sales tax revenue goes toward schools and education, the idea of maintaining the current sales tax system but exempting all types of e-commerce seems as perverse as it is absurd. The solution is to level the playing field between old and new businesses by eliminating state sales taxes altogether and replacing them with a more sensible and fair source of revenue.

Here's a concrete alternative. Why not replace our fifty separate state sales tax systems with a single and simple national consumption tax, whose proceeds are rebated to the states on a per capita basis? Unlike regressive sales taxes, a personal consumption tax can be made highly progressive by exempting a certain amount—say, the first $15,000 of consumption—so that the average cost of basic necessities like housing, food, and transportation would be free from taxation. At the same time, such a system would remove all tax collection burdens from businesses and ensure a level playing field for both "brick" and "click" industries.

A person's annual consumption could be calculated based on a simple formula: income minus savings and investment equals consumption. For example, if, after income taxes, you made $45,000 in a given year, saved $10,000, and spent the remaining $35,000, then with the $15,000 deduction, your taxable consumption would be $20,000. Naturally, the exemption level should be increased somewhat for each dependent. Because the sales tax does not differentiate between individuals with dependents and those without, our system would become more family-friendly in the process of becoming more progressive. A consumption tax designed for the new economy should also be education-friendly, given today's need for constant skills upgrading. Accordingly, education expenses might be viewed as investments rather than as consumption, and thus exempted from taxation.

In fiscal year 1997, all state and local sales taxes raised a combined $262 billion. A national consumption tax as described above, set at a 10 percent rate, would raise approximately the same amount of money, enabling us to replace all sales taxes. If there were a generous exemption at the bottom, the rich would pay higher consumption taxes than the middle-class, as a rule, and the truly poor would pay no consumption tax at all. The personal consumption tax we propose would also serve a public purpose by creating a bias in the tax code in favor of savings. To the extent that consumption taxes encouraged higher savings, they could increase the pool of capital available for investment and strengthen our overall economy in the process.

Raised nationwide, the consumption tax revenues would be distributed to the states on a per capita basis. For convenience, the Internal Revenue Service might collect the money, although the federal government would receive none of it; an independent agency might even be established to administer the distribution of the funds. For this system to work, Washington would have to distribute the money with few or no strings attached, and the states would need to reduce their other taxes by the amount that they receive as their share of the national consumption tax. Needless to say, conditioning the provision of new federal funds to states on the basis of the corresponding elimination or reduction of state sales taxes would be a powerful incentive for compliance.

The advantage of wealthy states over poor ones under our system would not be entirely eliminated—wealthy states would still raise more money, with minimal taxes, than could poor states at the same rates. But geographic differences in state and municipal spending per capita would be significantly reduced, to the benefit of the nation as a whole. Critics may complain that rich states would end up subsidizing poor states. But there are no rich states and poor states; there are only rich people and poor people. Rich people happen to be concentrated behind one set of arbitrary lines, while poor people are clustered behind another set of lines on a map. A system that appears to be "unfair" to particular states turns out to be very fair when applied to the population as a whole. It makes no difference to revenue sharing where the rich and poor are clustered, or whether they are intermingled evenly in every county and every state. Does a millionaire in New York City really have more in common with the people of upstate New York than with residents of New Jersey, right across the river?

In sum, replacing state and local sales taxes with a national consumption tax rebated to the states would not only provide an elegant solution to the Internet tax problem, but it would also render our whole tax system more efficient and progressive, and create a powerful new incentive for increased personal savings.

Sales taxes, however, are not the only ones that should be eliminated in the Information Age. So should corporate income taxes, for a variety of reasons. First, corporate income taxes, like state sales taxes, are classic examples of "stealth taxation." All economists agree that corporate income taxes are ultimately paid by individuals, not by corporations. Given that corporations are really just elaborate pass-through vehicles, all corporate taxes eventually fall on corporate shareholders, employees, and customers. Politicians tend to like these taxes, though, precisely because they are not visible to the public. But crafty politics may lead to poor policy.

In an increasingly global economy, differences in corporate tax rates between countries distort markets and corporate behavior, usually disadvantaging the countries with the highest tax rates. Indeed, the very process of globalization is undermining the rationale for corporate income taxes, because it encourages companies to locate their operations in a manner that lessens their corporate tax load.

Today, more and more companies are able to do what once only the largest multinationals could: minimize their tax exposure by moving from jurisdiction to jurisdiction. For instance, many companies incorporate in tax-free havens, like the Dutch Antilles, while others set up dummy companies as partners. Meanwhile, multinational corporations with activities in many countries have an incentive to structure their internal organization to minimize tax exposure, through complex tax-planning schemes that cycle the majority of corporate income through low-tax jurisdictions. In a world in which capital and corporations are highly mobile, imposing a domestic tax on corporations only serves to decrease their incentives to base their operations in—and run their worldwide income through—that particular country. As just one example, the decision of many insurance companies to make the island of Bermuda their headquarters costs the U.S. Treasury Department an estimated $4 billion a year.

Corporate income taxes have even more distorting effects in domestic policy. Routinely, members of Congress use the tax code to dole out favors to specific companies and industries, a practice that has led to an ever more complicated and counterproductive maze of corporate tax loopholes. This, in turn, has given rise to significant popular resentment, and to frequent demands for doing away with what has come to be called "corporate welfare."

More damaging still are state-level corporate income taxes, which states continually manipulate in order to compete against one another in zero-sum contests to attract businesses, factories, or facilities to their jurisdictions. The only real winners in this game are the small number of corporations (and their shareholders) that can extort ever more lucrative deals and concessions from the states courting them, even though the number of new jobs and benefits promised in such deals seldom materialize. The elimination by the states of their own corporate income taxes would be a major step toward ending these self-defeating practices and forcing states to compete with one another on the basis of their public services and quality of life.

One of the major goals of intelligent tax reform in the Information Age should be to make the individual the focus of taxation; another should be to make taxes as transparent as possible. Both of these goals could be achieved by replacing all corporate income taxes, which currently raise approximately 10 percent of federal revenue and 6.5 percent of state tax revenue, with revenue generated from individual income taxes. Doing so would allow decisions by corporations about where to locate their headquarters and facilities to be based on economic factors rather than on tax considerations. In fact, many companies would probably decide to return much of the income they had previously cycled through lower-tax jurisdictions back to the United States, following the abolition of federal and state corporate income taxes.

Naturally, new legislation would be required to ensure a smooth transition from corporate income taxes to individual income taxes. For instance, stronger legislation would be needed to prevent individuals from sheltering their incomes in dummy corporations set up as holding companies. Likewise, the United States and the European Union would need to enhance their restrictions on their citizens' ability to shelter individual assets in foreign tax havens, but such policies would be prudent even under the current system.

Many liberals will be quick to object that eliminating corporate income taxes would skew the tax system even more against the interest of working people and permit corporations to evade their responsibilities. But they would be wrong on both counts. If the public wants to shift a greater part of the tax burden to the wealthy or those benefiting most from corporate profits, then we should increase taxes on capital gains and passive income. Doing so would eliminate the middleman (the corporation), end the double taxation of capital, and put the tax burden where it belongs—on shareholders. Incidentally, shareholders would see greater returns on their investments, which would make it more difficult for them to argue against raising the capital gains tax.

In the final analysis, individuals pay all taxes anyway; we might as well be honest about the subject. A corporation is merely a group of shareholder-owners and employees whom the law protects from personal financial liability for corporate debts beyond the value of the corporation's assets. Indeed, a corporation is much like a dragon in a Chinese New Year's parade—there isn't really a dragon at all, just a group of people shuffling along inside a papier-mâché shell. In the twenty-first century, we should tax the people, not the dragon.


The anchor of our nation's tax system in the Information Age should remain the progressive income tax, because it represents the fairest and most efficient means of collecting public revenue. Its core principles are timeless: Individuals should be taxed on the basis of their total incomes, and wealthier individuals should incur higher tax rates. Unfortunately, however, the progressive income tax has evolved into an ever more convoluted, complicated, and problematic mess over the years. Our challenge, then, is to preserve its essence while radically simplifying its form.

In 1998, when *Money* magazine asked forty-six professional tax preparers to calculate taxes for a hypothetical family, every response was wrong. But the respondents were in good company; in 1999, according to a U.S. government audit, the civil servants who staffed the IRS telephone hotline gave out nearly 10 million incorrect answers to taxpayer questions. And our personal income tax is only becoming more complicated each year. In large part, this is because Congress and the White House have mastered the art of camouflaging their pet programs or giveaways through an elaborate set of loopholes in the form of tax expenditures and tax credits—all of which share the dubious distinction of being largely invisible to the average American. Democrats, in particular, have in recent years adopted a strategy of stealth social reform by means of dozens of narrowly targeted tax credits out of fear that more transparent programs would be less easily enacted or more easily repealed. In his 2000 budget, for instance, President Clinton proposed no fewer than twenty-seven new tax credits, five new exclusions, and three new deductions.

To their credit, Republicans have been the most ardent advocates of simplifying the income tax in recent years. But while they are correct in calling for a major overhaul of the current system, most Republican proposals for doing so are unconscionably skewed to the well-to-do, who are the last ones who need tax relief in the new economy. By contrast, Democrats, out of a defensive impulse to protect the increasingly weakened progressive features of our current system, usually oppose necessary rethinking of the personal income tax on principle. The current debate would seem to suggest that the goals of tax simplicity and fairness are somehow mutually exclusive. But this false dichotomy is just an artifact of old thinking. There is no reason why we could not design a radically simplified yet progressive income tax for the twenty-first century.

If the idea of greatly simplifying our tax code sounds familiar, it is because Republicans have been using it for years to sell their proposals for a so-called flat tax. The implication, of course, is that the goal of tax simplicity requires us to do away with today's progressive rate structure. Nothing could be farther from the truth. To understand why, we need to clear up some popular misunderstandings. Much of the confusion surrounding the idea of a flat tax, as well as much of its superficial appeal, stems from a poorly understood distinction between the concepts of a tax base and a tax rate. Indeed, typical flat tax proposals call flattening both the income tax base and rate, which can naturally lead to confusion between the two. The former refers to what is taxed, while the latter refers to how much it is taxed. As it turns out, virtually all of the complications in our current tax code stem from how the tax base is figured, not from how the tax rate is set. Accordingly, flattening the tax base makes eminent sense, while flattening the tax rate does not.

The first premise of a greatly simplified progressive income tax structure for the twenty-first century should be the elimination of the vast majority of income tax deductions, credits, and exemptions now in place. These subsidies and loopholes are responsible for most of the complications and distortions in our current tax system. Wipe these away, and volume upon volume of our incredibly unwieldy tax code could be moved to the historic records section of the National Archives. But our argument for eliminating most of these deductions is not only based on the goal of tax simplicity, it is also based on the ideal of equity.

The overwhelming share of benefits from today's tax expenditures flow to the wealthiest families in the United States. What the political scientist Christopher Howard calls "the hidden welfare state" consists of tax expenditures of all sorts, including tax deductions, tax credits, preferential tax rates, tax deferrals, and the exclusion of elements of income from taxation. In 1995 the visible welfare state (including Social Security and Medicare) cost nearly $900 billion; the hidden welfare state, operated through the tax code, added up to almost half that amount, around $400 billion. And this hidden welfare state is remarkably regressive, meaning that the more income you make, the more tax subsidies you receive. In 1994, for instance, taxpayers making more than $100,000 a year received 44 percent of the home mortgage interest tax expenditure, while taxpayers making between $30,000 and $50,000 received only 10 percent of the benefits, and those making $10,000 to $30,000 received less than 2 percent. Is this sensible social policy? Why should the government require all taxpayers to provide subsidies to rich homeowners without providing similar benefits to poor citizens who rent? Similar disparities undermine the legitimacy of our nation's other large tax expenditures.

What is more, the very poorest Americans, because they do not earn enough to pay income taxes in the first place, do not benefit from tax expenditures at all. The one exception to this rule is the means-tested Earned Income Tax Credit—the only targeted, refundable tax credit in the federal tax code. Unlike a typical tax deduction, the value of which increases with income, a tax credit is a single sum subtracted from the taxes you owe the government, and is therefore the exact same amount of money for everyone regardless of income. If the tax credit is refundable, then low income workers who are too poor to pay income taxes can nevertheless receive a check in the amount of the credit from the state or local government.

Most of today's tax deductions, expenditures, and credits—which total $700–800 billion a year—should be eliminated. By doing away with most of the hidden welfare state, the bulk of today's most troubling tax distortions would disappear, and calculating your taxes would become much easier. The minority of today's tax expenditures that serve a genuine public purpose could be replaced by a few consolidated, refundable tax credits earmarked to specific middle-class necessities, such as housing, child care, and lifelong learning. For instance, the mortgage income deduction, which chiefly benefits the affluent and increases with income, could be replaced with a refundable tax credit in a single, fixed amount that all Americans could use either for rent payments or mortgage payments.

The advantages of eliminating the majority of our current tax expenditures and replacing them with a small number of universal, refundable tax credits are numerous. First, most of the perverse incentives that now plague our tax code would disappear, leaving in their place a far more equitable system. All American taxpayers—rich and poor—would receive identical tax credits, but these would naturally be worth more to the poor, who need them most. Second, our tax code would become far simpler, more transparent, and user-friendly. The only party that would lose as a result of this radical simplification would be the army of tax accountants who would suddenly find themselves out of jobs. Next, thanks to this greater transparency, politicians could no longer camouflage their pet programs from public view by means of elaborate tax loopholes, meaning social policy would have to be pursued by other, more honest, means. Finally, the elimination of countless costly tax subsidies and expenditures would free up considerable resources that could be redirected toward other public purposes. For instance, if just half of today's tax expenditures were to be purged, then the savings to our citizens would exceed $300 billion a year.

In addition to eliminating, or consolidating and transforming, today's tax subsidies, a second principle of fair and intelligent tax reform for the twenty-first century should be treating all forms of income the same. Unfortunately, we do just the opposite today by providing preferential treatment, in the form of lower tax rates, to capital gains, interest, dividends, and other forms of passive income. As we shall see, there is little justification for maintaining this bifurcated system that taxes wage income at a higher rate than nonwage income.

In the past, those who have argued for reducing the capital gains tax have often premised their case on the complaint that capital is being taxed twice—once through the corporate income tax, and then again through capital gains. This has always been a dubious argument, given that labor is also being taxed twice: once through the payroll tax, and again through the personal income tax. And even if this argument were valid, its proponents would have to concede that a clear advantage of our proposal to eliminate corporate income taxes altogether would be the abolition of the double taxation of capital. If both federal and state corporate income taxes were eliminated, as we suggest, then there would be no rationale for taxing capital gains income differently from other forms of income, other than the short-term self-interest of the small number of people who own the majority of financial assets in America.

Those who argue that capital gains should be subject to preferential tax rates betray a fundamental misunderstanding of the basic nature of the new economy. As we discussed, the great winners in the economic boom of the 1990s were those who had significant assets in the financial markets. The outpacing of wage growth by the increase in capital assets seems to be a defining feature of our time. The need for individuals to own sizable financial assets in order to reap the true benefits of the new economy is precisely why we proposed ways to broaden ownership of financial capital in the previous chapter. Given this dynamic, however, continuing to favor capital owners over the less fortunate members of society, who derive the entirety of their income from their wages, is as misguided as it is unjust. Why should the wealthiest members of society see their advantage further compounded by means of the tax code?

Underlying the debate over whether to tax capital gains at the same rate as wages is a seldom-articulated distinction between earned income and unearned income. On a philosophical and moral level, there is a clear difference between income derived from one's own direct labor and toil—sweat equity, as they say—and the passive income derived from watching the value of one's assets accumulate. Throughout American history, hard work has always been heralded as the surest path to upward mobility. Contrary to popular mythology, however, capital ownership has continually proved to be the surest road to riches. This in an inevitable feature of capitalism— one that we must accept. But what we should not accept is a further reinforcement of capital's advantage over labor through our tax code, particularly at this point in our nation's history. On what basis should someone who works hard for a living be penalized to a greater degree through the tax code than the beneficiaries of trust funds who sit back and merely watch their assets accumulate? As a matter of principle, any simple yet fair tax system for the Information Age should be premised on treating all forms of income equally. No distinctions should be made for tax purposes between income derived from wages, financial markets, real estate investments, corporate dividends, or other sources.

Nor should income received from inheritance be exempt from taxation. Today, inheritances worth less than $675,000 are exempt from taxation—and conservatives propose abolishing inheritance taxes altogether. It is hard to justify this windfall, which has the effect of reinforcing hereditary class advantages. It would be more in line with the American ideal of self-reliance to tax inheritances at the same rate as income, with an exemption no larger than the gift tax. In a dynamic capitalist economy, ambitious individuals should be allowed and encouraged to enrich themselves by means that promote the wealth of society in general. But a democratic society, even as it encourages individual entrepreneurialism, should discourage the formation of dynasties.

When we unite these two principles described above—treating all forms of income equally, and replacing most or all current tax expenditures and deductions with a small number of targeted and refundable tax credits—we have a formula for a radically simplified and highly transparent new progressive income tax. Conservatives are correct when they claim that our Byzantine tax code, which now fills countless volumes, could be boiled down to a single, user-friendly page for the vast majority of Americans. But liberals should also take comfort in realizing that when it comes to taxation, simplicity need not be the enemy of fairness.


In addition to overhauling the ways we raised public revenues in the twentieth century, we should also consider whole new sources of public revenue in the twenty-first century. And the most promising are a wide range of "public assets"—highly valuable resources that the American people already rightfully own. America's public assets include, among others: the electromagnetic spectrum, the trees in our national forests, minerals under our public lands and the grazing rights upon them, and the commercial value of government-sponsored research and contracts. By charging fair market value for the private use of these public assets, the American people could raise surprising amounts of new revenue over the next decade.

The use of public assets to finance public programs is nothing new. The land-grant college legislation introduced after the Civil War enabled states to fund their own universities by selling publicly owned lands. In the twentieth century, a good example of this type of thinking can be found in the state of Alaska, where the former Republican governor, Jay Hammond, used public revenues from North Slope oil sales to establish a permanent fund on behalf of all Alaskans, which by 2000 distributed nearly $2,000 a year to each Alaskan citizen.

Regrettably, the United States now gives away most of its public assets for free or at greatly subsidized prices—enriching a few private interests and effectively defrauding the public in the process. In 1994, for example, in what Interior Secretary Bruce Babbitt called "the greatest gold heist since the days of Butch Cassidy," the government turned over public lands containing more than $100 billion worth of gold to a Canadian-based company—for less than $10,000. This type of blatant giveaway is actually mandated by the 1872 Mining Rights Law, which, despite its outdated provisions and highly deleterious effects, has yet to be repealed.

Another telling example is the case of Network Solutions, Inc. Network Solutions was a tiny company until the government transformed it into one of the most lucrative new monopolies of our time by giving it an exclusive contract to sell and distribute addresses to the World Wide Web. After receiving this contract in 1992, Network Solutions's stock value skyrocketed, and in 2000 it was sold to VeriSign for the sum of $21 billion. But to whom does this sudden wealth rightfully belong: the U.S. government and the public who provided the basis upon which it was created, or to the small number of shareholders who have reaped the benefits so far? Similar questions emerge when publicly sponsored research and development give rise to highly profitable pharmaceutical and technological breakthroughs, as is now so often the case. Doesn't the public have a right to recoup at least some of the financial returns on its investments?

There are countless other examples of valuable public assets that have been handed over to private interests for free or for firesale prices, often at great environmental costs. For instance, logging on public lands is so heavily subsidized that the government doesn't even recover its own expenses, let alone reap a reasonable profit on behalf of the public, as it should. Artificially low natural resource prices not only lead to pollution and waste, they can actually hold back technological innovation. But while the most valuable public assets of the past were on or beneath the ground, those of the future will not be. In fact, what could well turn out to be the greatest new sources of public revenues in the Information Age lie above us: the rights to the electromagnetic spectrum, and the rights to carbon emissions.

A curious thing recently occurred in Britain. In early 2000, the British government set out to auction part of its electromagnetic spectrum to private interests, and projected approximate revenues of $3 billion. By the time the bidding was done, however, the British taxpayers found themselves receiving $35 billion for the rights to use that particular bandwidth, which amounted to a full order of magnitude more than initially expected. By comparison, when the U.S. Congress was debating whether to sell or give away part of our nation's spectrum back in 1996, the initial projected price was assumed to be $70 billion. Through unfortunate political compromises, it was ultimately given away instead of auctioned. But had it been auctioned, how much could it realistically have raised: $140 billion? $280 billion?

Although the electromagnetic spectrum giveaways of 1996 were a missed opportunity, there will be many other portions of the spectrum up for grabs as wireless communication expands exponentially. In fact, many industry analysts are beginning to realize that auctioning the rights to the spectrum may be the best way to overcome today's artificial bandwidth scarcities—created through past spectrum giveaways—that threaten our competitive position in wireless technologies. Auctioning the rights to the spectrum could not only raise hundreds of billions of dollars in new public revenues, it could also help ensure that our spectrum is fully utilized for the benefit of all Americans.

Even larger sums of money will be at stake in the way we choose to reduce our emissions of carbon dioxide—the main pollutant responsible for global climate change. According to economists, the most efficient way to solve the problem is by establishing a system of tradable carbon emissions under which the United States would cap its annual emissions at a certain level and allow companies to buy and sell the limited number of carbon permits on the open market. The trillion-dollar question—quite literally—is whether the initial rights ought to be given away for free to polluters, or auctioned at fair market value. The economic forecasting firm DRI/MacGraw-Hill estimates that if the United States were to meet the carbon reduction goals it originally agreed to during the 1997 Kyoto Protocol, then the total value of the domestic carbon permits will range between $140 billion and $300 billion per year. This is a tremendous amount of money that could flow into our public coffers. Alternatively, all the proceeds could go to a small number of polluting industries, in what would amount to a corporate giveaway of a magnitude not seen since the original railroad land grants. Needless to say, auctioning the rights would be infinitely more fair than giving them away to polluters.

This is not to suggest that all Americans would suddenly receive a free lunch; implementing a system of tradable carbon emission permits would inevitably increase energy costs for most Americans. But this is as it should be. We should pay more for the pollution associated with our energy choices, since this would provide us with a strong incentive to consume less polluting energy: either by better insulating our homes, changing our lifestyles, or switching to cleaner energy sources. The real question is not whether the public will get a free lunch, but whether we will receive a fair deal in the process of solving global warming or a wildly unfair one. Economists agree that whether carbon permits are given away for free to polluters or auctioned at fair market value, the price of energy to consumers will be the same in either case. The catch, however, as the Council of Economic Advisers explains in their 2000 *Report to the President*, is that "allocating permits to firms would result in handing over assets valued in the tens to hundreds of billions of dollars annually . . . [which] would provide these firms with significant windfall profits and allow them to enjoy higher profits under climate policy than without climate policy." "On the other hand," they explain, "if the government sells the permits, it will receive revenue in the tens to hundreds of billions of dollars annually."

Assessing a fair-market value for the private use of these various public assets—in particular on the electromagnetic spectrum and carbon permits—could yield trillions of dollars in new public revenues in the coming decades. Since these new revenues belong to the American people, they ought to be returned to the American people, either by paying down the national debt or by cutting existing taxes.

In addition to modernizing our electoral and tax systems, it is also imperative that we modernize our education system. Public education is probably the most important way in which we, as a nation, invest in our collective future. This is particularly the case in the Information Age, as our nation's human capital becomes ever more important to our collective success and well-being.

To appreciate how attitudes about the importance of education have changed over the years, we may want to recall the words of Frederick Winslow Taylor, the most influential theorist of business management in the early twentieth century: "Now one of the first requirements for a man who is fit to handle pig iron is that he shall be so stupid and phlegmatic that he more nearly resembles in his mental makeup the ox than any other type." Likewise, Henry Ford favored "the reduction of the necessity of thought on the part of the worker." No management theorist or corporate leader would utter such sentiments today. To the contrary, most would agree with Daniel Bell, who has argued that "if industrial society is based on machine technology, post-industrial society is shaped by an intellectual technology. And if capital and labor are the major structural features of industrial society, information and knowledge are those of the post-industrial society." Marc Tucker, a leading expert on American education, has observed that the present-day system of primary and secondary education in the United States "was installed in the 1920s not to ensure high-quality results, but to enable the country to build a mass-production education system that would ensure minimum quality with high rates of efficiency. It is no more suited to the modern requirement for high quality than the industrial management systems rejected in the 1980s in the search for quality in the business world."

The sad irony is that the quality of America's education system has declined at the precise moment that the premium on knowledge is rising most rapidly. Here are two statistics that say more about the sorry state of U.S. education today than all the rhetoric in typical education policy debates. First, a full 95 percent of America's high school seniors score worse than their counterparts in other developed countries when tested for basic reading, math, and science. Second, an ever-growing number of scientists and engineers in the United States are foreign-born; the percentage of foreign born Ph.D.s and engineers jumped from 1.3 percent twenty-five years ago to roughly 25 percent in the 1990s. The fact that high-tech companies continually lobby Congress to admit even more skilled immigrants proves that the ability of our educational system to supply educated and motivated workers is failing to keep up with demand.

At the beginning of the twenty-first century, the United States suffers from a fundamental imbalance between an excellent university system and a troubled and class-stratified system of K-12 education. America's best colleges and universities are the finest in the world. The weakness is to be found in American primary and secondary schools. In effect, this means our public schools, since a full 89 percent of American K-12 students attended public schools in 1999. To be even more precise, the weakness is found in *some* of our public schools: Many of our suburban public schools are top-notch, whereas many of our inner-city schools have become islands of despair.

The weakness of our educational system has not escaped the attention of our political leaders on all sides of the ideological spectrum. They have proposed a wide range of cures: from smaller class sizes to more frequent student testing, from greater teacher accountability to higher teacher salaries, and from charter schools to school choice. Of these, the most promising yet controversial is school choice. Offering parents greater discretion over where to send their children to school would not only add a healthy dose of accountability to the school system and empower parents at the expense of school bureaucracies, but would also provide those children now stuck in our very worst schools a practical way out.

While the idea of school choice has been promoted chiefly by conservatives in recent years, in the 1960s the idea of vouchers appealed to liberals who wanted to give poor children the chance to attend good suburban schools. Today, for this very reason, a majority of African-Americans support the idea of school choice. The opposition comes from an unlikely alliance of unionized schoolteachers, who make up a very powerful lobby in the Democratic Party, and affluent suburbanites, many of them Republican voters, who are satisfied with their own neighborhood public schools. Their arguments, however, seem increasingly weak. The Democratic Party in particular finds itself in an awkward position by being officially opposed to school choice, while so many of its leading figures—including Bill Clinton, Al Gore, Edward Kennedy, and Jesse Jackson—have all sent their own children to expensive private schools. On what grounds can they claim that other families should be denied similar options?

Recent studies provide empirical evidence of the many benefits that can derive from school choice. Perhaps the most comprehensive inquiry into the subject was conducted by Caroline Hoxby of Harvard University, whose research reveals that school choice not only improves student performance (as measured by test scores and students' future earnings), but can also reduce spending on education in the process. Interestingly, Hoxby's research also found that greater school choice actually reduced the demand for private education: "policies that reduce choice . . . are likely to increase the share of students in private schools and reduce the share of voters who are interested in the general well-being of public education." While one can debate whether school choice should be limited to charter schools or extended to private and parochial schools as well, there is little question that greater school choice, in some form, could greatly improve the quality of America's education system.

To his credit, President George W. Bush made school choice one of the core themes of his presidential campaign, and has since proposed increasing federal spending on public education. But his actual proposal for school choice—premised on the idea of helping poor children escape failing schools by offering them a voucher of $1,500—reveals just how far we are as a nation from the possibility of a serious and fair system of genuine school choice. The $1,500 voucher he proposes is less than a quarter of the actual cost of educating the average child in America today; how are parents to come up with the rest? This dilemma helps expose what may be the biggest problem plaguing America's education system and the one that neither political party dares address: the large inequities in per pupil funding across the country.

George W. Bush is now the third president and the second Bush to claim to be our "education president." Yet neither he nor anyone else can plausibly claim that title when less than one-tenth of school funding comes from federal sources, and when vast disparities in per-pupil spending exist because of the antiquated link between school funding and state and local taxes. As a result, America's education debate is as surreal as it is hypocritical.

Our nation's leaders speak and act as though the future of American education will be determined in Washington, and routinely promise to make education reform one of their major priorities in office. Yet the actual role of the federal government in education policy remains minuscule. This means that all the grand pronouncements and national debates about vouchers, charter schools, national standards, class size, and teacher salaries are disingenuous to the degree that they presuppose a basic parity in school funding and a substantial federal role in financing education—neither of which actually exists. As long as the federal government contributes next to nothing to schools and the level of per pupil funding is determined by the vagaries of local financing, the national politics of education will continue to be a politics of symbolism. If we are serious about improving our education system, then we have little choice but to consider a genuine solution: equalizing school funding on a national basis.

The primary source of school funding in the United States has long been local property taxes, recently supplemented by aid from state governments. Other countries do not go about financing education the way we do. Among OECD countries in 1995, central governments accounted for an average of 54 percent of funding for primary and secondary education, seven times the rate in the United States, while regional and local governments split the rest. In the United States, by contrast, the federal government supplied only 8 percent of educational funding, with the rest divided between local and state governments. This link between education and localism in the United States is a relic of our colonial and rural past.

The United States does not suffer from a lack of overall school funding; to the contrary, we spend a greater share of our national income on K-12 education than any other advanced industrial democracy, with the exceptions of Canada and Denmark. What the United States suffers from is extreme variation in school funding across localities, rooted in our tradition of funding schools primarily by local property taxes. For example, per pupil spending on education in 1998 varied from an average of $4,000 in Mississippi to more than $9,000 in New Jersey, even after adjusting for cost-of-living differences. And disparities like these are also common within single states. In Virginia, for instance, average per pupil spending in Hanover County in 1997 was only one half of spending per pupil in Arlington County. Needless to say, such a wide chasm in the amount of money dedicated to each child translates into lower teacher salaries and hence less-qualified teachers, larger class sizes, and inferior facilities for schools on the losing side of this highly unequal playing field. These deep inequities only compound the disadvantages of class, culture, and poverty that already afflict our nation's inner cities, creating an environment that is even less hospitable to the process of learning.

The perverse design of America's current school funding mechanism is easy to illustrate. Suppose you have an impoverished inner city with a per pupil taxable property base of $60,000, neighbored by an affluent suburb with a per pupil property tax base of $300,000. The inner city would have to levy a painfully high 10 percent property tax to raise the same $6,000 per student that the suburb could raise through a mere 2 percent property tax. To make matters even worse, the state or local property and sales taxes that are the backbone of today's school funding system are extremely regressive in their own right, meaning that they disproportionately burden the less-well-off. The lower your income, the higher a share of your income typically goes to these taxes. When it comes to school finance, then, low-income Americans are doubly punished. Poor districts must impose higher tax rates to obtain the same amount of money that affluent districts can raise with low rates, and those higher taxes are often in the form of regressive property and sales taxes.

Recognizing these problems, a growing number of states have begun to equalize funding for local public schools on a statewide basis. Since 1971, when the California Supreme Court, in *Serrano v. Priest*, announced that the use of local property taxes to finance primary education violated the equal protection clause of the California constitution, forty-four of the fifty states have been sued by plaintiffs on similar grounds. The supreme courts of nineteen states have followed California's lead in holding that state constitutional provisions mandate the revision of public school finance to meet basic standards of equity. As a result of these lawsuits and the state legislation they inspired, by 1998 the proportion of educational funding provided by the states (48.4 percent) surpassed that provided by local districts (44.5 percent).

The logic behind these reforms was stated by the Vermont Supreme Court: "The distribution of a resource as precious as educational opportunity may not have as its determining force the mere fortuity of a child's residence." While these state-level reform efforts are encouraging, they do not go far enough and can sometimes lead to unintended disaster. Indeed, the experience of California illustrates the danger of equalizing education funding on a state basis without reducing or eliminating the link to property taxes. As Californians discovered in the wake of *Serrano* v. *Priest*, affluent property owners can all too easily be tempted to take part in revolts against increases in property taxes when such revenues are suddenly diverted to pay for schools in other districts. Many analysts blame Proposition 13, which restricts the ability of Californian localities to raise property taxes, for the decline of the state's once-great K-12 system.

If a child's education should not depend on "the mere fortuity of a child's residence" in this or that county within a state, then surely it also should not depend on the child's residence in this or that state in the United States. If it is unjust and inefficient for school quality to vary wildly between rich and poor neighborhoods within a state, it is equally unjust and inefficient for school quality to vary between rich and poor states. "Most of the resource inequality cannot be solved at the state level," education analysts David Grissmer and Ann Flanagan have observed in a report for RAND. "States spending the least are southern and western states that also have a disproportionate share of the nation's minority and disadvantaged students. Only the federal government can address this issue of interstate inequality in school spending."

A proposal to equalize school funding nationally is radical—in the sense that it tackles the root of the problem of national disparities in school funding—but it is the only way to ensure that all students across the country have access to a quality education on a relatively equal basis. We believe that the question of national equalization of funding ought to be debated before other more familiar, but arguably premature, proposals like national school choice and national school standards. After all, how could any national system of school choice be equitable if per pupil funding is not equalized first? Likewise, how can national standards be applied meaningfully and uniformly if educational resources remain so uneven?

Our federal government, like those in virtually all other advanced nations, should pick up most or all of the tab for K-12 education—on the condition that state and local governments reduce their taxing and spending on education commensurably. Where would the money come from to cover the roughly $300 billion now spent by state and local governments on schools? The Nixon administration, for instance, considered creating a new federal sales or value-added tax to fund public schools, thereby reducing reliance on local property taxes (this idea was never acted upon). A federal sales or property tax, however, would be just as regressive as the state and local versions, and thus suffer from the same political liabilities. A regressive tax, be it national, state, or local, that falls heavily on middle-class and working-class voters is far more likely to trigger a tax revolt that succeeds at the polls than a progressive tax that falls disproportionately on the well-to-do, who for all their grumbling may fail to find many allies among the majority of the electorate. One way to achieve the goal of progressivity would be by paying for schools with revenues from the federal income tax.

We recommend yet another approach: equalizing school funding nationwide by means of a progressive national consumption tax of the kind that we discussed earlier in this chapter. Raised nationwide, revenues from this consumption tax could be distributed to the states on a per pupil basis. This would enable states and localities to employ other means, for example state income or property taxes, to cover the other functions now paid for through state and local sales taxes, which our progressive national consumption tax would replace.

In order to avoid subsidizing the failure of entrenched school bureaucracies, it would be best to allocate the money directly to students rather than to schools. The allocation of funds on a per pupil basis would also be simplest and most beneficial in a system that permitted some kind of school choice—either among public charter schools or among public and private schools. In addition, the goal of equalizing access to educational opportunity would require certain variations in the distribution of national funds to reflect regional differences in the cost of living. The same dollar buys more in New Mexico than in New York.

Critics might object that our proposal would lead to a loss of local control over school curricula and standards, but this danger is easily exaggerated and the opposite is more likely to be the case. First, in areas from highway construction to welfare, there is a long tradition of combining federal funding with local discretion. Our proposal for national equalization of school funding merely applies this logic to the area of education. Nevertheless, it would be wise to collect and administer the national school funds by means that would prevent Congress from micromanaging the way the money is spent. In this way, national equalization could easily enhance local control, defined as parental choice rather than as the autonomy of local officials.

Far from breaking with our nation's heritage, equalizing school funding is the logical next step in the evolution of American public education. With each successive wave of economic transformation, since the initial Industrial Revolution of the 1800s, federal government support for education has expanded. In the first industrial era of the early nineteenth century, the public or common school became widespread, while the U.S. government founded the land-grant university system. Even so, in nineteenth-century America, the formal education of most Americans was limited to grades one through eight. In 1890, for example, fewer than 5 percent of teenagers went to high school, and an even smaller number went to college. In the second industrial era, which began in the late nineteenth century and lasted until the late twentieth century, a combination of compulsory school attendance laws with child-labor laws removed children from factories, fields, and mines and put them in classrooms. Then in the first half of the twentieth century, high school attendance became the norm rather than the exception.

The final decades of the twentieth century saw a debate over statewide equalization of school funding, which should now be succeeded in the first decade of the twenty-first century by a long-overdue debate about nationwide equalization. The best way to equalize school funding can and should be debated. But the goal should be clear: to ensure that every American child's access to quality education no longer depends, as it now does, on accidents of geography.

It is highly unlikely that the various proposals we have put forth in this chapter and the previous one for reinventing our nation's social contract and public sector would ever be implemented in tandem. Indeed, most are meant to be considered on their own merits. Nevertheless, we believe it is important to point out that our various proposals, when considered in combination, are meant to be revenue neutral. Because the total costs and savings of our proposals roughly balance each other out, they could be implemented without any significant change in the overall size of government relative to the economy.

The national consumption tax that we propose would raise approximately the same amount of revenue as the state sales tax system it would replace. In a similar fashion, our radically simplified progressive income tax, by broadening the tax base but maintaining the current rate structure, would raise several hundred billion dollars in additional public revenue per year, which could in turn be used to offset the elimination of the corporate income tax and to turn every newborn into a trust-fund baby from birth, after which there still might be over $100 billion remaining. Our proposals for charging fair market value for the private use of public assets could generate up to another $100 billion per year. These additional resources, finally, when combined with a redirection of the roughly $125 billion our federal government now spends annually on Medicaid, should suffice to cover the public safety net component of the universal and mandatory health insurance proposal we put forth.

These numbers are merely estimates; more precise figures would of course depend on more detailed policy proposals, which are beyond the scope of this book. But these estimates do illustrate that successfully reinventing our republic for the twenty-first century need not require an overall change in the relative size of our public sector. It would, however, require significant changes in the principles that guide our public sector and in the allocation of authority and responsibility between our different levels of government.

Many of the reforms that we suggest, like increasing the federal role in education and solving the Internet tax problem by means of a national consumption tax shared among the states, involve a shift in responsibility from the state and local level to the national level. Some critics might object that this undermines American federalism. To the contrary, we believe that our proposals are in keeping with the mainstream of American constitutional thought.

From the beginning of the American republic, there have been two schools of thought about the relationship between the states and the national government. The states' rights school has held that the United States is a loose confederation of quasi-sovereign states under a federal government that has minimal powers. This was the doctrine of the Anti-Federalists, who opposed the replacement of the Articles of Confederation by the present U.S. Constitution in 1789; of the Confederates, who tried to justify the unilateral secession of the southern states from the Union; and of twentieth-century segregationists, who denied that the federal government had the power to defend the civil and political rights of U.S. citizens against the deprivation of those rights by state and local governments. The states' rights school has been defeated again and again, by the ratification of the U.S. Constitution, by the triumph of the Union in the Civil War, and by the success of the civil rights revolution in the 1950s and 1960s.

The mainstream interpretation of American federalism has held that the federal and state governments are coordinate authorities, each of which is answerable to the American people. While the Constitution, in very general terms, provides for a basic division of labor between the federal government and the state governments, the drafters of the Constitution left the details to later generations. They understood that a document that was too rigid could never last for many generations, especially as conditions change, sometimes radically. The U.S. Constitution is an impressionistic sketch that can inspire a variety of broadly similar structures, not a blueprint specifying everything in advance.

This is the view found in the *Federalist Papers*, the authoritative description of the Constitution coauthored by Alexander Hamilton, James Madison, and John Jay (which they published under the collective pseudonym "Publius"). Although their interpretation is not the only one, it deserves a great deal of weight, because Madison and Hamilton had taken part in the Constitutional Convention, and because Madison, who became the fourth president of the United States, was later known as "the Father of the Constitution."

In Number 14, Publius predicts the increasing nationalization of American society by improving technology and commerce: "the intercourse throughout the union will be daily facilitated by new improvements. Roads will everywhere be shortened, and kept in better

order; accommodations for travelers will be multiplied and melio-
rated; and interior navigation . . . will be opened throughout. . . ." Although Americans in the eighteenth century tended to favor local
and state governments, Publius in Number 46 discusses the possibility that "the people should in the future become more partial to
the federal than to the State governments. . . ." In that event, writes
Publius, "the people ought not surely to be precluded from giving
most of their confidence where they may discover it to be most due."
According to Publius, it will be up to the voters, in any particular
era, to decide the details of the changing division of labor between
the federal government and the state governments. Only the American people can decide "whether either, or which of them, will be
able to enlarge its sphere of jurisdiction at the expense of the other."

In Number 32, Publius goes so far as to envision something like
modern revenue-sharing or the use of federal grants by the states: "I
am of opinion that there would be no real danger of the consequences, which seem to be apprehended to the State governments,
from a power in the Union to control them in the levies of money,
because I am persuaded that the sense of the people, the extreme
hazard of provoking the resentments of the State Governments, and
a conviction of the utility and necessity of local administrations, for
local purposes, would be a complete barrier against the oppressive
use of such a power." In other words, Publius foresaw the kind of
combination of federal funding and local discretion in spending that
we propose in the area of education. Indeed, in Number 36, Publius
envisions the states, rather than the federal government, as having a
minimal revenue base. "A small land tax will answer the purposes of
the States," presumably because the new federal government would
have assumed so many other responsibilities.

This view of American federalism as something pragmatic, flexible, and evolving over time in harmony with the wishes of the American people is not the view of the Confederates and the states' rights
segregationists of yesteryear. It is, however, the view of the central

tradition of American political thought and practice that runs from the framers of the Constitution through Lincoln to Franklin D. Roosevelt and his heirs in both parties. Even today, in spite of the hostility to the federal government on the part of the right wing of the Republican Party, this doctrine of flexible federalism has bipartisan support. Indeed, in the 1990s, the Republican congressional majority preempted state policy in various fields, ranging from marital law (discouraging gay marriage in the Defense of Marriage Act) to the enforcement of child support and eligibility of illegal aliens for welfare. What is more, the American business community often prefers a single federal policy to fifty conflicting state policies. As one observer has noted, "business interests now look to preemptive acts of Congress not just to set baselines (floors) below which state policies must not fall but to secure compulsory *ceilings* on the possible excesses of zealous states."

Cooperative federalism, then, can be popular as well as practical. When it comes to the division of labor among different levels of government in the twenty-first century, we ought to be guided by the philosophy that Abraham Lincoln set forth in a speech in the U.S. House of Representatives in 1848: "[L]et the nation take hold of the larger works, and the states the smaller ones; and thus, working in a meeting direction, discreetly, but steadily and firmly, what is made unequal in one place may be equalized in another. . . ."

All of the proposals we have put forth in this chapter share a common goal: renovating America's public sector in order to maximize both equity and choices among our citizens. In the electoral realm, this requires broadening voter choices, in a number of innovative ways, while reforming and ultimately replacing today's rigid two-party system. Like our antiquated democratic procedures, our tax code needs a combination of radical and incremental reform. As we have seen, state sales taxes and corporate income taxes should be abolished altogether, while the progressive income tax should be maintained but greatly simplified. The federal tax base should also be augmented by auctioning our public assets, rather than giving them away for free. As for the critical challenge of educating the next generation, two reforms above all others would help provide all American children a high-quality education in the Information Age: broadening school choice and equalizing school funding on a per pupil basis.

In our opinion, a government worthy of the Information Age would not only allow all its citizens to vote and receive public services on-line, but it would also enable voters to choose alternatives to today's Democratic and Republican Parties. It would collect revenues in a way that was fully compatible with the new realities of e-commerce and globalization, and offer most citizens the simplicity and elegance of filing their tax returns on a single page. And it would no longer discriminate against any of its citizens—least of all its children—on the basis of where they live.

During the 1990s there was a great deal of talk, but noticeably little action, about "reinventing government." We have attempted to provide a compelling vision of how to adapt our democracy to the new challenges of Information Age America.

# Four

•

# UNITY AND COMMUNITY IN THE TWENTY-FIRST CENTURY

"Americans of all ages, all stations in life, and all types of disposition, are forever forming associations," the French philosopher Alexis de Tocqueville observed in his famous 1835 tract, *Democracy in America*. "There are not only commercial and industrial associations in which all take part, but others of a thousand different types—religious, moral, serious, futile, very general and very limited, immensely large and very minute. . . . Nothing, in my view, deserves more attention than the intellectual and moral associations in America."

What Tocqueville described as "the intellectual and moral associations in America" constitute the third sector of American society—the realm of community or civil society. This third sector is far more complex and diverse than the other two realms of the market and the government. For instance, it includes an enormous variety of associations with different goals and different claims on the individual, ranging from globe-spanning religious institutions that comprise many smaller organizations to philanthropic foundations, charities of all kinds, and membership associations as undemanding as amateur softball teams and bird-watching clubs. At the same time, most Americans also share a broader sense of national community—reinforced by common customs, freedoms, cultural narratives, and a common language. It is this broader sense of community that fosters national unity even as it gives force and meaning to the concepts of American citizenship.

America's civil society sector has grown more inclusive over time. From the late eighteenth century to the early twenty-first century, our national community has evolved from one in which citizenship was limited to white Christian men of predominantly British descent into a highly diverse melting pot in which descendants of British colonial settlers are a minority. Equality in the community realm, however, has often lagged behind equality in the market and the state. Nonwhite Americans and women were granted at least nominal political and economic rights for generations even as they were excluded from fashionable clubs, schools, and neighborhoods. As recently as the 1960s, elite social clubs that discriminated against people on the basis of race and gender dominated the upper echelons of American community, and restrictive covenants in many neighborhoods prevented blacks, Jews, and sometimes Catholics from moving in. Until the Supreme Court in *Loving* v. *Virginia* (1967) struck down anti-miscegenation laws, roughly half the states banned marriage among U.S. citizens of different races—denying the right to exercise the most basic and intimate kind of voluntary association.

As these examples suggest, civil society can be a realm of exclusion and humiliation, as well as a realm of integration and personal fulfillment. Fundamental questions of civil rights have divided our nation since its very inception, giving rise to an all-out Civil War in the nineteenth century and a great deal of social unrest in the twentieth. The racial and ethnic bigotry that has resulted in the mistreatment of various minority groups—our nation's perennial shame—represents the dark side of our community sector. The Ku Klux Klan and other vigilante groups enforcing the norms of the dominant local majority, and the Social Register, attempting to create an American aristocracy, have been as much a part of the history of American community as the United Way and public libraries.

More typical, fortunately, has been the beneficial side of our communal institutions, be they secular or religious. Often, in fact, it has been voluntary institutions in the communal sphere that have come to the rescue of our citizenry in times of great need. When the first wave of industrialization in the United States created massive social dislocation, our community sector responded by creating a whole wave of caregiving institutions like the Salvation Army and church-based missions. Other institutions like the Boy Scouts and Girl Scouts helped assimilate enormous populations of immigrants and rural children to middle-class norms, while bowling and other amateur sports provided working-class and rural Americans with new forms of recreation and interaction. The community sector came to the rescue again after World War II, when the internal combustion engine and electrification created the car-based suburb. To combat isolation and anomie, voluntary organizations created a flourishing suburban culture, characterized by Little League and more recently soccer teams, and by giant villagelike churches and synagogues.

In considering the future of our community sector in the twenty-first century, then, two overarching questions rise to the surface: What forms will community institutions take in the century ahead? And, how inclusive will the community sector be as a whole?

The first question is almost impossible to answer—except after the fact. The Tocquevillian associations of American community, if they are genuine, are the products of spontaneous effort on the part of motivated individuals and groups, not the results of a master plan designed by visionary intellectuals and imposed from the top down by government officials. What is more, their sheer diversity, in both form and goal, is limited only by the boundaries of the law and the imagination. Among other factors, technological change can lead to unprecedented changes in the community sector, as it does in the market and the government. Before the invention of the TV, nobody could have predicted the appearance of television evangelists; before the spread of the personal computer and the World Wide Web, nobody could have envisioned the proliferation of on-line virtual communities such as Internet chat rooms.

This suggests that when reformers propose policies intended to preserve and revitalize America's community, we must be skeptical. It is not that their concerns are not legitimate. Indeed, our sense of community is under attack on many fronts. For example, the segmenting effects of new technology and new media make it ever more difficult for Americans to feel that they share a common frame of reference. The speed and occupational mobility that are hallmarks of the digital age make it more difficult for people to know their neighbors and to identify with a particular geographic community. The number of Americans now living alone, as well as the number who express feelings of loneliness, are skyrocketing. Then, too, institutions that once provided a common bond, like the military draft, have vanished and not been replaced. Even our sports stadiums are not what they used to be: many are now branded with corporate names, and separate entrances and private booths now separate the members of the elite overclass from the general public.

Naturally, these challenges to our community life and national cohesion lead elected officials and aspiring social reformers to propose community-enhancing cures of all kinds. For instance, we frequently hear calls for expanding or reinvigorating civil society. Embedded in many of these community-building plans, however, is a seldom noticed contradiction: Our ability consciously to promote a vibrant national community is extremely limited. Unlike the economic realm, which is organized primarily by markets, or the governmental realm, which is structured by rules of law and detailed policies, the communal realm is shaped by forces that cannot be easily identified or manipulated. Indeed, the community is the realm of society that is most resistant to models and schemes, a fact that explains why so many well-intentioned plans for improving our nation's community life fail to achieve their intended results.

The problem is as much conceptual as practical. For centuries, philosophers have debated the legitimacy of different approaches to social change. Some, like the Marquis de Condorcet, Auguste Comte, Karl Marx, Jeremy Bentham, and other rationalist philosophers of the Enlightenment tradition, have sought to reform existing institutions in light of an abstract ideal or goal by deducing first principles of social order. Pragmatists, like John Dewey and Richard Rorty, have rejected grand master plans and called for ceaseless experimentation in the design of institutions. Skeptical thinkers, like David Hume, Edmund Burke, Isaiah Berlin, and John Gray, have criticized the notion that society can be redesigned by either abstract reason or pragmatic experimentation. Society, they have argued, is not a mechanical construction but an organic entity, based on gradually evolving traditions. The task of reformers is to water and fertilize—and now and then prune—a growing plant.

This "Burkean" approach to society has significant limitations, particularly in the sectors of the economy and government, where the pressure of changing circumstances forces business organizations to rely on pragmatic planning and experimentation, and government officials to engage in rational reform, to the best of their abilities. In the realm of community, however, suspicion of grand attempts at social engineering and emphasis on the spontaneous generation of social order are much more justified. Indeed, political philosopher Francis Fukuyama has argued that while particular kinds of "social capital" are disrupted by technological and economic change, over time "the stock of social capital is constantly being re-plenished." If one era's community institutions fade, then their pur-pose may be better served by new institutions, which may only now be emerging.

Since our community sector evolves organically instead of inten-tionally, the best policy for nurturing new voluntary institutions is often to let them adapt on their own, with minimal outside interven-tion. This is particularly the case in a country like the United States, with its long tradition of accomplishing by voluntary association much of what is done by governments in other nations. Does this mean that those concerned about the well-being of our national community as a whole should do nothing? No. Rather, it means that the best way to strengthen our community sector may be an indirect strategy of removing or reducing the most serious social divisions in the community while relying on the resilience, entrepreneurialism, and goodwill of Americans to do the rest.

What, then, are the foremost threats to an inclusive and cohesive American national community in the decades to come? Perhaps the biggest question in the coming century is whether the United States will evolve into a highly integrated nation that shares a common iden-tity and destiny, or into a mere collection of rival groups that share lit-tle more than a territory and a set of political institutions. At the beginning of the twenty-first century, the integrity of the American community is threatened by three great divides: the racial divide, the generational divide, and the genetic divide. The racial divide is the oldest and deepest in American society. The generational divide is a recent phenomenon, caused by the burdens that the graying of the American population will impose on the working-age public. The ge-netic divide is a social division that does not yet exist but might be created by the abuse of the rapidly developing technology of genetic engineering. (The class divide is another enduring problem in the United States, but because many of our proposals for reforms in the market and government sector seek to ameliorate class inequality, we will not treat that subject separately here.)

Each of the three divides presents distinct dilemmas that require distinct solutions. Whether the United States thrives or fails in the twenty-first century will depend in large part on whether we as a people can prevent the racial, generational, and genetic divides from fissuring our hard-won and still fragile sense of an American community that transcends the smaller communities of ethnicity, class, religion, and region. If we can remove these fundamental roadblocks, we may be pleasantly surprised by just how well our community sector thrives in the decades ahead, and brings out the very best in all Americans.

Let us begin with the oldest and most destructive divide in America's community, the racial divide. Although much progress has been made in recent decades toward tearing down racial boundaries and ensuring civil rights for all Americans, much still remains to be done. At the dawn of the Information Age, we Americans must ask ourselves whether we aspire to be a truly unified nation—or several. We must decide whether our public policies should seek to emphasize our similarities, based on common citizenship, or our differences, based on biological factors of race. As we shall see, the argument has never been stronger for adopting a race-neutral, citizen-based approach to civil rights.

By the year 2000, California had become the first "postminority" state in the nation—meaning that non-Hispanic whites no longer made up the majority of the state's population. By 2100 the nation as a whole will reach a similar majority-minority profile, in which the number of whites will be outnumbered by the total number of Americans of other races. For the most part, this will be the result of intermarriage and today's historically high level of immigration, which, if maintained, is projected to lead to a full doubling of America's population by the end of the century.

Demography may be destiny, but it is a destiny that can be shaped and altered by our choices. It is within our power as a nation to decide whether we are going to be an integrated nation of individuals with different ancestries, or a balkanized multinational state, in which the government assigns every citizen to this or that arbitrarily defined racial category, favoring some while discriminating against others. It is also within our power as a nation to decide, by way of our immigration policies, both the general size of our future population and the relative mix between a high-skilled and low-skilled population and workforce. Over the long term this may be the most important choice of all.

Just as we have argued for citizen-based reforms in the realm of the economy and government, so we believe that reforms in the realm of community should be citizen-based. Our ultimate goal is to help foster an ever evolving but ever more integrated nation in which common citizenship and common democratic values outweigh racial and other divisions. When it comes to civil rights, we argue for a combination of color-blind public policies and strong antidiscrimination laws, which, in our opinion, offers the best hope for integrating our remarkably diverse population into a dynamic yet cohesive whole. With regard to immigration, we advocate an immigration policy geared to the nature and demands of an Information Age based on a more even balance between high-skilled and low-skilled immigrants. These policies would not only help to unite our nation, they would restore the original vision of America's greatest civil rights leaders.

In 1964 and 1965, the U.S. Congress, under the moral inspiration of Martin Luther King Jr. and his allies and the political leadership of President Lyndon Johnson, finally abolished the centuries-old racial caste system. Civil rights reformers disagreed about the next stage. Some, like Martin Luther King Jr. and Bayard

Rustin, favored abolishing racial labels based on biological origins altogether, and pursuing race-neutral approaches to combating poverty among all races. In 1963, for instance, King proposed including poor white citizens among the beneficiaries of a Bill of Rights for the Disadvantaged. "The moral justification for special measures for Negroes is rooted in the robberies inherent in the institution of slavery," King observed. "Many poor whites, however, were the derivative victims of slavery. . . . To this day the white poor also suffer deprivation and the humiliation of poverty if not of color." King concluded: "It is a simple matter of justice that America, in dealing creatively with the task of raising the Negro from backwardness, should also be rescuing a large stratum of the forgotten white poor."

Unfortunately, this race-neutral, need-based approach lost out, by the 1970s, to a race-based, need-neutral approach to civil rights. The emphasis of public policy shifted from antipoverty programs that helped all disadvantaged Americans to "affirmative action" or racial preferences that benefited affluent as well as poor members of racial minorities, while excluding disadvantaged whites. To build political support for these new group-based preferences, liberals in the 1960s and 1970s extended preferences to Latin American immigrants and women. Broadening the scope of affirmative action in this way won political allies for the program, at the price of destroying its moral legitimacy. Today, a majority of the beneficiaries of affirmative action—a program originally intended to help the descendants of American slaves—are middle-class white women and voluntary immigrants from Latin America and their children who arrived in this country after the Civil Rights Revolution in the 1960s and cannot claim to have suffered under the pre-1960s forms of institutionalized racism.

Inevitably, this incoherent regime of selective preferences created a backlash. In the past decade, the preference system has been trimmed back by federal courts as well as state governments. There is now a growing consensus that the race-conscious policies of the past thirty years have polarized the American people, without significantly reducing socioeconomic disparities among American racial and ethnic groups. Moreover, high levels of racial intermarriage and recent genetic discoveries are rapidly rendering our system of racial classification obsolete. For these and other reasons, it is high time to reconsider the rejected alternative of a one-nation civil rights policy based on individual rights rather than group identity.

Our pseudoscientific system of five official races—whites, blacks, Latinos, Asian and Pacific Islanders, and Native Americans—dates back only to the 1970s, although the black and white categories originated centuries earlier. This oversimplified schema, promulgated by the federal government for the past three decades, does not correspond to the way Americans actually think about themselves. For instance, Korean-Americans do not necessarily feel a sense of affinity with Malaysian-Americans, even though the federal government shovels them into the same nonsensical category of "Asian and Pacific Islanders." It is equally nonsensical to treat recent immigrants from Hungary, fourth-generation Italian-Americans, and tenth-generation Anglo-Americans as members of a single community: "non-Hispanic whites."

In any event, the growing number of interracial marriages is blurring the lines between our official races and producing a new version of the American melting pot. A century ago, the term *melting pot* described the amalgamation of old Anglo-Americans and new European-Americans into a single new ethnic community as a result of intermarriage and cultural syncretism. Israel Zangwill, an English Jew, popularized this option in his 1908 play *The Melting Pot*, in which a character declares: "America is God's crucible, the Great Melting Pot where all the races . . . are melting and reforming! . . . Germans and Frenchmen, Irishmen and Englishmen, Jews and Russians—into the crucible with you all! God is making the American." As Zangwill predicted, the once-powerful European diaspora cultures faded away in a few generations. By the end of the twentieth century, most white Americans had ancestors from more than one European nation.

In the words of John Dewey: "Such terms as Irish-American or Hebrew-American or German-American are false terms, because they seem to assume something which is already in existence called America, to which the other factors may be hitched on. The fact is, the genuine American, the typical American, is himself a hyphenated character. . . . He is not American plus Pole or German. But the American is himself Pole-German-English-French-Spanish-Italian-Greek-Irish-Scandinavian-Bohemian-Jew—and so on." This fusion of racial categories and ancestries will only intensify in the years ahead, as newcomers from Latin America and Asia grow in number and influence.

Recent immigrants from Latin America and East Asia are intermarrying with the post-European white majority at a remarkable rate—one in two Asian-Americans, one in three Latinos. The younger Americans are, the more likely they are to be in transracial marriages. In 1990, for example, only 53 percent of married black Americans under the age of twenty-five were in black-black marriages—compared to 84 percent of blacks over the age of sixty-five. Nothing short of a complete reversal of today's high intermarriage rates can prevent the formation, at different rates in different regions of the country, of a mixed-race majority in the United States in the long run. The golfer Tiger Woods—who jokingly describes himself as "Cablinasian," by which he means a fusion of Caucasian, black, Indian, and Asian—may well be a forerunner of the "average American" in the centuries to come.

Even in the absence of rising transracial marriage rates, advances in genetic research are undermining American traditions of racial classification. Our familiar racial categories, in fact, reflect premodern pseudoscience. For centuries, Europeans invoked biblical authority to divide all human beings into three races alleged to have descended from one of the three sons of Noah—Japheth, Ham, and

Shem. (The terms *Semitic* and *Hamitic* reflect this primitive notion.) The influence of the biblically derived three-race schema influenced the eighteenth- and nineteenth-century European and American anthropologists who arbitrarily divided humanity into the "races" labeled "Caucasian," "Mongoloid," and "Negroid"—categories reflected by U.S. census labels for generations.

Genetic research has demolished old ideas about racial classifications by proving that all human beings are 99.9 percent identical in their genetic makeup, and by revealing unsuspected patterns of relationships among human populations. According to genetic evidence, the Italian nation is a hodge-podge of different groups; northern Italians have links to Central Europe and southern Italians to North Africa. Likewise, the idea that Old World nations like the Japanese, Germans, Poles, and others correspond to "races" has been discredited. If the idea of race is a myth even in fairly homogeneous countries like those of Europe and East Asia, it breaks down altogether in the United States, where European, African, and American Indian populations have been mingling to some degree from the beginning of the colonial era in the seventeenth century.

Instead of recognizing and celebrating the growing number of Americans of mixed races, our government has only made matters worse by premising the 2000 Census on the even more absurd "one-drop rule." According to this rule, an American citizen who has any "minority" ancestry whatsoever will be automatically assigned by the federal government to that "minority." Today, the federal government treats someone with one Asian ancestor and fifteen white ancestors as 100 percent Asian and Pacific Islander.

As this example suggests, our arbitrary system of racial labels is collapsing under the weight of its own absurdity and complexity. The assignment of American citizens to this or that "race" by the federal government should come to an end. Subnational ethnic and racial identities should be a matter of voluntary affiliation, neither encouraged nor discouraged by law. In the twenty-first century, American citizens, whether native or naturalized, should be classified by the government as members of only one nation—the American nation—and only one race—the human race.

The abolition of racial labels should be accompanied by the abolition of race-based public policy. As early as 1871, Frederick Douglass, the abolitionist who had escaped from slavery, dismissed the radical black nationalist Martin Delany's call for racial quotas as "absurd." Douglass wrote: "According to the census, the colored people of the country constitute one-eighth of the whole American people. Upon your statistical principle, the colored people of the United States ought, therefore, not only to hold one-eighth of all offices in the country, but they should own one-eighth of all the property, and pay one-eighth of all the taxes of the country. . . . Now, my old friend, there is no man in the United States who knows better than you do that equality of numbers has nothing to do with equality of attainments." As an alternative to feel-good tokenism, Douglass favored bringing about genuine "equality of attainments" between black and white Americans by means of social reform.

The legitimate goals of affirmative action, like increasing the presence of blacks and Latinos in higher education, the professions, and politics, can and should be pursued—but by race-neutral methods like better primary education for all Americans. In his classic autobiography *Hunger of Memory* (1982), Richard Rodriguez pointed out the essential flaw of affirmative action as a tool of social mobility: "Those least disadvantaged were helped first, advanced because many others of their race were more disadvantaged. The strategy of affirmative action, finally, did not take seriously the educational dilemma of disadvantaged students. They need good early schooling!" Measures to combat racial separation by class and subculture, like school choice and the equalization of school funding, would also help lower-class whites, who remain a majority of the nation's poor.

The era of preferences for favored groups and penalties for disfavored groups should be replaced, then, by a new era of identical individual rights for all Americans. What is more, the realm of individual rights should be expanded, by banning discrimination against gay and lesbian Americans in employment and housing, if not in family law. Tragically, many liberals have opposed amending the Civil Rights Act to protect gays and lesbians for fear that such an amendment would eliminate group preferences as the price of protecting the rights of gay citizens as individuals. White racism, like nonwhite racism, will continue to exist. To prevent racist sentiments from being translated into action, antidiscrimination laws should therefore remain in place, to help all victims of racial discrimination—nonwhite and white alike.

In the twenty-first century, the United States has the potential not only to live up to the vision of a color-blind nation shared by Frederick Douglass and Martin Luther King Jr., but to become the most racially mixed and integrated nation in the developed world. For this to happen, we need to abandon the system of racial classifications and preferences that, at this stage in our nation's history, only serves to reinforce racial differences instead of diminishing them, and to polarize our nation instead of unifying it.

Discussing the downsides and unintended consequences of our current system of racial preferences is controversial. But there may be no topic more difficult to discuss in our country today than our immigration policy—so wedded are many Americans to predetermined views on both sides of this issue, and so quick are they to accuse their detractors of malevolent intentions. Yet when it comes to the long-term profile and health of the American nation—meaning the very size of our population, our educational and economic makeup, and our race relations—no single other factor may be as important. Indeed, immigration is by far the largest source of U.S. population growth, and if today's historically high rates of immigration continue, our total population may more than double by the end of the century.

The reason the immigration debate is so contentious is that any policy choice inevitably involves significant trade-offs. There is simply no such thing as a win-win immigration policy; whatever choice is made, there will always be winners and losers, both domestically and internationally. For instance, high levels of low-skilled immigrants (most of America's current immigrants fall in this category) tend to benefit domestic employers and capital owners, as well as the poor from abroad who come to our shores. However, the same policy also tends to depress wages for America's current working poor, and to increase the disparity between our educational and economic haves and have-nots. In studying this matter, the National Academy of Sciences concluded that increased immigration tends to disproportionately depress the wages and economic circumstances of low-skilled and low-income workers, while benefiting the wealthiest Americans.

Immigration is now the chief factor contributing to the growth of poverty in the United States. Between 1979 and 1997, as much as 75 percent of the increase in the size of the total American poor population resulted from immigration. Sadly, one of the most significant factors blocking recent immigrants and the native poor from joining America's economic mainstream is the arrival of subsequent waves of low-skilled immigrants. According to the Urban Institute, an increase of 10 percent in immigration reduces the wages of the immigrants already here by as much as 9 to 10 percent. The fact that large-scale immigration tends to benefit the wealthy while lowering the wages of the working poor also helps explain some of the most significant economic trends of recent decades. Surely it is not just coincidental that the broad-based upward mobility and growing middle class this country enjoyed during the 1950s and 1960s occurred at a time of relatively low immigration, or that the shrinking middle class and increased economic polarization evident throughout the 1980s and the early 1990s corresponded with a period of relatively high immigration.

There is also a genuine risk that relying too heavily on immigrant labor (whether of the low-skill or high-skill variety) encourages our citizens and leaders to divert their attention from much needed domestic reforms. For instance, it is generally easier to import low-skilled workers from abroad than to employ many of the native-born poor, just as it is easier to import engineers from abroad than to help fix our educational system, which is clearly failing to produce a sufficient number of highly skilled workers. Yet ignoring domestic reforms will only raise domestic tensions.

These are not the only trade-offs implicit in any immigration policy. Reacting to a government projection that the U.S. population will double again by the end of the twenty-first century, Colorado's former Democratic governor Richard Lamm and former Republican senator Alan Simpson of Wyoming published a joint article in the *Washington Post* in June 2000 asking some difficult questions: "How will America be better off with 571 million people? What amenities that we now enjoy will be improved? What about urban congestion, open space? Will 571 million people help our educational system? What will it mean with regard to crime, and our quality of life?"

Given all these trade-offs, our collective challenge is to forge an immigration policy that reflects our nation's perennial values and long-term objectives, while balancing the often conflicting interests of various sectors of our society. There is no question that America's preeminent position in the world today owes a great deal to our embrace of newcomers from around the globe. The fact that the fertility rate of native-born Americans is below replacement levels, moreover, may mean that some amount of immigration will be necessary to prevent the U.S. population from shrinking. For a number of reasons, then, we believe that the United States for the foreseeable future should continue to welcome some immigrants into our community. The big questions, however, are: Where and how do we draw the line? And what should be the relative mix between low-skilled and high-skilled immigrants?

The most obvious starting point is to rethink the present mix of skilled and unskilled immigrants. The United States is alone among the industrial democracies in having an immigration policy that is biased against educated immigrants. Because of an emphasis on family reunification, 65 to 70 percent of visas are now allotted to family members of U.S. citizens and lawful permanent residents, many of whom are poor and uneducated. In 1996, fully 35.8 percent of immigrants had less than a high school education; by comparison, only 9.7 percent of U.S.-born citizens lacked a high school diploma. Today, Canada, with a system that awards points to skilled immigrants, brings in people with better qualifications from the same countries that send the United States their unskilled workers.

In the nineteenth and twentieth centuries, a policy of expanding labor-intensive farm and factory production by importing vast numbers of unskilled workers may have made sense (although even then, immigration reduced the economic prospects of the native white and black poor). But in a knowledge-based economy, in which the educational attainments of our citizenry are among the most important determinants of our nation's economic success, a policy of flooding the American labor market with uneducated workers is simply self-defeating. Paradoxically, our nation's leaders continuously extol the virtues of building a highly educated workforce while simultaneously backing an immigration regime that brings about precisely the opposite effect.

An immigration policy geared to Information Age America would favor skilled immigrants over unskilled immigrants. Throughout American history, the United States has benefited from the talents of immigrant scientists like Albert Einstein; immigrant inventors like Alexander Graham Bell, Guglielmo Marconi, and An Wang; and immigrant businessmen like Andrew Carnegie. In the twenty-first century, we should build on this tradition by tipping the balance in favor of educated and enterprising newcomers from other lands.

Limiting family-based immigration to spouses, minor children, and parents of citizens and lawful permanent residents—a reform suggested by the U.S. Commission on Immigration Reform headed by the late Barbara Jordan—would greatly reduce the proportion of unskilled to skilled immigrants. An immigration policy that favors skilled immigrants would reduce the immigrant-caused growth of poverty in the United States. At the same time, a skill-based immigration policy would reduce the rate of U.S. population growth. Economically successful people of all races tend to have fertility rates at or below replacement.

Needless to say, too heavy a reliance on well-educated foreign workers to fill our domestic jobs could backfire by reducing the incentives to improve our own schools and universities, or to upgrade the skills of our current population. To reduce this risk and ensure that American citizens as well as recent immigrants remain first in line for the new jobs of the future, it may well be advisable to gradually lower our overall level of immigration from today's historic highs, while encouraging more Americans to choose careers based on math and science. (Between 1986 and 1996, the percentage of bachelor's degrees in the United States conferred in natural, health, and computer science and engineering actually declined from 28 percent to 24 percent.)

The proposed establishment of a "guest worker program," which would bring great numbers of poor workers from Mexico and other countries into the United States for a limited amount of time, would be a step in the wrong direction. If companies in some industries like agribusiness were allowed to pay foreign guest workers less than the minimum wage, soon companies in other industries would demand the same right to replace American citizens demanding decent wages with more compliant foreign workers. The problem of illegal immigration would also increase, for the simple reason that many of the guest workers would have an economic incentive to abandon their assigned jobs in order to seek higher wages as permanent resident undocumented workers.

Illegal immigration will always be a problem to some degree. For the most part, proposals for reducing illegal immigration focus on the "supply side"—controlling the southwestern border and strengthening security in airports and marine ports. This is necessary but far from sufficient. For political reasons—chiefly the opposition of unscrupulous American employers to regulations requiring them to check the citizenship of their workers—there has been very little attention paid to "demand side" reforms. But information technologies of the kind routinely used by credit card companies and banks make it easy to devise a highly secure system of digital employment records that employers could be mandated to use. If a computerized employee database were combined with stiff penalties for employers who hire illegal immigrants, such a system would send a strong message to all employers. And if employment opportunities for illegal immigrants dried up in the United States, as a result of sanctions on employers who violate the law, word would quickly travel back to the source countries, discouraging many potential illegal immigrants in the first place.

Employers of low-paid labor often make the self-serving claim that reducing the pool of unskilled workers in the United States would cripple the economy. But tighter labor markets and higher wages would encourage technological innovation and diffusion, by creating greater incentives for the substitution of new technologies for labor. The economist Lester Thurow argues that a major reason for low productivity in the U.S. service sector is an overabundance of low-wage labor: "If wages are falling, it is profitable for companies to move to lower-cost, lower-productivity, labor-intensive methods of production. The guard at the parking lot becomes cheaper than the automated fare collection machinery." We have everything to gain from encouraging labor-saving productivity breakthroughs—instead of artificially retarding them by maintaining high levels of low-skilled, low-wage immigration.

Of course, there are some labor-intensive occupations—particularly in caregiving fields like nursing—that will never be automated. As our society ages, there may come a time when we once again need to increase the number of unskilled immigrants to satisfy the demand for such jobs. For the foreseeable future, however, a policy that raises our proportion of skilled immigrants and gradually lowers our overall immigration levels would not only boost our competitiveness, productivity, and living standards, but would disproportionately help the poorest American workers of all races, who suffer the most as a result of today's irrational and outdated immigration regime. In fact, the new approaches to civil rights and immigration that we propose would reinforce one another—doing far more to help all of the neediest Americans get ahead, while promoting rather than retarding racial integration in the process.

While the racial divide represents the oldest fissure in the American national community, the generational divide represents the most recent. By the generational divide we mean political conflict among Americans on a generational basis. This relatively new phenomenon in our politics threatens to grow in significance in the decades ahead.

The late twentieth century in the United States saw the emergence for the first time of the elderly as a special-interest group. The American Association of Retired Persons (AARP) became one of the most powerful lobbies in American politics. And the special-interest politics of the elderly shows all the pathologies typical of special-interest politics of all kinds. For instance, the elderly lobby has frequently combined the language of grievance and victimhood with demands for ever-increasing entitlements, such as the addition of government-paid prescription drug benefits. Unfortunately, the gray lobby tends not to present the interests of the elderly as one of many competing interests that must be balanced, but rather as demands that must be satisfied, no matter what the cost to society at large.

The emergence of special-interest politics of the elderly is the unwelcome result of a welcome development—the increasing health and longevity of our population. Within a few years, for the first time in our nation's history, there will be fewer Americans aged twenty to twenty-nine than people fifty-five to sixty-nine. And by 2020, the younger group may shrink to be 40 percent smaller than the older group. Between 1950 and 1992, the life expectancy for white men at age sixty-five rose by 21 percent; for white women, by 25 percent. Thanks to this increased longevity, by the 1990s, more than 40 percent of Americans between the ages of fifty and fifty-nine had living family members from four or more generations. Indeed, the number of Americans now living beyond the age of one hundred has mushroomed to more than seventy thousand. And advances in genetic therapy and biomedical research will only extend average life spans further.

The fact that American citizens are enjoying longer lives should be cause for celebration. Unfortunately, however, several factors cloud what ought to be a joyous development: the competition for resources among the growing number of elderly citizens and the shrinking number of young Americans; the coming crisis of caregiving that will manifest itself when the members of the baby boom generation reach their final years; and a much neglected but equally important phenomenon, the spatial and geographic segregation of Americans by age. All three of these trends are exacerbated by the new reality of generational voting blocs, and more specifically, by the fact that today's elderly tend to vote in high numbers, while the young tend to do just the opposite. Unless these potential problems are redressed relatively soon, the promise of an aging America may turn very sour.

The most frequently discussed source of intergenerational strife stems from the impact of our changing demographic profile on our social welfare programs for retirees. When Bismarck introduced government pensions in Germany in the 1870s, hardly anybody lived long enough to qualify for one. Likewise, when Social Security was introduced by Franklin Roosevelt, the initial number of recipients was too small to be politically significant; indeed, the pension age was five years older than the standard life expectancy. But medical advances and declining birthrates have combined to change all of that: As mentioned, the latest projections are that our Social Security system will start paying out more than it takes in as of 2016, and become insolvent as of 2038. The prognosis is even more alarming for Medicare, the other main entitlement program for retirees.

These fiscal problems of course are compounded by the political problem that the elderly tend to vote as a bloc for politicians who promise to defend and increase their retirement and health care benefits. One of the results is that the rate of growth of entitlements for the elderly is outstripping the rate of growth of the economy as a whole. Because the size of government in relation to the economy is unlikely to expand, additional growth in spending on the elderly will have to come at the expense of spending on other social needs, including spending on child care and education. Overspending on one generation of retirees could therefore lead to dramatic underspending on the generations that follow, which would compromise our collective future.

While there has been much public debate about the coming strains on our Social Security and Medicare systems, there has been relatively little debate about the broader caregiving crisis to come. After all, the huge cohort of baby boom retirees will not only require their monthly pension contributions, but also unprecedented amounts of time-consuming and expensive individual care in their final years. And the strain that the new demand for eldercare will place on society at large will be increased by the diminishing ability of families to provide such care. The decrease in birthrates and increase in life expectancies are turning the pyramidal family of the past into a vertical family that is both tall (a growing number of generations) and narrow (a shrinking number of people in each generation).

Between 1987 and 1996, the number of nursing homes increased by 20 percent. Already by 1997, 22 percent of U.S. families were providing care for an elderly relative. Needless to say, these pressures will increase dramatically as a result of the graying of the baby boom generation and the changing nature of the American family.

The need to provide unprecedented amounts of individualized care for the elderly, especially for nonfamily members, can be expected to deepen tensions between working-age citizens and retired citizens. Young parents struggling to raise their own children, and perhaps to care for their own parents or grandparents, will resent the demand of single-issue lobbies representing the elderly for more government resources for eldercare. For their part, the elderly will feel that they have earned a right to a high standard of care by their contributions to society during their working lives. Each cohort will naturally be tempted to look out for its own interests, which will be in opposition to one another.

Finally, the emerging generational divide is widened further by our bizarre system of residential segregation by age. In today's America, one neighborhood may consist predominantly of young working families, while another is inhabited almost exclusively by retirees. There are even entire states—Florida and Arizona come quickly to mind—dominated by retirees. This age apartheid encourages irrational political behavior by retirees, demanding that unseen working-age people somewhere else support them, as well as by working adults, who rebel against supporting old people with whom they have no sense of connection. It also encourages geographically concentrated age groups to vote against the interests of the generational minorities in their own vicinity; for example, elderly voting blocs typically oppose new local spending initiatives for public education. Obviously, if the young and old lived among one another, there would be a greater inclination to realize that a community involves trade-offs and cooperation across generations.

What can be done about the generational divide? Fortunately, a great deal. We have to remember that the generational divide is not the result of bad motives on the part of elderly or nonelderly voters. It is simply another case where the rational pursuit of self-interest by many individuals, without any coordination, results in collective problems. The answer, then, lies in changing the norms, incentives, and barriers that cause today's generational divide in order to permit a healthier and more complementary relationship among all generations to emerge.

The single most important remedy may be a wholesale reconception of the process of retirement. Today's norms, which enshrine sixty-five or sixty-seven as the standard retirement age, are not only anachronistic but perverse. When individuals routinely live into their nineties and even hundreds, why should we maintain social, employment, and legal conventions that suggest that these individuals should cease to be productive members of the workforce for the final twenty-five to thirty-five years of their lives? To the contrary, we have everything to gain from encouraging all American citizens to remain healthy and productive members of society for as long as they can. In the twenty-first century, the whole timing of retirement should be at the discretion of the individual; perhaps we should retain a minimum age for retirement, but certainly not a maximum age.

Given the option, many healthy Americans may well choose to remain in the workforce well into their seventies if not eighties. This would not only enhance our nation's overall prosperity and provide a new pool of highly seasoned and experienced workers, but it would also decrease the fiscal burden on our entitlement system, since most of those who continue to work would not require government aid while doing so. Alternately, many Americans may choose to devote their later years to giving back to society in a variety of ways, by caring for the very young, the very needy, or the very old. Indeed, retirees could well turn into the new army of volunteers that our community sector so needs.

While many fret about the fiscal implications of the baby boom's mass retirement, history may show these worries to be far outweighed by all the potential economic and civic contributions of a large pool of healthy and publicly minded senior citizens. There should be little question as to the potential for a virtuous cycle: The longer America's senior citizens remain productive members of society, the more they will contribute to the public good, and the less they will impose on the public purse. Indeed, the *Journal of Gerontology* reported in 1999 that Americans over age sixty-five who volunteered a minimum of forty hours a year were a full 67 percent more likely to live longer than their counterparts who did not. But for this virtuous cycle to replace today's vicious cycle, we must eliminate our fixed retirement age and enable America's septuagenarians, octogenarians, and even nonagenarians to remain in the workforce for as long as they choose, or to take up new vocations as part of America's armies of compassion.

If one way to lessen the entitlement burden that is widening the generational divide is to do away with a fixed retirement age, then the second is to reinvent our entire approach to social welfare. As we argued in Chapter 2, America needs a new social contract for the twenty-first century. By increasing the degree to which pensions and health care are paid for by compulsory savings, rather than transfer payments from today's workers to today's retirees, we could solve the very design problem that turns demographic variances between generations into fiscal time bombs for all involved. It is not a moment too soon to begin moving from our Industrial Age social contract to one adapted to the Information Age.

Another major barrier standing in the way of intergenerational harmony is physical, resulting from outmoded zoning laws. As we have noted, our system of generational apartheid segregates neighborhoods by age as ruthlessly as racial apartheid used to segregate neighborhoods by race. A typical American may grow up in a middle-class suburb, and spend the college years in an "apartment city" surrounded by tens of thousands of single young people, before moving to a neighborhood for young couples with "starter" homes, followed by a more prosperous middle-class neighborhood for families with children, and finally by a neighborhood where virtually everyone is old. This bizarre pattern, in which each stage of life is accompanied by a physical migration, is not the result of "market forces," inasmuch as real estate is one of the most heavily regulated industries in the United States. Rather, this generational apartheid is the result of ill-considered zoning regulations and development policies that mandate that all housing in a particular neighborhood be similar, and that the functions of dwelling, work, and education be kept far apart.

The New Urbanist movement, which advocates mixed-use land policies in the construction of new suburbs and the revitalization of urban cores, has shown that many Americans, given the chance, prefer to live in the equivalent of a premodern small town or an old-fashioned urban neighborhood, in which people of all ages and various income groups live among each other and mingle on a daily basis. Except in "greenfield" developments, however, realizing this ideal will require substantial revisions of zoning laws—by, for example, allowing families to build "granny flats" adjacent to their homes, which could also be used by children in college or low-income workers. Needless to say, the opportunities for the elderly to contribute to community can only be maximized if they reside among younger neighbors, instead of being warehoused among hundreds or thousands of other old people.

Changing our nation's retirement norms, our basic social contract, and our residential zoning laws could do a great deal to alleviate what is fast becoming a festering generational divide in our political and community spheres. But no matter how successful such policies are, how integrated our generations become, and how long our senior citizens remain healthy and productive members of society, there would still be one big challenge left unaddressed: how to care for the growing number of senior citizens in their final years. Americans in the twenty-first century will have obligations to a growing number of living parents and grandparents—and great-grandparents, and perhaps even great-great-grandparents. Because men still tend to die earlier than women, the burden may fall disproportionately on widowed women taking care of their own widowed mothers and other elderly relatives. Making matters worse, baby boomers and the successor generations will have fewer children to help them. As a result, they will depend more on care by nonfamily members.

Providing America's shrinking families with the help they need for their growing number of elderly members will be a joint responsibility of the state and the community. If the burden falls primarily on the state, however, it will only exacerbate the fiscal burdens and political tensions already caused by our aging society. Fortunately, there is an alternative that is particularly suited to the American context. In the democracies of continental Europe, citizens are accustomed to turning to the central government for family-reinforcing goods like child care, early education, and eldercare. But throughout our history, we Americans have looked to charities and volunteerism to perform many of the tasks that are performed in other societies by a paternalistic government. It may be, then, that American philanthropic institutions like charities, foundations, and churches could once again come to the rescue of the broader society—this time helping to meet the unprecedented need for the provision of quality eldercare in the coming century.

Is it realistic to expect the nonprofit sector—staffed, in part, by healthy retirees—to play a significant role in care for the needy elderly? One of America's most unique and heartening virtues is the strong philanthropic impulse of our citizens. Indeed, Americans donate far more money to charities, both per capita and overall, than any other nation on the planet. In 1999, for instance, approximately 70 percent of our citizenry donated to charities of some sort. The combined total in charitable giving in that year was $190 billion, of which approximately 75 percent came from individuals, 10 percent from foundations, 8 percent from bequests, and 6 percent from corporations.

The strong American tradition of volunteerism is as encouraging as our tradition of charitable giving. In 1999, for instance, 49 percent of Americans reported that they volunteered for a community purpose, compared to only 19 percent of citizens of France and 13 percent of citizens of Germany. And there is reason to hope that volunteerism levels could increase further in the coming decades, particularly if the large number of relatively healthy senior citizens decide to enter the voluntary sector. In the mid-twentieth century, the primary source of volunteers who led most secular and religious caregiving initiatives and community-minded efforts were women. But their mass entry into the paid workforce in the decades since has led to an overall decline in volunteerism and civic activism. In the decades ahead, it may well be Americans in their seventies and eighties and nineties who rise to the occasion, providing much of the care for Americans in their hundreds and beyond. Of course, this would require not just a new army of volunteers but also a significant expansion of charitable funding.

Fortunately for our nation as a whole—and potentially for our neediest citizens—we can expect a generational wealth transfer of enormous proportions over the next half-century, a significant portion of which will go to charitable causes. Researchers John Havens and Paul Schervich predict a total wealth transfer of between $41 trillion and $136 trillion over the next fifty-five years. By 2025, it is estimated that charitable giving alone could surpass $1.2 trillion per year (in inflation-adjusted dollars). To put this figure in context, this is nearly twice as much money as our government currently spends on all domestic discretionary programs. As this example suggests, America's philanthropic largesse could go a very long way toward alleviating the coming crisis of eldercare as well as many other social problems—provided that this level of giving does materialize, and that a significant portion is directed toward helping the neediest and oldest Americans.

There are many explanations for America's exceptionally high rates of philanthropic giving: cultural reasons, historic reasons, and tax reasons. Culturally, our nation's deep belief in equality of opportunity and upward mobility, reinforced by wave after wave of immigrants coming to our shores to reap the American dream, gave rise to a spirit of public generosity that often takes the form of private giving rather than government spending. This is the American way. The fabulous amounts of wealth accumulated by a small number of individuals during what Mark Twain called the Gilded Age of the late nineteenth century, led to the first Golden Age of philanthropy, and the establishment of several large foundations—like the Carnegie, Rockefeller, and Ford Foundations—that still exist to this day and have profoundly influenced American society and the world at large. This legacy has already inspired many of the new cyberelites of recent decades to follow in the footsteps of their predecessors and establish large foundations of their own: most notably the Packard, Hewlett, and Gates Foundations. The charitable tax deduction, first enacted in 1917, has also played a significant role in encouraging philanthropy by rewarding contributors with tax breaks in proportion to their generosity (although such deductions only accrue to those who itemize on their tax forms).

In order to encourage a steady and expanding stream of philanthropic funding in the twenty-first century, and help leverage it toward the areas of greatest need, we propose both maintaining the charitable tax deduction and simultaneously reforming it in some important ways. On the first point, we believe that the centrality of philanthropic giving to our nation's social and moral health justifies an exception to our previously stated goal of eliminating most income tax deductions. In our opinion, the charitable tax deduction is particularly defensible because, in contrast to the vast majority of other current tax deductions, its benefits accrue to Americans of all income levels (both those who give, and those who receive charitable services). If the deduction were eliminated, we fear that the very source that feeds so much of our civil society would dry up.

That being said, we also believe that our charitable tax code should be amended to reflect the fact that some types of charitable activities are more valuable to society as a whole than others. For instance, it would be tragic if an excessive amount of philanthropic resources in the twenty-first century went to a narrow range of elite institutions—such as private universities or the opera—that disproportionately benefit the wealthy. If this were to occur, the public interest rationale for maintaining the charitable tax deduction would dissolve.

Unfortunately, the nonprofit sector as it exists today in the United States is not particularly well positioned to play a greater role in relieving the burden of care for the elderly that would otherwise fall on the government. First, relatively few of today's growing number of nonprofit and community organizations are of a strictly caregiving nature. Second, there has been a significant social stratification in the realm of community organizations. With the possible exception of certain religious denominations, most branches of civil society that are thriving today are of an elite nature. At the turn of the twenty-first century, elite-oriented charitable organizations—such as the opera, private universities, environmental groups, and soccer leagues—are thriving. But many of the communities and constituencies most in need—particularly the young, the old, and the inner-city poor—are not receiving the caregiving resources they deserve.

One way to redress this situation is to redirect some of the philanthropic resources on which our communal institutions depend. Currently, about 43 percent of philanthropic contributions flow to religious institutions, 14 percent to educational institutions (mostly higher education), 9 percent to health, 9 percent to human services, 6 percent to arts and culture, and 3 percent to environmental causes. Clearly, the majority of philanthropic dollars does not go into direct services for the neediest Americans. How could a larger share of philanthropic dollars be redirected toward relieving the strain on families in the area of caregiving without undermining the philanthropic impulse or freedom of choice of individual donors?

The United States now recognizes two broad types of nonprofit institutions: those that focus on lobbying and those that are primarily charitable in nature. Contributions to the former are not tax deductible, while contributions to the latter are. We propose expanding this binary system into a trinary system by distinguishing between two types of tax-exempt organizations: the minority (like the Salvation Army or a church soup kitchen), which are entirely dedicated to providing direct care to the neediest, and the majority (like most religious institutions, universities, membership organizations, or the opera), which do serve the public interest but not as directly. In our opinion, the strictly caregiving organizations should receive even more favorable tax treatment, to reflect their greater importance to the well-being of our society as a whole. Accordingly, we propose that donations to this new type of caregiving organization be rewarded through tax deductions worth 150 percent of the value of the contribution (as opposed to the current rate of 100 percent for all other charities). Naturally, new regulations would need to be enacted to ensure that the charities benefiting from this special deduction were devoted solely to caregiving for the neediest populations, and to prevent both donors and nonprofit organizations from gaming the system.

Such a policy, if it proved effective, could become one of the most innovative and important means of addressing the crises of senior care that we will face in the coming decades, while at the same time helping the chronically poor of all ages, many of whom risk being left behind in the new economy. Given the amounts of likely philanthropic giving in coming years, the results could be dramatic. Not only would many Americans choose to connect their own philanthropic and economic interests with those of the neediest citizens, but this new wave of funding could inspire a whole new array of caregiving organizations. In fact, many of today's religious and secular nonprofit organizations would likely create caregiving offshoots of their own to take advantage of the preferential tax treatment, while allocating more of their resources to alleviating human suffering of multiple types. Ideally, a new spirit of entrepreneurship, volunteerism, and innovation might arise in the caregiving sector. Along with the other reforms we propose, this might help turn what is now shaping up to be a vicious generational divide into a virtuous intergenerational collaboration.

If the racial divide is a threat to American community inherited from the past, and the generational divide is a threat of the present, the genetic divide may be the greatest threat to community in the future. By the *genetic divide* we mean the ability of elites to upgrade the genes of their offspring, thereby creating a profound division between the majority of ordinary citizens and a minority of genetically superior individuals.

It is always difficult to predict the social impact of new technologies, and it could be argued that any serious discussion of a genetic divide is premature at this stage, but we believe it is not, for several reasons. First, the scientific community is actively debating this subject; for example, the American Association for the Advancement of Science issued a major report in September 2000 that assessed the scientific, ethical, religious, and policy issues relating to inheritable genetic modifications in humans. In addition, political thinkers and commentators have begun to speculate about how advances in human genetic engineering could alter today's political coalitions. We believe the American public and our elected officials should join in this debate in order to guide the unfolding genetics revolution before it surprises us with unpleasant and unintended consequences.

What makes the genomics revolution so contentious is that it could ultimately allow us to manipulate the very essence of our human nature, which took some 3.5 billion years to evolve through natural selection. Of course, research in genomics will not start out with that goal in mind; nevertheless, that is precisely where it may lead us. Now that the human genome has mostly been sequenced, the next major step will be a proliferation of readily available genetic tests to determine a patient's predisposition to a wide range of illnesses. By 2001 there were already 450 genetic tests in development. This will pave the way for a new wave of medications that are custom-tailored to a patient's genetic profile. Next will come genetic therapy, the practice by which the genetic disposition of a living human being is altered to cure various gene-based illnesses. Then may come the day that replacement organs are routinely grown in vitro. None of this is as far off as some may think. For example, it is quite likely that a human being will be cloned somewhere in the world in the next several years (in our opinion, cloning of actual human beings, as opposed to mere human tissues or human organs, should be banned).

For all the novelty of these various genetic developments, however, the real turning point will come with the advent of germ-line modification. The basic difference between germ-line engineering and other types of genetic therapy is that in the former the modification is passed on to all future generations. This distinction can be illustrated by the difference between cosmetic surgery on the one hand, and, on the other, changing a person's look through altering his or her basic genetic blueprint: The former goes with you to your grave, while the latter is handed down to all your descendants. Germ-line manipulation will be acutely contentious. Many religious traditions will oppose it on the grounds that human nature is sacred and ought never to be tampered with. By contrast, others will argue that the ability to eliminate debilitating illnesses prior to birth implies a moral obligation to do so.

The debate over human germ-line engineering is unlikely to fall along conventional liberal-conservative lines. Instead, the public may soon be divided into four distinct camps by two distinct debates: the debate between prohibitionists and legalizers, and a debate among the legalizers between egalitarians and elitists.

The first debate hinges on whether research in germ-line modification should be prohibited altogether or allowed to proceed, under government regulation. Both the Left and the Right will have their own prohibitionist wings. The prohibitionist wing of the Left is represented today by those American and European liberals who are opposed to the use of genetic engineering in farming. This "Green" Left can be expected to oppose even the most benign forms of germ-line engineering as a fundamental misuse of technology. The antigenetics Left will find allies among fundamentalist Christians, Jews, and Muslims, who believe that it is blasphemous for human beings to "play God" by altering the basic genomes of humans or other organisms.

The "legalizers," by contrast, will include progressives who are comfortable with the use of high technology to improve the human condition and right-wing libertarians who, unlike religious conservatives, celebrate economic dynamism and scientific progress. Whether they are on the Left, Right, or center of the political spectrum, the legalizers will agree that the potential of germ-line engineering to improve human health should be cautiously explored.

In making their case to outlaw all human germ-line modification, the prohibitionists can cite the damage done by eugenics enthusiasts in the early twentieth century. Long before it was tainted by association with genocidal Nazi policies, eugenics was favored by many progressives in the United States and Britain like Theodore Roosevelt, Oliver Wendell Holmes Jr., H. G. Wells, and George Bernard Shaw. However, the genetic basis of inheritance was not understood until the 1930s, and the structure of DNA and RNA was not deciphered until the 1960s. Unfazed by their ignorance of the mechanisms of heredity, state governments in the United States in the first half of the twentieth century sterilized not only thousands of "idiots" who suffered from only slight mental retardation but also many ordinary people who were victimized because of their racial ancestry or their poverty. That kind of abuse of eugenics by authorities blinded by social prejudices, prohibitionists could argue, could happen again.

This is an argument that deserves to be taken seriously. But practically every institution in American society has been abused, at one time or another, in the service of caste or class. The potential for abuse is an argument for regulation, not for prohibition. In any event, it is doubtful that anyone in the twenty-first century United States would favor reviving the horrifying practice of compulsory sterilization of the allegedly unfit, or anything that might remotely resemble racial or class genocide. Those who did would be marginalized and dismissed by mainstream proponents of reasonable genetic intervention as well as by its adversaries.

Ultimately the decisive factor in the debate over whether germline modification in some form should be allowed will be the drive to improve human health, and particularly that of unborn children. On what grounds could one tell prospective parents that they could not make use of such a treatment to turn what would otherwise be a terminally ill child into a healthy one? In addition to this humanitarian argument in favor of some form of germ-line engineering, there may also be an economic one. All other things being equal, democratic nations that used biomedical means to eliminate certain kinds of terrible birth defects from their populations, thereby freeing resources for other uses, would have an advantage over other nations that prohibited such procedures. Indeed, taxpayers burdened by the costs of providing for an ever-expanding population of elderly people are unlikely to be enthusiastic about also paying for the treatment of terrible physical and mental handicaps that could have been prevented through genetic interventions.

The alternative to prohibition would be the legalization and regulation of certain forms of germ-line intervention. When it comes to providing a regulatory framework for such procedures, the legalizer school can be expected to divide into elitists and egalitarians. These two schools, within the larger school of legalizers, will propose quite different answers to the dilemmas created by two kinds of germ-line engineering: therapy and enhancement. Germ-line therapy can be defined as the genetic elimination of undesirable traits. Germ-line enhancement, by contrast, is the genetic addition of desirable traits.

Human germ-line therapy, if it becomes practicable, is likely to be the least controversial form of germ-line engineering. Indeed, few would oppose the elimination or modification of genes that cause severe mental retardation, deformity, blindness and deafness, and chronic, crippling illness. The argument that many severely retarded and handicapped people are able to lead decent lives is not an argument against eliminating the genetic origin of their afflictions. The fact that individual lepers were able to lead adequate lives in some cases was not an argument against eliminating leprosy. Leper colonies are a thing of the past. Some day, schools for the blind and deaf and mentally retarded and congenitally insane may be unknown as well.

Although germ-line therapy should be permitted, if it becomes practical and safe, we believe its scope should be strictly limited. Once we go beyond the area of gross mental and physical handicaps into the more complex area of temperament, the danger of social prejudice grows (as the era of state-sponsored sterilization in the U.S. proved). Different societies, and different classes and subcultures within the same society, assess "normal" behavior differently. For instance, what seems to be "hyperactive" behavior to one group may be normal behavior to another.

Consider the debate over Ritalin. Many parents, out of deference to doctors and school authorities, have consented to prescribe this drug to young children—mostly boys. Critics of the widespread use of Ritalin claim that boys are being punished for having temperaments that are genetically hardwired to be different from those of girls. In effect, little boys in the United States are being drugged on a massive scale to make their behavior more like that of little girls. At least the use of the drug can be stopped. But what if boys had been genetically engineered to eliminate their allegedly undesirable boy-like behavior? A reform intended to keep young boys in their seats in the second grade might accidentally have eliminated a generation of leaders whose accomplishments were inextricably linked to male aggression and plain fidgetiness.

We simply do not know enough about the link between the personality traits we value and the personality traits we dislike to safely eliminate the latter. The claim of nineteenth-century European Romantics that genius, illness, and madness are linked has been refuted already by medical advances. The tubercular artist of nineteenth-century cliché has vanished along with tuberculosis, but fine art continues to be made. Homer and Milton were blind, but eliminating blindness will not eliminate poetry. On the other hand, many have suggested a link between creative genius and some forms of manic-depressive behavior (the "melancholy" of tradition). A population wired to be perky, industrious extroverts might also be a population bereft of certain kinds of intellectual creativity. Germ-line therapy, then, should be limited to the most extreme mental and physical handicaps. Tampering with the genes that influence temperament should be forbidden, at least until much more is known about the biological basis of personality and achievement.

Reaching a consensus about the scope of legitimate germ-line therapy would not, by itself, create a consensus about its availability. On this issue the two opposing sides within the camp of legalizers will be elitists and egalitarians. These two sides will not necessarily correspond to "Right" and "Left"; the elitist camp might include members of the libertarian Left, while conservative populists who do not oppose germ-line modification on religious grounds might join the ranks of the egalitarians.

The debate about access to germ-line therapy will likely mirror the familiar debate over access to general health care. The elitists will argue that access to it should be rationed by the market (i.e., by wealth); whereas the egalitarians will argue that access should be rationed directly or indirectly by the government on the basis of need, among all citizens, without regard for individual income or wealth. In some debates about political philosophy, both sides have a plausible case, but not in this one. Even today, the rich tend to be healthier than the poor, as a result of environment and upbringing and financial endowments. But at least the incidence of genetic illness is distributed more or less randomly across classes (with the exception of those illnesses concentrated in particular ethnic groups, like Tay-Sachs disease in the Jewish community or sickle-cell anemia among black Americans). If access to germ-line therapy were rationed by wealth, then genetically based diseases would be found almost exclusively among the poor—the very people whose families lack the resources to deal with severe handicaps.

The same egalitarian logic that supports universal access by all citizens to germ-line therapy, if and when it becomes practical and safe, leads to the conclusion that germ-line enhancement should be either prohibited altogether or provided on an equal basis to all citizens. Germ-line enhancement, as we defined the term above, is the use of genetic technology to endow individuals with heritable traits they do not possess, or to enhance desirable traits they do possess. In theory, parents or a despotic state could decide to make children smarter, stronger, better-looking, more energetic, or all of the above.

In the very distant future, egalitarians might consider universal programs of germ-line enhancement (along with similar universal programs for ability-enhancing drugs or bionic prostheses like computer implants in the brain). But genomics is in its infancy now, and the potential for disaster is enormous.

To begin with, it is not clear what abstract intellectual or behavioral traits ought to be enhanced. As we have already observed, "desirable" traits like leadership or creativity may well depend on "undesirable" traits like aggression, egocentrism, and depression. Moreover, the traits that promote individual success change as society changes. Different types of characters have risen to the top in Greek city-states, the Roman empire, medieval Europe, eighteenth-century colonial British America, and the twenty-first-century United States. Enhancement germ-line engineering might saddle children with intellectual aptitudes, behavioral traits, or physical attributes that were considered desirable by their parents' generation but which were rendered archaic by the passage of a few decades. Consider fads in education, for instance, which have followed a cycle in the United States. One generation favors loose, unstructured play, then there is a reaction in favor of discipline and memorization. What if children born in the former period had the imaginative areas of their brains enhanced, while the latter era produced cohorts of children with prodigious memories and submissive personalities? Higher education shows the same faddishness. In the 1980s and 1990s, Wall Street offered college graduates the preferred career, then Hollywood, then dot.coms. It will always be easier for individuals to reprogram their minds when society changes than it would ever be for them to reprogram their genes.

Even if it were available to all citizens, then, germ-line modification for the purpose of enhancement might be a bad idea because of the potential for unwise decisions on the part of parents. But the greatest argument against such procedures is the danger that the powerful or wealthy few would try to use them to convert their families into genetic dynasties.

In one perspective, the history of politics is little more than the attempts of successive ruling classes to monopolize power, wealth, and prestige, and to prevent their overthrow by outsiders—rival aristocrats, bourgeois rebels, workers, slaves, and barbarians—who want a greater portion of these goods for themselves. Many ruling elites have claimed to be naturally superior to those whom they rule, but the viciousness with which most aristocracies and oligarchies have repressed their subjects proves that few have believed their own rhetoric.

For all its promise, germ-line modification technology comes with a grave threat—perhaps the greatest threat that the human species has faced since it attained its present form roughly one hundred thousand years ago. That is the possibility that, for the first time, an elite could become in practice what elites have often claimed to be in propaganda: a master race whose superiority resulted not from the combination of greater resources and opportunities with ordinary human endowments but from genuine mental and physical superiority.

The most dramatic and horrifying attempt by a modern society to create a genetic elite took place in Nazi Germany. But the Hitler regime was inspired by pseudoscientific mythology, not science. The Nazis knew of no way to promote their insane schemes of enhancement eugenics other than mass murder of alleged undesirables—Jews, Slavs, homosexuals, and the handicapped—and pro-natal policies encouraging fertility among the supposed Aryan-German "master race." But suppose Hitler and his followers had been able to directly modify the genome? Can anyone doubt that the Nazi oligarchy would have carried out its program of attempting to create a genetic aristocracy in the laboratory?

Human germ-line enhancement may produce a similar threat even when it is not sponsored by a dictatorship. In democracies like the United States, elites based on wealth rather than on political power might try to use such technology to convert the passing advantages of money into the permanent advantages of genes. The democratic political culture of the United States has not prevented a series of wealthy elites—from the southern planters to the northeastern members of the Social Register in the Gilded Age to today's overclass parents sending their children to Power Preschools—from doing everything possible to rig the rules of society in favor of their offspring. If they could rig the rules of nature in favor of their children, many of these elite families would.

For this reason, when it comes to germ-line intervention, the strict libertarians who favor a free market in biotechnology may be as much a threat to the future of humanity as Nazi-like totalitarians. A master caste produced by a laissez-faire policy in a marketplace for reproductive technology would be as menacing as a master caste produced by design by a dictatorial government. The danger would be nothing less than speciation—the fissioning of the human race into two or more species. If speciation were to correspond to national or other political boundaries, the result would likely be endless war and conflict, initiated, possibly, by unmodified humans fearing subjection by their modified neighbors. If speciation occurred within a society, among classes that had artificially been transformed into genetic castes, the result would be either endless insurrection by the lower classes or a new form of slavery—a form of slavery all the more sinister because the masters would be innately superior to their slaves not only in rhetoric but in reality.

The case for prohibiting germ-line engineering to enhance individual attributes, then, is as powerful as the case for legalizing a minimal version of it for therapeutic purposes. The two can and should be distinguished. Opponents of germ-line intervention will claim that there is a "slippery slope" leading from germ-line therapy to germ-line enhancement, but like most slippery-slope arguments this one is unconvincing. There is an enormous and obvious difference between eliminating a gene that causes blindness or mental retardation and attempting to create an aristocracy of posthuman or superhuman beings. Rejecting the latter enterprise does not require us to reject the former.

Let us sum up our tentative conclusions, while noting that these are general principles to guide public debate on these matters in the decades ahead, rather than specific policy proposals, which would be premature at this stage. We have argued from a technology-friendly egalitarian perspective for rules governing the emerging field of germ-line intervention. If it becomes practicable and safe, then germ-line therapy should be legalized—but only on two conditions. First, it should be limited to the elimination of only the grossest kinds of mental and physical defects—preferably by methods that do not require abortion. Second, this minimal version of germ-line intervention should be accessible to all citizens on the basis of need rather than wealth.

Germ-line intervention for enhancement purposes, by contrast, should be prohibited altogether. Even a universal program of germ-line enhancement might result in disaster, because of the folly of misguided parents or ignorant public authorities. More important, the danger that political or economic elites might use these tech-nologies in attempts to turn their descendants into a new species of humankind, capable of permanently subordinating everyone else, makes it imperative to prohibit germ-line enhancement for the fore-seeable future.

For a ban on germ-line enhancement to be meaningful, it would have to be adopted on both a national and international basis, which of course raises quite a number of challenges for global governance. An individual nation that successfully proceeded with a mass up-grade of its gene pool might produce a competitive disadvantage on the part of all other nations, something which in turn could lead to a wave of international conflict. Preventing a genetic divide must therefore be both a national and international priority over the com-ing century. The cost of doing otherwise could be our nation's next civil war, or a new international genetic arms race—either of which would be disastrous.

Throughout this book we have maintained that the very nature of the Information Age argues for a broadening of individual choices: voting choices, educational choices, retirement choices, employment choices, and lifestyle choices. We also believe that women deserve the right to make their own reproductive choices, in the context of legal contraception and abortion. At the same time, however, we argue that certain types of reproductive choices—such as the ability of parents to engineer designer babies through germ-line modification—should be limited at all cost. In making this distinction, we are guided by the conviction that the well-being and unity of our nation must always supersede the individual rights of its citizens, in the cases when these come into direct conflict. In this case, the unregulated use of genetic engineering could undermine the egalitarian ethos that underlies the principles of our democracy and the promise of the American dream.

If America musters the will and the foresight to prevent the racial, generational, and genetic divides from tearing it apart, then the result could be an efflorescence of our community sector. Not only would we have the most dynamic economy and strongest military in the world, but we would have the most integrated and diverse population of any advanced nation. The United States, which set an example to the world of the twentieth century through its commitment to democracy, could set an equally powerful example in the twenty-first century as the most integrated melting-pot nation on the globe, unified across the lines of race, generation, and class.

This accomplishment could—and should—give rise to a renewed American sense of patriotism. A purely sentimental patriotism degenerates all too easily into xenophobia and jingoism; a purely intellectual patriotism is too weak to preserve a sense of community. What is needed is a critical patriotism, a patriotism of both the heart and the head. Such an approach can find an example in a famous toast by Stephen Decatur at Norfolk in April 1816: "Our country! . . . May she always be in the right; but our country, right or wrong." Carl Schurz, the great immigrant German-American senator, improved on this in Chicago on October 17, 1899: "Our country, right or wrong. When right, to be kept right; when wrong, to be put right."

# Five

•

# THE POLITICS OF
# THE RADICAL
# CENTER

Forty years after he drafted the Declaration of Independence, Thomas Jefferson warned later generations of Americans against being paralyzed by reverence for their great predecessors:

> Some men look at constitutions with sanctimonious reverence, and deem them like the Ark of the Covenant, too sacred to be touched. They ascribe to men of the preceding age a wisdom more than human, and suppose what they did to be beyond amendment. I knew this age well; I belonged to it, and labored with it. It deserved well of its country. It was very like the present, but without the experience of the present; and forty years of experience in government is worth a century of book-reading; and this they would say themselves, were they to rise from the dead . . . Laws and institutions must go hand in hand with the progress of the human mind.

What Jefferson said of our political Constitution applies to all sectors of American society. As conditions change and as knowledge increases, it is necessary to revise not only the institutions of the market, the government, and the community, but also the assumptions and the political alliances that maintain them. Skepticism about misguided radicalism is healthy; in the last century, we saw what horrors could be unleashed by ideologues willing to stop at nothing, even mass murder, to bring about their various versions of heaven on earth. But the negative examples of utopian extremists should not be invoked to dismiss and deride the achievable projects of commonsensical reformers. In the words of George Bernard Shaw, "Reformers have the idea that change can be achieved by brute sanity."

Indeed, it is reformers rather than reactionaries who have a better claim to the label of conservative. Who are more conservative— those who would sacrifice the part to save the whole, or those who would prefer to lose the whole rather than to alter it in any way? The true patriots in American history have always understood that when conditions change it is necessary to pursue perennial goals by new means. Renovation is conservation by means of innovation.

This basic lesson is particularly apparent in the United States, which has been founded not once, but three times. The first founding, of the Revolutionary War era, was followed by the second founding, during the Civil War and Reconstruction, which was followed by the third founding, of the New Deal era. Each of our informal republics that emerged from these successive revolutions was guided by its own reinvention of the realms of the market, the state, and the community. And each of these versions of our republic lasted sixty to eighty years before it gave way in the next period of comprehensive change. The last American founding took place half a century ago, between the 1930s and the 1950s (with a belated echo in the 1960s). Can the fourth founding of the United States be far away?

At the beginning of the twenty-first century, it is clear that the third republic of the United States, whose framework was established in the New Deal era between the presidencies of Franklin Roosevelt and Lyndon Johnson, is rapidly growing obsolete as a result of technological, demographic, and other types of change. As we have seen, many of the institutions of our society have become outmoded and counterproductive, including the health care and Social Security systems that are the basis of our social contract; our methods of electing public officials, raising tax revenues, and managing schools; and even our basic approaches to civil rights and immigration. These institutions are not evil. They are merely passé. Indeed, many of the structures, rules, and customs that impede progress today promoted progress in the past.

In the preceding chapters, we have sketched a new, Radical Centrist agenda for reinventing our public, private, and communal sectors. The goal is a fourth American republic that realizes our nation's perennial goals of liberty, equality, and unity in the new conditions of the twenty-first century. In this final chapter, we speculate about the politics necessary to build this new America. As we shall see, the record of American history suggests that major political changes have often been catalyzed by military or economic crises, although there are more hopeful precedents for broad-based reform in times of relative peace and prosperity. As to the potential constituency for change, we argue that there is a large base of independent-minded and alienated voters who, along with enlightened business leaders, may support a forward-looking political agenda that does not fit comfortably into today's Democratic and Republican Parties. The American people are well ahead of their political leaders.

A striking and sobering fact about major change in American history is that it has tended to be widely spaced in time and associated with cataclysms: the Revolutionary War, the Civil War and Reconstruction, the Great Depression, World War II, and the early cold war. Major political change in the United States, in short, tends to be revolutionary, not evolutionary. Political and social transformations are usually clustered in waves, separated by periods of stability lasting for decades or even generations. Periods of dramatic renovation of the polity as a whole are separated by long periods of modest, incremental reform within the system established during the last wave of major change.

One phenomenon responsible for the wavelike nature of change is technological progress, which, as Joseph Schumpeter and others have observed, tends to occur in concentrated bursts of invention. Demographic change—in the form of changes in family structure, age ratios, fertility, or immigration patterns—is more incremental, but its cumulative effects on society can be just as profound.

Institutional change usually lags behind social and economic change. For decades, sometimes generations, needed reforms are bottled up by the opposition of groups with an interest in perpetuating an anachronistic status quo. Then a crisis—secession from Britain, the Civil War, the Depression and World War II—provides an opportunity. The logjam breaks; the river bursts through. In a relatively short time, reformers in Congress, the presidency, and the courts enact the long-delayed reform agenda. Between 1861 and 1875, the dominant Republican Party hurriedly rushed into law dozens of proposals, ranging from federal railroad subsidies to national banking reform, that the Whigs and Federalists of earlier eras had proposed but could not enact. Likewise, most of the programs enacted into law during the New Deal, from Social Security to farm price supports, were inspired by proposals dating back to the late nineteenth century.

During these rare creative crises, American reformers often invoke the imperatives of national security. Lincoln's Emancipation Proclamation was issued as a war measure. The Truman administration's G.I. Bill expanding access to higher education was justified as a reward for American veterans. (Unwise reforms, like the federal Prohibition of alcohol, which originated as a war measure during World War I, are frequently enacted in this way as well.)

Each of the three American foundings has come to an end when all parties accept the rules of the new system and agree to abide by them. Often this "ratification" of the institutional revolution takes the form of the election of a president representing a faction that had bitterly fought against the reforms only a few years before. The founding of the first republic, for instance, was ratified when Thomas Jefferson became president in 1800. Many of Jefferson's supporters had fought against the adoption of the 1787 federal Constitution, but when he captured the presidency, they changed their strategy to one of working within the system rather than working to undermine it. A presidential election also marked the ratification of the second republic of the United States, which arose from the carnage and chaos of the Civil War and Reconstruction. In this case, southern Democrats acquiesced in naming the northern Republican Rutherford B. Hayes as president in return for the end of Reconstruction in the South. From that time on the southern elite would work using the new rules of Lincoln's second republic. Then the election of 1952 marked the ratification of the third republic, whose framework was built by Franklin Roosevelt and his successor Harry Truman beginning in 1932. Throughout the thirties and forties, many Republicans had bitterly denounced the New Deal for creating a tyrannical federal government. As president, however, Eisenhower signaled the acquiescence of the Republican majority by refusing to undo any major New Deal program.

During the three or four generations that separate foundings in American history, the major parties and political interest groups usually accept the basic rules established in the last period of radical change. These periods of ordinary politics that stretch for decades between periods of extraordinary politics can be frustrating for those who are more interested in overhauling outdated institutions than in tinkering with them. It is therefore encouraging to observe that some significant and enlightened reforms have taken place during periods of peace and prosperity.

The state-by-state extension of suffrage to all white men, for instance, took place in the relatively quiet "Era of Good Feelings" of the 1820s and 1830s. The civil rights revolution (which was, in effect, an aftershock of the New Deal era) took place during the prosperous economic years of the 1960s, before all the political unrest surrounding the Vietnam War reached a boiling point. The enactment of major environmental legislation also took place during the relatively quiet period of the last several decades. As yet another example, the earned income tax credit, one of the most successful American antipoverty initiatives, was enacted and expanded between the 1970s and the 1990s, a period otherwise sterile in significant social legislation.

So where are we today in "political time"? Must we await another painful national crisis—economic, social, geopolitical, or environmental—to muster the will for long-overdue reforms? Or will the historic opportunity provided by America's longest economic boom and sole superpower status provide a new opening for enlightened reform?

Clearly, the first years of the new millennium are not one of the great ages of political reform, like 1782–1800, 1860–76, or 1932–68. Rather, the first years of the twenty-first century in the United States can be compared to the first years of the twentieth. Then, as now, the challenge was to adapt American society to a new phase of technological civilization—the second industrial era in the 1900s, the Information Age in the 2000s. Then, as now, it was becoming clear that systemic change, not merely incremental reform, was in order.

But then as now systemic change was not yet possible. The reformers of the late nineteenth century like the Mugwumps and the Populists shared a vague sense that things were not right, but they failed to correctly analyze the situation. The Mugwumps, ignoring the transformation of the industrial economy, tended to assume that most problems resulted from political corruption. Their favored reforms were important but limited to the democratic process, like the secret ballot. The Populists, by contrast, feared industrial progress and sought to preserve an America of family farms. Like the Mugwumps, they tended to blame the side effects of industrialization on elite conspiracies rather than on structural change. Populists therefore favored this or that crackpot panacea—the nationalization of the railroads, or a currency based on bimetallism. The parallel with the 1990s and the first years of the twenty-first century is almost exact. The contemporary equivalent of the old Mugwumps were obsessed with campaign finance reform and gimmicks like term limits, to the exclusion of more important reforms. And the hard-core Populists of our time, represented by Patrick Buchanan, sought to restore an earlier economic and social order by means of industrial protectionism.

By the 1900s, the intellectual and political leaders of what was to become the Progressive movement—thinkers like Herbert Croly and politicians like Theodore Roosevelt—had moved beyond the late-nineteenth-century combination of moral outrage and cure-all gimmicks. They realized that the changes for the worse in American society were not primarily the result of the machinations of evil individuals or sinister elites, but of long-term trends in industrial society. The challenge was not to reject technological and economic progress, but to channel it to minimize the bad effects and share the benefits with all Americans. The earlier generation of malcontents had offered various unrelated proposals; the Progressives began to hammer out a program that would be realized to a large degree in the New Deal era of 1932–68.

Although epochal change would not occur until the 1930s, the Progressives and their Populist allies managed to enact a number of significant reforms in the realms of the market, the state, and the community. In the realm of the market, antitrust legislation, worker safety laws, consumer protection laws, the regulation of the professions, and the abolition of child labor were all legacies of Progressive reform. In the political sphere, the Progressives gave women the vote, sponsored the secret ballot and the city manager form of municipal government, reformed civil services at all levels, and amended the Constitution to provide for direct election of senators. And as we have also seen, during the Progressive era there was an explosion of creative institution-building in the American community sector that produced new, important voluntary organizations like the YMCA, the Salvation Army, and amateur sports leagues.

If our analogy proves to be accurate, then perhaps the best that we can hope for are incremental reforms over the next several years, followed by more fundamental reforms over the next several decades, as hurried responses to national emergencies. This would be better than a continuation of the bipartisan paralysis and the politics of recrimination that we have witnessed since the early 1990s, but clearly inferior to a whole-scale, preemptive adoption of much-needed reforms. In prosperous and quiet times, the forces of self-interested preservation will often defeat the forces of renovation.

If there is cause for greater hope, however, it is to be found in what may be an emerging coalition of voters and business interests who are already predisposed to consider a Radical Centrist agenda and the principles on which it is based—increased individual choice and citizen-based reform; greater personal responsibility and the concept of big citizenship; and a new approach to governance premised on a true safety-net philosophy and cooperative federalism.

The potential for a new, broad-based reform constituency in American politics is most evident in the declining support for the two major parties, identified as they are with mid-twentieth-century liberalism and mid-twentieth-century conservatism. As we have seen, Americans are increasingly boycotting our two dominant parties in several ways. After peaking in the early 1960s, rates of voting have reached historic lows. At the same time that voter turnout has plummeted, an unprecedented number of Americans have ceased to identify with either of the two established parties.

What explains this recent political dealignment? The answer, we believe, is that the plurality of the American public wants a political program that neither major party is capable of offering, because each is controlled by extremes in its own camp. Indeed, recent political developments confirm that conventional liberalism and conventional conservatism simply do not correspond with the views of most Americans.

In the last years of the twentieth century, the old Right and the old Left discovered, to their shock, that they are frequently out of sync with American public opinion. During the crisis over the shutdown of the federal government in 1995, the would-be counterrevolutionaries of the Republican Congress discovered that the American people do not want to radically downsize government; they are generally comfortable with a strong and energetic state, as long as it is solvent and efficient. The conservatives were shocked again during the impeachment of President Clinton. While the public disapproved of Clinton's adulterous affair in the White House, most Americans did not share the reactionary moral traditionalism of the leaders of the Republican Right. In a similar fashion, President George W. Bush was surprised by the public outrage that followed his early efforts to roll back environmental protections.

For their part, liberals were equally dismayed by public attitudes at the millennium. Both polls and statewide ballot initiatives demonstrated public opposition to the liberal panacea of racial preferences for favored minorities. The public was adapting to an era of growing integration and racial intermarriage, but liberals had not caught up. Likewise, liberal attempts to rally public support by "saving Social Security," a tried-and-true technique in the 1970s and 1980s, were as ineffectual by 2000 as the efforts in the 1900s of politicians in the Lincoln Republican tradition to "wave the bloody shirt" and rally voters by denouncing the Confederacy. Proposals to privatize part or all of Social Security no longer frightened the majority of voters. They had adapted to the new era of widespread ownership of stocks and bonds, even if liberals had not.

For good or bad, the Information Age has changed the nature of American democracy. In most high-profile matters, the public is no longer a passive bystander—its voice is heard through almost instantaneous public opinion polls, focus groups, and various public interest organizations. As Newt Gingrich and congressional Republicans discovered in the mid-1990s, those who veer from the new center pay the price, as Mr. Gingrich did with his political life. America's silent majority is no longer so silent.

These armies of disaffected, independent-minded voters, together with a large number of centrist Republicans and Democrats, are neither conservative nor liberal in the traditional sense. Polls show there are majorities of Americans who are socially tolerant yet supportive of law and order, fiscally conservative yet accepting of government intervention to ensure economic fairness and security, committed to racial unity yet skeptical of race-based affirmative action, concerned about the strength of our economy yet equally concerned about the health of our environment, and deeply committed to both electoral and educational reform. Needless to say, Americans who share all of these views do not feel at home in either of today's major parties.

Strong public support for bold reforms like doing away with our antiquated and unfair electoral rules, abolishing racial preferences, providing universal health care, and preventing harmful global climate change suggests that the public is just not interested in business as usual. Rather, many Americans want a new agenda worthy of the Information Age. Public opinion data reveals high levels of support for many of the policy proposals advocated throughout this book.

Most Americans want more electoral choices, and would therefore be inclined to support the proposals we have advanced for choice voting. The strong grassroots support for equalizing school funding within states would likely translate into strong support for doing so nationally. Polls and recent ballot initiatives confirm that the American public is ready to move from a race-based approach to civil rights to a new-citizen-based approach that focuses on need rather than ancestry. Judging from the popularity of individualized retirement accounts and public discomfort with further advantages for the well-to-do, it seems reasonable to infer that our proposal for progressive privatization of Social Security is closer to the public's preferences than either the straight privatization plans of conventional Republicans or the steadfast opposition to any privatization by conventional Democrats. There are also indications of strong backing for the idea of shifting from an employer-based social contract to a citizen-based one, and in so doing achieving universal health care without the limitation of choice a single-payer system would impose. Even when it comes to preventing a genetic divide—an issue that lies in the future—polling reveals that the majority of Americans tend to agree with our guarded support of therapeutic uses for germ-line engineering as well as our steadfast opposition to germ-line enhancement.

Although these examples help illustrate the existence and general orientations of a potential Radical Centrist constituency in America, it would be a mistake to take them too literally. The fact that a majority of Americans supports each of these policies independently does not imply that there is a uniform constituency that would support all of these policies in combination. Those who support adding a personal savings element to Social Security, for example, may disagree on how to fund public schools. Likewise, even though polling results reveal a significant level of support for several of the policies advocated in this book, many of the bolder proposals we put forth have yet to be polled in a serious way. We simply do not know where the public stands on inaugurating a new era of universal capitalism, or creating a new category of caregiving charitable organizations. Our policy recommendations, after all, are based not on polling results but on principled arguments about the public interest.

With these caveats noted, however, we are encouraged by the sheer size of a potential new force in American politics. According to one survey in March 2000, when asked to assume that an unnamed third-party candidate had a chance to win the presidential election, 27 percent picked the third-party candidate—compared to 28 percent who said they would vote for a Democrat and 26 percent who said they would vote for a Republican. At least some of the constituencies that are alienated from conventional liberalism and conservatism may be the foundation of the next era in American politics.

Those devoted to renovating the American republic and advancing a Radical Centrist agenda might also find significant support among the newly wealthy and influential elites of the technology sector. As individuals and executives, business elites in all sectors are equally self-interested. But it is possible to speak of forward-looking and backward-looking industries. A forward-looking industry is one that is a laboratory for the technologies, forms of corporate governance, and employer-employee relationships that, in time, will be adopted by most or all sectors of the economy.

Each of the three successive technological revolutions—the First Industrial Revolution, the Second Industrial Revolution, and the Information Revolution—was pioneered in a small number of industries before spreading to the rest of the economy. During the transition from one phase of technological society to another there is inevitably a period in which the economy is partly modernized and partly backward. In such situations, groups with a vested interest in the old order, which may include both ordinary people and elites, often try to use their political power to block technological or political change, while both the workers and the elites in the new, advanced sectors of industry form a constituency for economy-wide reform.

This happened in the United States in the nineteenth century, when populists and elites in the agrarian sector fought against the emerging manufacturing sector, whose beneficiaries included industrial workers as well as industrial capitalists. In the pivotal presidential election of 1896, many industrial workers joined with their employers to rally behind the Republican William McKinley in order to defeat the Democratic and Populist candidate William Jennings Bryan, the symbol of America's agricultural past. The triumph of industry over agriculture ensured the modernization of agriculture by industrial techniques pioneered in the manufacturing sector.

During the Second Industrial Revolution of the early twentieth century, a similar split appeared—not between agriculture and industry, but between labor-intensive first-phase industries and capital-intensive second-phase industries. Corporate support for Franklin Roosevelt's New Deal came disproportionately from capital-intensive industries associated with the then-new technologies of the second industrial era, like electric power companies and oil companies. Because their major input was capital, in the form of high technology, these companies were not threatened by New Deal reforms of labor law, wage policies, and working conditions that forced labor-intensive industries to improve the way they treated their workers or go out of business. In the long run, the technologies of the second industrial era transformed all sectors of the economy, just as the technologies of the first industrial era had done earlier, to the benefit of all Americans.

The new elites of Silicon Valley and other centers of the digital economy may or may not lend their aid to a general program of American renewal. They are, however, more likely to do so than other business elites, for two reasons. As advocates of new technology, they can only profit from the rapid spread of the information revolution to every economic sector. And as leaders in a relatively clean industry that depends on educated workers rather than on un-skilled labor or the wasteful use of natural resources, they and their enterprises are not threatened by reforms that would provide a cleaner environment and a smarter workforce.

The new high-tech elites have everything to gain from helping to improve the quality of education throughout the country. Several have already begun to throw their newfound political muscle behind the cause of school reform. To these pragmatic engineers, reforms such as equalizing school funding and broadening school choices may seem like obvious solutions to the problems bedeviling our schools. Likewise, because many of the relatively clean industries of the future are now forced to subsidize many of the polluting activi-ties of the extractive industries of the past (either directly or indi-rectly), it is feasible that the former might join a new coalition against the latter on issues such as global warming and energy effi-ciency. In a similar fashion, those at the forefront of wireless com-munications may be more likely to push for periodic auctioning of the electromagnetic spectrum, much of which has been given away for free to broadcasters in the past. Hence the industries of the fu-ture may turn out to be the most ardent supporters of the proposals we have put forth for reclaiming our nation's public assets.

More broadly still, businesses of all types and sizes will recognize the value of a new social contract that provides greater flexibility to industry and greater security to individuals, by linking all benefits di-rectly to individuals rather than to employers. If the distinction be-tween full-time and contingent workers ceases to be meaningful, not only will employers and employees be better off but also the public is likely to be more tolerant of the disruption of careers and commu-nities that accompanies creative destruction in the marketplace. En-lightened business leaders should also be strong supporters of replacing our antiquated patchwork of state sales tax regimes with a progressive national consumption tax whose revenue is rebated to states. Doing so would not only level the playing field between e-commerce and the brick-and-mortar retailers, but it would also lessen the administrative burden on companies and create a powerful new incentive for personal savings, which would result in greater capital formation. If businesses lead on these types of issues, politicians will have to follow.

The most obvious overlap between a Radical Centrist agenda and that of the business community is the repeal of the corporate income tax. This is not only an inefficient tax but one that leads to perverse consequences in an increasingly globalized economy. Unlike many pro-business conservatives and antibusiness liberals, we do not confuse business with the wealthy, or treat "corporate" as a synonym for "rich." Under the reforms we have proposed, rich individuals would pay more in taxes than they currently do, to make up for the windfall they would receive from the elimination of the corporate income tax. In our opinion, freeing industry to go about its business in as unencumbered a manner as possible is fully compatible with requiring affluent individuals—as individuals—to pay their fair share of the costs of the public sector. Certainly, the businesses of the future will act mostly out of self-interest, just like their predecessors did. But their enlightened self-interest as economic institutions is likely to overlap with much, though clearly not all, of the reform agenda advocated in these pages.

The final element of a potential new coalition of the Radical Center is the large number of Americans who were young adults at the turn of the century, and who will be leading our nation by the middle of the century. Commonly referred to as members of Generation X (born between 1964 and 1978) and Generation Y (born between 1979 and 1999), this 130-million-strong group of current and future voters has already distinguished itself in the political arena for being even more disengaged and dealigned than their baby boomer parents. Not only do today's young adults vote at lower levels than pre-ceding generations did at similar ages, but an ever higher percentage identify themselves as political independents.

As if this were not sufficient evidence of the contempt that the next generation of Americans holds for the political status quo, they also register the highest level of support of any generation for chang-ing the rules that lock in our current two-party system. When one considers that these will be the voters and leaders of tomorrow, it seems clear that, at a minimum, they will destabilize the current po-litical order, and at a maximum, they may become the leading cham-pions of a new political program, if not one or more new parties.

The most likely explanation for why today's young adults are so politically disengaged and unaligned is that they are behaving in a perfectly rational manner: They realize that the current system does not accurately reflect their concerns or priorities, regardless of which of the usual suspects they vote for. Survey data reveals that the top concerns of today's young adults include economic insecurity, envi-ronmental conservation, lack of access to health care, education reform, fiscal discipline, and campaign finance reform. From a dis-tance, they intuitively know that today's politicians are doing remark-ably little to address most of these concerns. Having come of age in the era of a "free-agent nation," members of Gen X and Gen Y are the least likely of any generation to have health insurance. The idea of severing the traditional link between employment and health in-surance, in favor of citizen-based universal coverage, should appeal to them greatly. But there are no politicians talking about this type of bold yet commonsensical solution.

This new generation of Americans—the first to have matured in the era of personal computers, and later, the World Wide Web—are also far more comfortable with, and supportive of, individualized choices in all spheres of their lives. To them, voting choices, educa-tional choices, retirement choices, lifestyle choices, and career choices are all best when maximized. Greater choices may have been frightening to some older generations, but to most in this new generation they are empowering. Twenty-something author Andrei Cherny describes his brethren as the "choice generation."

There is little question that today's young adults hold the key to the future of American politics; the question is whether and when they will choose to exercise the generational political muscle. Anecdotal evidence, including the popularity of senator John McCain among young people and the election of third-party governor Jesse Ventura in Minnesota, which was mostly due to an unexpectedly high turnout of first-time young voters, suggests that when the right type of political leaders come along, today's young adults will come out and do their part.

English poet and social thinker Samuel Coleridge observed that the only infallible form of prophecy is to learn the attitudes of those between the ages of twenty and thirty. Using that test, we can confidently predict a politics of the future that is strikingly different and more open to new ideas than the politics of today.

What is impossible, however, is to predict when and exactly how an emerging coalition of the Radical Center—composed, perhaps, of many of today's alienated voters, young adults, and enlightened business leaders—will transform American politics. Essentially, there are two ways in which a new Radical Center could succeed: by forming its own political party, or by taking over one of the two dominant ones. A necessary precondition for the former path is reform of our existing electoral system so as to weaken our two-party duopoly and permit the gradual ascension of a serious third party. Such reforms are most likely to start at a state level, where electoral laws can most easily be changed.

As long as the existing voting system is maintained, change will have to come within the two-party system, as it has since the Republican-Democratic duopoly began in the 1850s. Fortunately, the two major parties are mere shells for a number of constituents whose identities and agendas have repeatedly changed. For example, between the 1960s and 1990s, the Goldwater-Reagan conservatives captured the Republican Party from the old midwestern Right and northeastern liberal Republicans, bringing in a majority of former white southern Democrats in the process. At the same time, the white new Left of the 1960s, allied with black civil rights activists, became the base of the Democratic Party, which today includes many former liberal Republicans. Whereas the South formed the base of the Democratic Party before the 1960s, it has become the base of the GOP. Broad-based social movements have been most successful when they seized an existing party; third parties, by contrast, have the greatest influence when they are organized around a single issue (the abolition of slavery in the 1850s and 1860s, the reduction of the federal deficit in the 1990s) and disappear when their goal has been achieved. This suggests that a Radical Centrist coalition might be more successful if it seeks to take over either the Democratic or the Republican Party, rather than attempt to found a formal third party. Indeed, since neither party has succeeded in building a majority over the past decade, each is ripe for transformation.

Whether we take advantage of today's peace and affluence to renovate our national home, or do so hurriedly in a slapdash and ill-considered manner in the midst of some prolonged emergency, remains to be seen. One thing, however, is clear. Comprehensive and thoughtful change in the way we Americans organize our economy, our government, and our community is long overdue. Sooner or later—in peace and prosperity or, perhaps more likely, during some prolonged crisis—there will be a fourth founding that establishes a fourth republic of the United States.

What is required of the next generation of American leaders is not impossible, merely difficult. In the scale of difficulty, modernizing our market, state, and community sectors for the Information

Age is a challenge comparable to those faced by the generations of American leaders who presided over the metamorphosis of agrarian America into the second American republic, and of this steam-age America into a third republic suited to the era of electricity, cars, and suburbs. They did it without examples to guide them; we can do it using their examples to guide us.

Among the traditions American leaders of the past have bequeathed to us is a tradition of renewal. To be true to their example, we must repair and in some cases replace their handiwork. To cling to it out of nostalgia, when they, if they were with us, might be the first to point out the need for innovative thinking, would betray the spirit of our predecessors, while harming those who succeed us. Change is unsettling and sometimes dangerous, but the alternative is stagnation.

National reinvention is not a threat to the American tradition. It *is* the American tradition.

# ACKNOWLEDGMENTS

In writing this book, we have benefited from the advice, criticism, and support of numerous colleagues and friends.

Our greatest intellectual debt is to Sherle Schwenninger, whose insights and expertise helped shape core sections of the manuscript. Maya MacGuineas provided invaluable assistance and inspiration on matters of fiscal policy. Our colleagues Steve Clemons, Michael Calabrese, and Gordon Silverstein also contributed in profound ways to our thinking. We cannot thank these five enough for their constant encouragement and their generous gifts of time and advice.

A number of individuals were kind enough to review early drafts of our manuscript and offer candid critiques as well as insightful comments. These include: James Fallows, Francis Fukuyama, Walter Mead, Diane Ravitch, Robert Kaplan, Jed Shilling, Phillip Longman, Peter Frumkin, Jonathan Koppell, James Snider, James Pinkerton, Eric Cohen, Tom Kalil, Jacob Hacker, David Friedman, Jill Gravender, Peter Derby, and Yasmina Zaidman. Our book benefited greatly from their help, for which we remain profoundly grateful.

We also owe thanks to a number of New America Foundation research associates and interns. First among these is Nikolai Slywka, to whom we are indebted for the diligent assistance, editorial skill, and critical insight he provided. Andrew Harig, Steven Wu, and Irene Hahn were also very helpful.

The entire staff of the New America Foundation, together with our financial supporters, our many brilliant Fellows, and our distinguished Board of Directors, provided the institutional base and intellectual community which made this project possible. We are deeply grateful to all of them.

We are especially indebted to Adam Bellow, our editor at Doubleday, as well as to William Thomas, editor-in-chief at Doubleday, for supporting us enthusiastically at every stage. Finally, we are very grateful to our agent, Kristine Dahl of International Creative Management.

# NOTES

## INTRODUCTION: DIGITAL DISJUNCTURE

1 *independents*: From national polls conducted throughout 2000 by the Gallup Organization. In a poll conducted January 25–26, 37 percent of respondents self-identified as independent, versus 32 percent Democrat and 30 percent Republican. In polls conducted on June 22–25 and December 13, the share of independents rose to 39 percent and 42 percent, respectively.

3 *"both political parties"*: David C. King, "The Polarization of American Parties and Mistrust of Government," in *Why People Don't Trust Government*, eds. Joseph Nye, Jr., Philip D. Zelikow, and David C. King (Cambridge, Mass.: Harvard University Press, 1997), p. 156.

3 *conservatives, liberals, and moderates*: Poll conducted by the Voter News Service and the *Los Angeles Times*, cited in "Election 2000 from A to Z," *Society* 38, no. 4, May/June 2001, p. 3.

9 *job tenure*: Lawrence Mishel, Jared Bernstein, and John Schmitt, *The State of Working America 2000/2001* (Ithaca: Cornell University Press, 2001), pp. 232, 234.

14 *"Continuity with the past"*: Quoted in Julius J. Marke, "How the Right to Counsel Developed," *New York Law Journal,* March 16, 1999, p. 5.

15 *Radical Center:* The phrase "the radical center" was used to describe disaffected white working-class Democrats by the sociologist Donald I. Wallace in *The Radical Center: Middle Americans and the Politics of Alienation* (Notre Dame: University of Notre Dame Press, 1976). Replying to Joe Klein's *Newsweek* cover story "Stalking the Radical Middle," September 25, 1995, John Judis distinguished between the political views of the working-class "radical middle" or "radical center," and the affluent "sensible center" in "Off Center," *The New Republic,* October 16, 1995, p. 4. Judis's analytical distinction is followed in Michael Lind, "The Radical Center or the Moderate Middle?" *New York Times Magazine,* December 3, 1995. In this book, we are not using the term *Radical Center* in this narrow sense, which changes in partisanship and demography already may have rendered obsolete. Rather, we use the term to describe a public philosophy distinct from liberalism and conservatism in the forms in which they have been familiar for the past generation.

## CHAPTER 1: THE FIRST THREE AMERICAS

34 *tripartite arrangement:* The market revolution occurred in the thirteenth century, and the state revolution occurred in the seventeenth century, but the separation of both from a relatively autonomous community sector characterized by religious freedom was the last element of the synthesis to appear. See Charles Tilly, *Coercion, Capital, and European States, A.D. 990–1990* (Oxford: Basil Blackwell, 1990); William H. McNeill, *The Pursuit of Power: Technology, Armed Force, and Society Since A.D. 1000* (Chicago: University of Chicago Press, 1982); Niall Ferguson, *The Cash Nexus: Money and Power in the Modern World, 1700–2000* (New York: Basic Books, 2001); Luciano Pellicani, *The Genesis of Capitalism and the Origins of Modernity,* trans. James G. Colbert (New York: Telos Press, 1994).

34 *"great transformation":* Karl Polanyi, *The Great Transformation: The Political and Economic Origins of Our Time* (New York: Beacon Press, 1980). See also Daniel Bell, *The Coming of Post-Industrial Society: A Venture in Social Forecasting* (New York: Basic Books, 1999 [1973]); David S. Landes, *The Unbound Prometheus: Technological Change and Industrial Development in*

*Western Europe from 1750 to the Present* (Cambridge, Mass.: Cambridge University Press, 1969).

36 *three previous American republics:* In *The Next American Nation* (New York: The Free Press, 1995), one of the authors, Michael Lind, used the metaphor of three republics to discuss the history of legal regimes governing race and civil rights in the United States, and identified the beginning of the third republic, "Multicultural America," with the Civil Rights Revolution. The legal scholar Bruce Ackerman, using a similar schema to describe eras of constitutional interpretation rather than racial regimes, suggested that a third republic was founded in the New Deal era in his trilogy *We the People* (Cambridge, Mass.: Belknap Press of Harvard University Press, 1991– ). For the purposes of the present study of transformations of American society in its entirety, it makes sense to identify the last major change with the New Deal era, as Ackerman does in his narrower study of constitutional law and theory. (These and other descriptions of American history in terms of successive "republics" are inspired, of course, by the example of France.)

37 *urban population in 1790:* Stuart Bruchey, *Growth of the Modern American Economy* (New York: Dodd, Mead & Company, 1975), pp. 2–3.

37 *Americans on farms in 1831:* John Judis, *The Paradox of American Democracy: Elites, Special Interests and the Betrayal of Public Trust* (New York: Pantheon Books, 2000), p. 248.

38 *inland waterways:* Bruchey, *Growth of the Modern American Economy,* p. 18.

38 *steamboats:* Ibid., p. 17.

38 *rise of cotton:* Peter J. Hugill, *World Trade Since 1431: Geography, Technology, and Capitalism* (Baltimore: Johns Hopkins University Press, 1995), p. 81.

38 *capital from Britain:* Ibid., p. 86.

40 *Whitney and Evans:* Bruchey, *Growth of the Modern American Economy,* p. 65.

40 *growth of textile industry:* Ibid., p. 35.

40 *steam power:* Ibid., p. 66.

40 *Pennsylvania coal:* Ibid.

40 *railroad construction:* Ibid., p. 52.

40 *Deere and McCormick:* Ibid., p. 54.

41 *horse-drawn machines:* Ibid.

41 *rise of manufacturing and construction:* Ibid., p. 44.

41 *Northeast manufacturing capability:* Ibid., p. 46.

41 *immigration from Western Europe:* Ibid., p. 39.

42 *"As I would not be a slave,"* Roy P. Bassler, editor, *The Collected Works of Abraham Lincoln, Volume II, 1848–1858* (New Brunswick: Rutgers University Press, 1953), p. 532.

42 *federal armed forces:* Bruce D. Porter, *War and the Rise of the State: The Military Foundations of Modern Politics* (New York: The Free Press, 1994), p. 264.

43 *federal civilian employees:* Ibid.

43 *Internal Revenue Act of 1862:* Ibid., p. 260.

43 *government spending:* Ibid., p. 266.

43 *state and municipal budgets:* Ibid., p. 265.

44 *corporate law reform:* Bruchey, *Growth of the Modern American Economy*, pp. 97–99. See generally Alfred Chandler, *The Visible Hand: The Managerial Revolution in American Business* (Cambridge, Mass.: The Belknap Press, 1977); idem, *Scale and Scope: The Dynamics of Industrial Capitalism* (Cambridge, Mass.: The Belknap Press, 1990).

44 *commercial banks:* Bruchey, *Growth of the Modern American Economy*, p. 89.

44 *new technologies:* Ibid., p. 101.

44 *"This American people":* Quoted in Daniel T. Rodgers, *Contested Truths: Keywords in American Politics Since Independence* (New York: Basic Books, 1987), p. 137.

45 *Madison:* Quoted in Drew R. McCoy, *The Elusive Republic: Political Economy in Jeffersonian America* (New York: W.W. Norton, 1980), pp. 255–256.

45 *"as Madison understood it"*: Ibid., p. 259.

46 *electrical transformers*: Vaclav Smil, *Energies* (Cambridge, Mass.: The MIT Press, 1999), p. 155.

46 *internal combustion engine*: Ibid., p. 160. The economist Joseph Schumpeter wrote: "We are just now in the downgrade of a wave of enterprise that created the electrical power plant, the electrical industry, the electrical farm and home and the motorcar." Joseph A. Schumpeter, *Capitalism, Socialism and Democracy* (New York: Harper Books, 1975), p. 70.

47 *Population due to immigration*: Bruchey, *Growth of the Modern American Economy*, p. 85.

47 *1930 Census*: Virginia D. Abernethy, *Population Politics: The Choices that Shape Our Future* (New York: Plenum Press, 1993), p. 198.

47 *Shift from farm labor*: U.S. Bureau of the Census, *Historical Statistics of the United States* (Washington, D.C.: U.S. Government Printing Office, 1975), pp. 139, 465.

49 *Progressive response to populists and industrialists*: John F. Walker and Harold G. Vatter, *The Rise of Big Government in the United States* (Armonk, N.Y.: M.E. Sharpe, 1997), p. 19.

49 *Progressive reform*: Ibid., p. 20.

51 *"People want"*: Franklin D. Roosevelt, "Message to Congress Reviewing the Broad Objectives and Accomplishments of the Administration," June 8, 1934, *The Papers and Addresses of Franklin D. Roosevelt: The Advance of Recovery and Reform, 1934, Volume 3*, compiled and collated by Samuel I. Rosenman (New York: Random House, 1938), p. 288.

51 *"I am fighting Communism"*: Quoted in Arthur M. Schlesinger Jr., *The Age of Roosevelt*, vol. 3, *The Politics of Upheaval* (Boston: Houghton Mifflin, 1960), p. 325.

52 *growth of federal government*: Walker and Vatter, *The Rise of Big Government*, p. 236.

54 *household electronics*: Herbert Stein and Murray Foss, *The Illustrated Guide to the American Economy*, 3rd edition (Washington, D.C.: The AEI Press, 1999), p. 258; and Forrester Research, Inc., www.forrester.com.

55 *"The age of steam"*: Vladimir Ilyich Lenin, *On the Development of Heavy Industry and Electrification* (Moscow: Progress, 1972 [1920]), p. 52. See Gerhard Mensch, *Stalemate in Technology: Innovations Overcome the Depression* (Cambridge, Mass.: Ballinger, 1979).

## CHAPTER 2: NEW ECONOMY, NEW SOCIAL CONTRACT

59 *Denis Papin*: Peter J. Hugill, *World Trade Since 1431: Geography, Technology, and Capitalism* (Baltimore: Johns Hopkins University Press, 1993), p. 125.

60 *"creative destruction"*: Joseph A. Schumpeter, *Capitalism, Socialism and Democracy* (New York: Harper Books, 1975 [1942]), p. 83.

62 *productivity after 1973*: Robert D. Atkinson and Randolph H. Court, *The New Economy Index: Understanding America's Economic Transformation* (Washington, D.C.: Progressive Policy Institute, 1998), p. 21.

67 *median job tenure*: Bureau of Labor Statistics, *Employee Tenure in 2000*, "Median Years of Tenure"; and Bureau of Labor Statistics, *Monthly Labor Review*, October 1963.

67 *contingent workers*: Cynthia M. Fagnoni and Kay E. Brown, "Contingent Workers: Income and Benefits Lag Behind Those of Other Workers," a report by the U.S. General Accounting Office, June 2000, p. 15.

67 *job dislocation*: See Walter Russell Mead, "The New Economy Takes Your Order," *Mother Jones*, March/April 1998.

68 *Tom Peters*: See his "What Will We Do for Work," *Time*, May 22, 2000, p. 66.

69 *number of uninsured*: Council of Economic Advisers, "Living in the New Economy," *Economic Report of the President* (Washington, D.C.: Government Printing Office, January 2001), Chapter 5, www.access.gpo.gov.

69 *United States spends twice as much on health care than OECD average*: Michael J. Graetz and Jerry L. Mashaw, *True Security: Rethinking American Social Insurance* (New Haven: Yale University Press, 1999), p. 129, fig. 7.3.

69 *health care coverage and economic inequality in 1997*: Ibid.

69 *decline in employer-provided health insurance*: James L. Medoff and Michael Calabrese, "The Impact of Labor Market Trends on Health and

Pension Benefit Coverage and Inequality," a report for the U.S. Department of Labor, February 28, 2001, A1.

70 *private pension coverage:* Ibid., A2.

75 *libertarian economist Milton Friedman:* Milton Friedman, "How to Cure Health Care," *The Public Interest,* Winter 2001, no. 142, p. 21.

77 *proportion of individuals whose employers paid the full cost of health coverage:* Medoff and Calabrese, "The Impact of Labor Market Trends . . . ," A3.

79 *FDR envisioned a fully-funded system:* see Daniel Patrick Moynihan, "Building Wealth for Everyone," *New York Times,* May 30, 2000, A27; and Sylvester J. Scheiber and Paul B. Shoven, *The Real Deal: The History and Future of Social Security* (New Haven: Yale University Press, 1999), pp. 36–37. Scheiber and Shoven include a quote from FDR, supplied by Frances Perkins, on the subject of a Social Security program that would eventually require government subsidies: "This is the same old dole under another name. It is almost dishonest to build up an accumulated deficit for the Congress of the United States to meet in 1980. We can't do that. We can't sell the United States short in 1980 any more than in 1935," p. 37.

79–80 *Singapore's safety net system:* See the website for Singapore's Central Provident Fund, http://www.cpf.gov.sg/cpf_info/home.asp; and Bruce F. Spencer, "Singapore Government Partially Restores Reduction in CPF Rates," *Employee Benefit Review* 54, no. 8 (February 2000), p. 42.

80 *"it is actuarially unsound:"* Quoted in Scheiber and Shoven, *The Real Deal,* p. 110.

81 *elderly will outnumber college-age Americans four to one in 2040:* Cited in Peter G. Peterson, *Gray Dawn: How the Coming Age Wave Will Transform America—and the World* (New York: Random House, 1999), p. 31.

81 *The great debate over Social Security:* Social Security reform is discussed from a variety of perspectives in World Bank, *Averting the Old Age Crisis: Policies to Protect the Old and Promote Growth* (New York, N.Y.: Oxford University Press, 1994); Scheiber and Shoven, *The Real Deal*; Henry Aaron and John B. Shoven, *Should the United States Privatize Social Security?* (Cambridge, Mass.: MIT Press, 1999); Dean Baker and Mark Weisbrot, *Social Security: The Phony Crisis* (Chicago: University of Chicago Press, 1999); Peter

J. Ferrara and Michael Tanner, *A New Deal for Social Security* (Washington, D.C.: Cato Institute Press, 1998).

82 *two-tier systems in Australia, Chile, and Britain:* Scheiber and Shoven, *The Real Deal,* p. 284.

82 *World Bank recommendation: Averting the Old Age Crisis,* p. 302.

82 *social democratic Sweden:* Scheiber and Shoven, *The Real Deal,* pp. 312–13.

83 *return on long-term government bonds:* Scheiber and Shoven, *The Real Deal,* p. 238.

83 *growth in payroll taxes:* Graetz and Mashaw, *True Security,* p. 104.

83 *increase in percentage of Americans eighty-five years or older:* Ibid., p. 105.

83–84 *Social Security insolvency:* John L. Palmer and Thomas R. Saving, "Status of the Social Security and Medicare Programs: A Summary of the 2001 Annual Reports" (Washington, D.C.: Social Security and Medicare Board of Trustees, March 2001), p. 7.

85 *implications of low savings:* Albert B. Crenshaw, "Sounding Alarms on Saving," *Washington Post,* June 6, 1999, H2.

85 *few or no pensions:* Medoff and Calabrese, "The Impact of Labor Market Trends," B1.

85 *rise in consumption; drop in savings:* Council of Economic Advisors, "Table B-30.—Disposition of personal income, 1959–2000," *Economic Report of the President* (Washington, D.C.: Government Printing Office, January 2001), H.Doc 107–2. See also: Richard Peach and Charles Steindel, "A Nation of Spendthrifts? An Analysis of Trends in Personal and Gross Saving," *Current Issues in Economics and Finance,* 6, no. 10, September 2000; Nicholas Kulish, "U.S. Savings Rate Hits an All-Time Low," *Wall Street Journal,* August 29, 2000, A2; Stephen S. Roach, "The Recession We Need," *New York Times,* January 4, 2001, A23.

86 *households with zero or negative net worth:* Edward N. Wolff, "Recent Trends in Wealth Ownership, 1983–1998," Working Paper No. 300, Jerome Levy Economics Institute, April 2000, www.levy.org.

86 *net financial assets of Americans:* Catherine P. Montalto, "Wealth of American Households: Evidence from the Survey of Consumer Households," a report for the Consumer Federation of America, February 13, 2001.

86 *credit card debt:* Ibid.; see also Kathy M. Kristof, "Study Says Parents to Blame for Kids' Misspent Youth," *Los Angeles Times,* April 13, 2001, A1.

88 *Robert Shiller and "macro markets":* Robert J. Shiller, "Wealthy Market? Yes. Healthy? Wise? No." *New York Times,* April 30, 2000, C4.

89 *Social Security dependence and income level:* Graetz and Mashaw, *True Security,* p. 102.

90 *beneficiaries of means-tested safety net programs:* The Administration for Children and Families, U.S. Department for Health and Human Services, "Total Number of Recipients of Temporary Assistance to Needy Families," *U.S. Welfare Caseloads Information,* www.acf.dhhs.gov/news/stats/welfare.htm.

91 *Maya MacGuineas:* see her articles "The Best of Both Bush and Gore," *Los Angeles Times,* October 22, 2000; "Social Security: The Liberal Case for Partial Privatization," *Washington Monthly,* April 2001.

93 *transition costs:* Based on calculations by fiscal policy analyst Maya MacGuineas, using data from *Report of the 1994–1996 Advisory Council on Social Security, Volume 1: Findings and Recommendations* (Washington, D.C.: U.S. Government Printing Office, 1997), and *Bipartisan Commission on Entitlement and Tax Reform,* Transmitted Pursuant to Executive Order No. 12878 (Washington D.C.: January 1995).

94 *working-class wage stagnation:* Lawrence Mishel, Jared Bernstein, and John Schmitt, *The State of Working America, 2000/2001* (Ithaca: Cornell University Press, 2001), pp. 115, 117; Ruy Texeira and Joel Rogers, *America's Forgotten Majority: Why the White Working Class Still Matters* (New York: Basic Books, 2000), pp. 81–82.

95 *middle class shrinking as proportion of population:* Mishel, Bernstein, and Schmitt, *The State of Working America,* p. 84.

95 *levels of wealth and income inequality:* Wolff, "Recent Trends in Wealth Ownership."

96 *richest 10 percent own approximately 90 percent:* Ibid.

96 *"Issues of equity"*: William J. McDounough, "Opening Remarks," *FRBNY Economic Policy Review* 1, no. 1 (January 1995), p. 2.

97 *"Nations are less disposed to make revolutions"*: Alexis de Tocqueville, *Democracy in America,* ed. J. P. Maier, trans. George Lawrence (Garden City, N.Y.: Anchor Books, 1969).

98 *"people are likely to become better stewards"*: Jeff Gates, *The Ownership Solution: Toward a Shared Capitalism for the 21st Century* (Reading, Mass.: Addison-Wesley, 1998), p. xxi.

98 *"contemporary capitalism"*: Ibid., p. xix.

99 *The Stakeholder Society*: Bruce Ackerman and Anne Alstott, *The Stakeholder Society* (New Haven: Yale University Press, 1999). For an early treatment of the stakeholding concept, see the policy report by Michael Sherraden, "Stakeholding: A New Direction in Social Policy" (Washington, D.C.: Progressive Policy Center, January 1, 1999).

99 *KidSave*: First proposed in 1998, KidSave was included in Kerrey's and Moynihan's "Social Security Solvency Act of 1999"; see Moynihan, ibid., and Matthew Miller, "Staking Each U.S. Citizen to a Share of the Wealth," *Seattle Times,* March 3, 1999, B4. In 2000, Kerrey put forth a slightly altered version of the program in legislative proposal S.3200, cosponsored by Senators Moynihan, Rick Santorum, Charles Grassley, and John Breaux. In this latest version, each child on the day of birth is granted an interest-free $2,000 loan that need not be repaid until the child reaches thirty. After 2005, the value of the loan would be indexed to inflation. The account holder would not be able to withdraw funds until age sixty-two, and assuming an 8 percent return the account would be worth about $250,000 when the holder was sixty-seven. KidSave garnered bipartisan support, including the accolades of the conservative Heritage Foundation. See David C. John, "KidSave: An Innovative Step Toward Better Retirement Security," Heritage Foundation Executive Memorandum, No. 74, October 27, 2000.

## CHAPTER 3: DIGITAL ERA DEMOCRACY

109 *7 percent of counties*: Susan Schmidt and Ben White, "State Officials Hear Warning in Court's Rebuke," *Washington Post,* December 14, 2000, A28.

110 *voting rates:* Office of Election Administration, Federal Election Commission, *2000 Voter Registration and Turnout,* Portrait of America table, "Presidential Election Voter Turnout, 1924–2000," www.fairvote.org/turnout/preturn.html; John Hill, "Voter Turnout Continues Falling in Both U.S., State," *Sacramento Bee,* December 22, 2000, A3.

111 *spending in 1994 elections:* Cited in the Center for Voting and Democracy, *Monopoly Politics 1998,* www.fairvote.org.

111 *party identification:* See, for instance, the national polls conducted by the Gallup Organization on December 13, 2000; February 9–11, 2001; and May 18–20, 2001.

111 *percentage of moderates:* The 50 percent figure comes from exit polls conducted by the Voter News Service and the *Los Angeles Times,* cited in "Election 2000 from A to Z," *Society* 38, no. 4 (May/June 2001), p. 3. See also: "One Nation, Fairly Divisible," *The Economist,* January 20, 2001, p. 24.

111 *party affiliation, ages eighteen to twenty-nine:* Ted Halstead, "A Politics for Generation X," *The Atlantic Monthly,* August 1999; Everett Carl Ladd, ed., "Party Identification by Social Group," *America at the Polls, 1998* (The Roper Center, University of Connecticut, 1999), p. 60.

114 *vote-swapping among "Nader Traders":* Helen Kennedy, "Liberals Devise Plan to Help Gore, Nader," *Houston Chronicle,* October 29, 2000, A4.

116 *divergence in voting patterns:* See Keith T. Poole and Howard Rosenthal, *Congress: A Political-Economic History of Roll-Call Voting* (New York: Oxford University Press, 1997), p. 292: "The degree of polarization of Congress is approaching levels not seen since the 1890s." See also idem, "D-NOMINATE after 10 Years: A Comparative Update to Congress: A Political-Economic History of Roll-Call Voting," *Legislative Studies Quarterly* 26, no. 1, February 2001, pp. 5–29; Jon R. Bond and Richard Fleischer, eds., *Polarized Politics: Congress and the President in a Partisan Era* (Washington, D.C.: CQ Press, 2000); Joseph S. Nye, Philip D. Zelikow, and David C. King, eds., *Why People Don't Trust Government* (Cambridge, Mass.: Harvard University Press, 1997).

121 *"[Lott] then filled the amendment tree":* Barbara Sinclair, "Partisan Imperatives and Institutional Constraints: Republican Party Leadership in the House and Senate," in *New Majority or Old Minority? The Impact of Republi-*

*cans on Congress,* eds. Nicol C. Rae and Colton C. Cambell (New York: Rowman and Littlefield, 1999), p. 37.

123 *budgeting on a two-year basis:* David Bauman, "Congress does double-take on two-year budgeting," *GovExec.com,* May 28, 1999.

124 *on-line voting in Arizona:* Associated Press, "Internet Voting Not Yet the Mouse That Roared," *Chicago Tribune,* March 13, 2000, A4.

125 *searchable federal websites:* On September 22, 2000, Firstgov.gov was launched, a Web portal that allows users to search all 27 million pages of the government's websites at no cost. The portal is the brain-child of computer science professor and entrepreneur Eric Brewer.

127 *Dole in 1996:* David Maraniss, "Image-Makers Produced Virtual Reality Convention," *Washington Post,* August 17, 1996, A1.

128 *Oliver Wendell Holmes Jr.:* Quoted in Dale Russakoff, "Tax Cheats: A Tradition of Omission; $80 Billion in Loss to Treasury Estimated," *Washington Post,* April 8, 1998, A1.

129 *federal tax revenues:* Herbert Stein and Murray Foss, *The Illustrated Guide to the American Economy,* 3rd edition (Washington, D.C.: The AEI Press, 1999), p. 212.

130 *John F. Due:* Quoted in Hal R. Varian, "Forget Taxing Internet Sales: in Fact Just Forget Sales Taxes Altogether," *New York Times,* March 8, 2001, C2.

130 *sales and excise taxes:* Michael P. Ettlinger et al., "U.S. Averages: Average State and Local Taxes in 1995," *Who Pays? A Distribution of the Tax Systems in All 50 States* (Washington, D.C.: Report published jointly by Citizens for Tax Justice and the Institute on Taxation and Economic Policy, 1996), Appendix I, p. 51.

131 *lost revenue by 2003:* National Governors Association, "Overview of Sales and Use Taxes and Electronic Commerce," analysis posted on-line, February 23, 2001, http://www.nga.org/nga/legislativeupdate.

132 *State and local sales taxes:* "United States State & Local Government Finances by Level of Government: 1996–1997," U.S. Census Bureau, www.census.gov/govs/estimate/97/97stlus.

134 *headquarters in Bermuda:* Bradley L. Kading, "The Future of Reinsurance Regulation," *CPCU Journal* 48, no. 2 (June 1995), p. 12.

135 *tax revenues from corporate income tax:* Table B-84, "Federal Government current receipts and expenditures, national income and product accounts (NIPA), 1959–2000"; Table B-85, "State and local government current receipts and expenditures, national income and product accounts (NIPA), 1959–2000," *Economic Report of the President* (Washington, D.C.: Government Printing Office, 2001).

137 *professional tax preparers:* Daniel J. Mitchell, "8 Billion Pages of Tax Forms," *Indianapolis Star,* January 4, 2000, A9.

137 *incorrect answers from IRS:* Ibid.

137 *2000 Budget:* Daniel J. Mitchell, "Making the Tax Code Even Worse," *Heritage Foundation Views,* February 10, 2000, www.heritage.org/views/2000/ed021000.html.

138 *"hidden welfare state":* Christopher Howard, *The Hidden Welfare State: Tax Expenditures and Social Policy in the United States* (Princeton: Princeton University Press, 1997).

138 *cost of visible welfare state:* Ibid., p. 27.

138 *cost of hidden welfare state:* Ibid., p. 25.

139 *home mortgage interest rate benefits:* Ibid., p. 28.

139 *$700 billion to $800 billion:* See, for instance, Office of Management and Budget, *Analytical Perspectives: Budget of the United States Government, Fiscal Year 2002* (Washington, D.C.: Government Printing Office, 2001), and Joint Committee on Taxation, *Estimates of Federal Tax Expenditures for Fiscal Years 2001–2005* (Washington, D.C.: Government Printing Office, April 6, 2001).

143 *public assets:* For a cogent study of public assets, see David Bollier, *Public Assets, Private Profits: Reclaiming American Commons in an Age of Market Enclosure,* report published by the New America Foundation, March 2001, www.newamerica.net.

143 *Alaska Permanent Fund:* Alaska Permanent Fund website, "19 Years of Dividends," http://www.apfc.org.

143 *"the greatest gold heist":* Quoted in Associated Press, "Babbitt Blames Old Mining Law in Ceding a Potential Windfall," *New York Times,* September 7, 1995, A20.

143 *1872 Mining Rights Law*: For a thorough discussion of the Mining Act of 1872, see Carl J. Mayer and George A. Riley, *Public Domain, Private Dominion: A History of Public Mineral Policy in America* (San Francisco: Sierra Club Books, 1985), Chapter 3. See also Dale Bumpers, "Capitol Hill's Longest-Running Outrage," *Washington Monthly*, January 1998, p.14. Further information can be found at the website of the Mineral Policy Center, an environmental organization: www.mineralpolicy.org.

144 *Network Solutions and VeriSign*: Lawrence M. Fischer, "Internet Registrar to Be Sold for \$21 Billion," *New York Times*, March 8, 2000, C2; Joanne Legomsky, "Finding Potential in Computer Security Stocks," *New York Times*, November 5, 2000, C9.

144 *spectrum auctions in Britain*: "The Price Is Right," *The Economist*, p. 21; see also in the same issue, "Battle of the Airwaves," pp. 57–58.

145 *1996 spectrum giveaway*: Editorial, "A Fix for the Broadcast Giveaway," *New York Times*, October 11, 2000, A34; Edmund L. Andrews, "The Political Battle Grows Over the Use of New Broadcast Technology," *New York Times*, March 18, 1996, D1.

145 *auctions to prevent artificial bandwidth scarcity*: Stephen Labaton, "FCC to Promote a Trading System to Sell Airwaves," *New York Times*, March 13, 2000, A1.

145 *DRI/MacGraw Hill*: Cited in M. Jeff Hamond, *Tax Waste, Not Work* (San Francisco: Redefining Progress, April 1997); see also idem, "Tax What We Take—But Not What We Make," *Sacramento Bee*, December 21, 1997, F1; Ted Halstead, "Lower Tax for Lower Emissions," *Journal of Commerce*, December 4, 1997, 6A; and Paul Overberg, "Carbon Tax Proposals Getting New Attention," *Gannett News Service*, May 21, 1992.

146 *"Allocating permits to firms"*: "Making Markets Work for the Environment," Chapter 7, *Economic Report of the President* (Washington, D.C.: Government Printing Office, 2000), box 7–4.

147 *"mass-production education system"*: Marc Tucker, "Developing a World-Class Education System," in *Restoring Broadly Shared Prosperity*, ed. Ray Marshall (Washington, D.C.: Economic Policy Institute, 1997), p. 115.

148 *foreign-born engineers and Ph.D.s:* Robert D. Atkinson and Randolph H. Court, *The New Economy Index: Understanding America's Economic Transformation* (Washington, D.C.: Progressive Policy Institute, 1998), p. 41.

149 *African-American support of school choice:* John H. McWhorter, "Why Don't Black Americans Give Bush a Chance?," *Washington Post,* December 31, 2000, B02; Edward J. Boyer, "Blacks Split over Vouchers," *Los Angeles Times,* September 3, 2000, A1; Floyd H. Flake, "Gore's Achilles' Heel," *New York Times,* March 12, 2000, sec. 4, p. 15.

149 *"policies that reduce choice":* Caroline Hoxby quoted in "The Difference That Choice Makes," *The Economist,* January 27, 2001, www.economist.com.

151 *government funding of education in Europe and the United States: Education at a Glance: OECD Indicators 1998,* cited in John A. Donohue, "The Case for Serious Federal Financing of America's Public Schools," in *Passing the Test: The National Interest in Good Schools for All,* ed. Michael Calabrese (Washington, D.C.: Center for National Policy, 2000), p. 65.

151 *per pupil spending disparities across states:* Ted Halstead and Michael Lind, "The National Debate Over School Funding Needs a Federal Focus," *Los Angeles Times,* October 8, 2000, M2; Anna Bernasek, "To Fix School, Discriminate on Spending," *Fortune,* September 4, 2000, p. 84; see also David Grissmer and Ann Flanagan, *The Role of Federal Resources in Closing the Achievement Gaps of Minority and Disadvantaged Students,* RAND report prepared for the Brookings Institute Conference on the Black-White Score Gap, February 1–2.

151 *Disparities within Virginia:* Table 91, "Revenues and Expenditures of Public School Districts Enrolling More Than 15,000 Students, by State: 1996–97," *Digest of Education Statistics* (Washington, D.C.: National Center for Education Statistics, 2000).

152 *Supreme Court rulings:* David Goodman, "America's Newest Class War," *Mother Jones,* September/October 1999.

153 *rise in proportion of state funding of education:* "Total Expenditures for Education in the U.S., Table 1," *FY 2001 Budget Summary Appendices,* Department of Education, Budget, http://www.ed.gov/offices/OUS/Budget01/BudgetSumm/.

153 *"The distribution of a resource":* Quoted in Goodman, "America's Newest Class War."

153 *"Most of the resource inequality"*: Grissmer and Flanagan, *The Role of Federal Resources*.

158 *"the intercourse throughout"*: Alexander Hamilton, James Madison, and John Jay, in *The Federalist Papers*, ed. Clinton Lawrence Rossiter (New York: Penguin Books, 1999).

159 *"the people should in the future become"*: Ibid.

159 *"the people ought not surely to be precluded"*: Ibid.

159 *"whether either, or which of them, will be able"*: Ibid.

159 *"I am of the opinion that"*: Ibid.

159 *"A small land tax will answer the purposes"*: Ibid.

160 *"business interests now look to preemptive acts of Congress"*: Pietro S. Nivola, "Does Federalism Have a Future?" *The Public Interest*, Winter 2001, p. 45.

160 *"[L]et the nation take hold of the larger works"*: Abraham Lincoln, *The Collected Works of Abraham Lincoln, Volume I, 1848–1858*, Roy P. Bassler, ed. (New Brunswick: Rutgers University Press, 1953), p. 480.

CHAPTER 4: UNITY AND COMMUNITY
IN THE TWENTY-FIRST CENTURY

163 *"Americans of all ages"*: Alexis de Tocqueville, *Democracy in America*, ed. J. P. Maier, trans. George Lawrence (Garden City, N.Y.: Anchor Books, 1969), pp. 513–517.

163 *on community and civil society*: Roger D. Putnam, *Bowling Alone: The Collapse and Revival of American Community* (New York: Simon and Schuster, 2000).

168 *"the stock of social capital"*: Francis Fukuyama, *The Great Disruption: Human Nature and the Reconstruction of Social Order* (New York: The Free Press, 1999), p. 282.

171 *"It is a simple matter of justice that America"*: Martin Luther King Jr., *Why We Can't Wait* (New York: Harper and Row, 1963), p. 142.

171 *extension of group preferences*: See generally Michael Lind, *The Next American Nation* (New York: The Free Press, 1995).

172 *"God's crucible"*: Israel Zangwill, *The Melting Pot* (New York: Arno Press, 1975), p. 33.

173 *"Such terms as Irish-American"*: Quoted in Horace M. Kallen, *Culture and Democracy in the United States* (New York: Boni and Livewright, 1924), pp. 131–132.

173 *transracial marriages*: See Steven A. Holmes, "The Politics of Race and the Census," *New York Times*, March 19, 2000, D3; Amitai Etzioni, "The Monochrome Society," *The Public Interest*, no. 137 (Fall 1999), p. 53; and Michael Lind, "The Beige and the Black," *New York Times Magazine*, August 16, 1998, p. 38.

174 *ancestry of Italians*: See Luigi Luca Cavalli-Sforza, *The Great Human Diasporas: The History of Diversity and Evolution* (New York: Perseus, 1996).

174 *2000 Census and the one-drop rule*: See Holmes, "The Politics of Race and the Census."

175 *Douglass to Delany*: Quoted in Robert S. Levine, *Martin Delany, Frederick Douglass, and the Politics of Representative Identity* (Chapel Hill: University of North Carolina Press, 1997), p. 232.

175 *"Those least disadvantaged"*: Richard Rodriguez, *Hunger of Memory: The Education of Richard Rodriguez* (New York: Bantam Books, 1982), p. 151.

176 *population doubling by 2100*: "Annual Projections of the Total Resident Population as of July 1: Middle, Lowest, Highest, and Zero International Migration Series, 1999 to 2100," U.S. Census Bureau, Population Division, Population Projections Branch, November 2, 2000.

177 *National Academy of Sciences on immigration*: cited in "Breaking-Up the INS," *San Diego Union-Tribune*, August 13, 1997, editorial.

177 *Impact of immigration*: Figure in Robert J. Samuelson, "America as Mexico's Economic Safety Valve," *Washington Post*, Thursday, July 20, 2000, p. A25.

178 *"How will we be better off with 571 million people?"*: Alan K. Simpson and Richard K. Lamm, "571 Million Americans," *Washington Post*, June 20, 2000, A23.

179 *visas for family members*: "Immigrants Admitted by Type and Selected Class of Admission, Fiscal Year 1998," Table 4, *1998 Statistical Yearbook of the INS* (Washington D.C.: Government Printing Office, 2001), p. 28.

179 *education levels of immigrants:* Lawrence Mishel, Jared Bernstein, and John Schmitt, *The State of Working America* (Ithaca: Cornell University Press, 1999), p. 183.

180 *declining number of bachelor's degrees in the sciences:* "The (Somewhat) Scientific American," *Scientific American,* December 2000, p. 36.

180 *"guest-worker program":* See Mary Beth Sheridan, "Mexico Proposes Immigration Pact to Cut Down Third-Country Passage," *Washington Post,* April 5, 2001, A3.

181 *"If wages are falling":* Lester Thurow, "Wages and the Service Sector," in *Restoring Broadly Shared Prosperity,* ed. Ray Marshall (Washington, D.C.: Economic Policy Institute, 1997), pp. 65–69. The availability of cheap labor retarded the industrialization of India, according to the economic historian David S. Landes, who quotes a British traveler's report of 1807: "In India it is seldom that an attempt is made to accomplish anything by machinery that can be performed by human labor"; in *The Wealth and Poverty of Nations* (New York: W. W. Norton, 1998), pp. 226–227. By contrast, in the United States, Canada, Australia, and New Zealand during their period of economic development, "through the efforts of entrepreneurs to counteract high wage costs and overcome labour scarcity [high wages] generated technological progress, which in turn supported and enhanced the high productivity which came in time to provide the basis upon which these high wages were paid." A. G. Kenwood and A. L. Lougheed, *The Growth of the International Economy, 1820–1980* (London: George Allen and Unwin, 1983), pp. 146–147.

183 *changing age distribution of United States:* Editorial, "Employment's New Age," *New York Times,* July 30, 2000.

184 *Social Security prognosis:* John L. Palmer and Thomas R. Saving, *Status of the Social Security and Medicare Programs: A Summary of 2001 Annual Report* (Washington, D.C.: Social Security and Medicare Board of Trustees, March 2001), p. 5.

184–85 *increase in nursing homes:* "The Changing American Family," *Economic Report of the President* (Washington, D.C.: Government Printing Office, 2000), p. 184.

185 *elder care rates:* Ibid., p. 174.

186 *elderly volunteers:* See Theodore Roszak, "The Aging of Aquarius: Retiring Boomers and the Politics of Compassion," *The Nation*, December 28, 1998, pp. 11–14.

187 (*Journal of Gerontology*) *report:* Cited in Lee Bowman and Scripps Howard, "Volunteering Enhances Longevity, Study Says," *The Plain Dealer*, March 4, 1999, A9.

188 *New Urbanism:* See Andres Duany, Elizabeth Plater-Zyberk, and Jeff Speck, *Suburban Nation*, (New York: North Point Press, 2000); and Peter Katz, *The New Urbanism: Toward an Architecture of Community* (New York: McGraw-Hill, 1993).

189 *charitable donations:* "1999 Contributions: $190.16 Billion by Source of Contribution," Giving USA/AAFRC Trust for Philanthropy, www.aafrc.org/CHAR.HTM.

190 *rates of volunteering:* Karl T. Greenfeld, "A New Way of Giving," *Time*, July 24, 2000, p. 48.

190 *wealth transfer through charitable giving:* John J. Havens and Paul G. Schervish, "Millionaires and the Millennium: New Estimates of the Forthcoming Wealth Transfer and the Prospects for a Golden Age of Philanthropy," report published by the Social Welfare Research Institute of Boston College, October 19, 1999.

192 *Philanthropic giving:* "1999 Contributions: $190.16 Billion by Type of Recipient Organization," Giving USA 2000/AAFRC Trust for Philanthropy, www.aafrc.org.

194 *Report by the American Association for the Advancement of Science:* Mark S. Frankel and Audrey R. Chapman, "Human Inheritable Genetic Modifications: Assessing Scientific, Ethical, Religious, and Policy Issues," American Association for the Advancement of Science, September 2000, www.aaas.org/spp/dspp/sfrl/germline/main.htm.

197 *sterilization:* See Stephen Jay Gould, *The Mismeasure of Man* (New York: W. W. Norton and Co., 1996).

198 *Ritalin use:* For a penetrating essay on the controversy surrounding Ritalin use and diagnoses of attention deficit hyperactivity disorder (ADHD),

see Arthur Allen, "The Trouble with ADHD," *Washington Post Magazine*, March 18, 2001, W8.

205–6 *Stephen Decatur:* Cyrus Townsend Brady, *Stephen Decatur* (Boston: Small, Maynard and Co., 1900).

206 *Carl Schurz:* Hans L. Trefousse, *Carl Schurz, a Biography* (Knoxville: University of Tennessee Press, 1982).

## CHAPTER 5: THE POLITICS OF THE RADICAL CENTER

207 *"Some men look":* Quoted in Edmund S. Morgan, "Back to Basics," review of Vincent Crapanzano, *Serving the Word: Literalism in America from the Pulpit to the Bench*, in *The New York Review of Books*, July 20, 2000, p. 47.

208 *"Reformers have":* Quoted in "Quick Fixes," *The Economist*, June 24, 2000, p. 14.

216 *reform of electoral rules:* The idea of replacing plurality elections with instant runoff elections has recently gained support in major mainstream media. See, for example, Editorial, "Spoiler-free Elections," *USA Today*, February 5, 2001, A12; William Raspberry, "Post-Traumatic Suggestions," *Washington Post*, January 1, 2001; Hendrik Hertzberg, "College High Jinks," *The New Yorker*, November 13, 2000, p. 69. Public interest in third parties and third-party candidates is remarkably high. According to a Shorenstein Center poll of December 15–19, 1999, 31 percent of voters agreed with the statement "The two-party system is seriously broken and the country needs a third party," compared to the 27 percent of eighteen- to twenty-nine-year-olds and the 25 percent of those over thirty who agreed that "The two-party system works fairly well." The Joan Shorenstein Center on the Press, Politics, and Public Policy, "Support of Two-Party System," www.vanishingvoter.org. According to a Portrait of America poll of January 23, 2001, more voters (29 percent) said they would support a hypothetical third-party candidate for Congress who had a chance for winning than said they would pick a Democrat (26 percent) or a Republican (24 percent). "Voters Rate Congress," www.portraitofamerica.com. See also Lydia Saad, "Public Supportive of Third-Party Movement in U.S.," Gallup Organization, Poll Releases, July 23, 1999, www.gallup.com; and Frank

Newport, "Americans Support Proposal to Eliminate Electoral College System," Gallup Organization, Poll Releases, January 5, 2001, www.gallup.com.

216 *health care reform:* According to a Gallup poll conducted in September 2000, 64 percent of Americans think "that it is the responsibility of the federal government to make sure all Americans have health care coverage," while 31 percent disagree, and 5 percent have no opinion.

216 *global warming:* A Gallup poll from March 2001 revealed that 63 percent of Americans worry about global warming either a "great deal" or a "fair amount." The Gallup Organization, "Gallup Poll Topics: Environment," March 5–7, 2001, www.gallup.com/poll/indicators/indEnvironment2.asp.

217 *public opinion of race-based civil rights:* Americans are overwhelmingly opposed to racial preferences. A Gallup poll conducted in late October 2000 showed that 85 percent of Americans would vote against, and only 13 percent for, a proposition mandating racial preferences in jobs and schools. The Gallup Organization, "Referendum 2000," November 1, 2000, www.gallup.com/poll/releases/pr001101.asp. A Zogby poll in January 2000 showed 77 percent of Americans, including 52 percent of Blacks, 71 percent of Hispanics, and 67 percent of liberals, opposing racial preferences in school admissions. Cited in Debbie Schlussel, "Forget About Merit: W's GOP Disses Affirmative Action Foes," News Archive of American Civil Rights Institute, August 7, 2000, www.acri.org/news/august.html. Although a December 1997 *New York Times* poll demonstrated broader support for racial preferences, with 52 percent in favor and 35 percent opposed, this same poll found that 53 percent of Americans favor and 37 percent reject the replacement of racial preferences with preferences for the poor. Cited in Richard D. Kahlenberg, "Class-Based Affirmative Action," *Boston Globe,* January 19, 1999, A11.

217 *popularity of IRA's and partial privatization of Social Security:* Eileen Ambrose, "401(k) Helped Many to Save for Retirement," *Baltimore Sun,* December 31, 2000, C1. According to a Gallup poll conducted in late October 2000, 66 percent of Americans favored, 30 percent opposed, and 4 percent were indifferent to a "law that would allow people to put a portion of their Social Security payroll taxes into personal retirement accounts that would be invested in private stocks or bonds." The Gallup Organization, "Gallup Poll Topics: Social Security/Medicare," October 25–28, 2000, www.gallup.com/poll/indicators/indsocialsecurity.asp.

217 *support for citizen-based social contract:* Potential public support for a citizen-based social contract must be inferred from answers to polls about more specific questions. For example, polls show that while Americans believe that government should ensure universal health care coverage by a large majority, the public is divided on the issue of adopting a single-payer government health care system. From this we infer that there would be substantial public support for a system based on mandatory health care savings that guarantees universal, portable health care coverage without requiring the government to nationalize the health insurance industry.

For polling data demonstrating consistent public support of the idea that government should guarantee universal health care coverage, see the Economic Policy Institute, "The Pulse on . . . Health Care," www.epinet.org. For polling data indicating public ambivalence about a single-payer health care system, see Center on Policy Attitudes, "Americans on Health Care Policy," Findings, August 30, 2000, www.policyattitudes.org.

217 *support for gene therapy:* In a poll by Portrait of America in July 2000, 68 percent of Americans believed medical researchers should pursue new treatments based on genetic research, while 79 percent believed that genetically engineered "designer babies" would be "bad for the human race" and 68 percent considered the creation of such babies to be morally wrong. "Americans OK with Some Genetic Research," July 13, 2000, www.portraitofamerica.com.

218 *March 2000 survey:* "Race for Congress Close: Strong Interest in Third Party," March 12, 2000, Portrait of America telephone survey, www.portraitofamerica.com/html/poll-793.html. We are indebted to Rob Richie of the Center for Voting and Democracy for drawing our attention to this survey.

220 *high-tech elites promote school reform:* Notable examples include Bill Gates, Tim Draper, Jim Barksdale, and Ron Unz.

222 *policy concerns of young adults:* Ted Halstead, "A Politics for Generation X," *The Atlantic Monthly*, August 1998; Jack Dennis and Diana Owen, "The Partisanship Puzzle: Identification and Attitudes of Generation X," Stephen Earl Bennet and Stephen Craig, eds., *After the Boom: The Politics of Generation X* (Lanham, Md.: Rowman and Littlefield, 1997).

223 *"choice generation":* A term coined by Andrei Cherny in *The Next Deal: The Future of Public Life in the Information Age* (New York: Basic Books, 2000).

# INDEX